Authentic Virtual World Education

Sue Gregory · Denise Wood
Editors

Authentic Virtual World Education

Facilitating Cultural Engagement and Creativity

Springer

Editors
Sue Gregory
School of Education
University of New England
Armidale, NSW
Australia

Denise Wood
Central Queensland University
Rockhampton North, QLD
Australia

ISBN 978-981-10-6381-7 ISBN 978-981-10-6382-4 (eBook)
https://doi.org/10.1007/978-981-10-6382-4

Library of Congress Control Number: 2017949499

Printed on acid-free paper

This Springer imprint is published by Springer Nature
The registered company is Springer Nature Singapore Pte Ltd.
The registered company address is: 152 Beach Road, #21-01/04 Gateway East, Singapore 189721, Singapore

Preface

Imagine an experience, so immersive that your heart beats faster, your blood pressure rises and you cannot wait to get to class to do it again. Such has been the attraction of the use of virtual worlds in higher education since their emergence in the 1980s and their ascendance to the peak of their popularity in 2007.

Now ten years later, the authors of this edited book take the reader on a journey of creative discovery as they share their research and teaching practice utilising virtual worlds as platforms for engaging their students in immersive authentic learning experiences across a broad range of disciplinary fields. The authors share their pedagogical approaches to harness the affordances of virtual worlds to introduce students to contemporary issues such as the environmental, social and economic challenges facing humanity in the twenty-first century, engaging with cultural diversity, the restorative effects of natural environments and sustainability.

The affordances of virtual worlds as authentic environments that can provide situated learning in simulated environments are showcased with practical examples drawn from fields as diverse as teacher education, law, languages, sustainability, computer architecture, business, international relations, health and the arts. The authors show how they are combining their teaching in virtual worlds with scholarship as they use their teaching and the virtual world platform as virtual laboratories for innovative research into new applications of technologies to support intrinsically motivating experiential learning as well as strategies for enhancing feedback and assessment within these learning environments.

The authors share both their successes and the challenges they have encountered and propose strategies for mitigating the issues that can arise when engaging students with media-rich online technologies. The insights provided by the authors are therefore applicable beyond virtual world technologies and will be of interest to educators, researchers and students across diverse disciplinary fields.

Armidale, Australia — Sue Gregory
Rockhampton North, Australia — Denise Wood

Acknowledgements

The editors wish to acknowledge all those who were involved in the development as well as the review and editing process of this collection.

First and foremost, we thank the chapter authors for sharing their expertise and insights through their excellent contributions.

We would also like to express our gratitude to the panel of assistant co-editors and reviewers (Dr. Lisa Jacka; the late Dr. Clare Atkins, who passed away during the production process and whose contribution in reviewing the book has been invaluable; Penny Neuendorf and Prof. David Parsons) who gave generously of their time to assist us in ensuring the quality of the book's content.

Special of notes of appreciation must go to Nick Melchior, Editor, who provided us with invaluable guidance and input whenever it was needed.

Finally, we recognise the assistance and support we received from the publishing team at Springer Nature. Their knowledge, dedication and efficiency in responding to our queries and requests for help have made working with them an absolute pleasure.

Sue Gregory
Denise Wood

Contents

Editors and Contributors

About the Editors

Sue Gregory is an Associate Professor, Chair of Research and a member of the ICT education team in the School of Education at the University of New England, Australia, where she is responsible for leading and driving research within the school and training pre-service and post-graduate education students on how to incorporate technology into their teaching. She is a long-term adult educator and, since 2008, has been teaching in Second Life, in which she has created and manages several inworld spaces including classrooms and a playground for students. Sue's research focus is on adult learning, authenticity, engagement, immersion, impact and the efficacy of virtual worlds for education; in particular, she has been examining student perceptions of their learning in a virtual world. Sue is chair of the Australian and New Zealand Virtual Worlds Working Group (VWWG) and recently led an Australian Government Office of Learning and Teaching (OLT)-funded project entitled "VirtualPREX: Innovative Assessment using a 3D Virtual World with Pre-Service Teachers".

Denise Wood is a Professor, Engaged Research Chair and Director of the Centre for Regional Advancement of Learning, Equity and Participation (LEAP) at Central Queensland University, Australia. She had led over AU$6 million in national funded research projects focusing on learning and teaching, and the innovative use of information and communication technologies, including virtual worlds, to enhance learning outcomes and the social and educational participation of people from underrepresented groups in Australia and South Africa. One of these projects, which is of particular interest to this publication, was an Australian Leaning and Teaching funded national project, "Facilitating flexible, enquiry-based experiential learning through an accessible, three-dimensional virtual learning environment (3DVLE)", the outputs of which included guidelines for academics teaching in virtual worlds about the affordances and features of virtual worlds for learning and teaching in higher education, case studies across a range of disciplinary fields and the development of an accessible virtual world viewer.

Contributors

Des Butler Queensland University of Technology, Brisbane, QLD, Australia

Vanessa Chang Curtin University, Perth, Australia

Debbie Corder Auckland University of Technology, Auckland, New Zealand

Ali Fardinpour Wise Realities, Curtin University, Perth, Australia

Helen Farley University of Southern Queensland, Toowoomba, QLD, Australia

Scott Grant Monash University, Melbourne, VIC, Australia

Sue Gregory School of Education, University of New England, Armidale, NSW, Australia

Lyn Henderson James Cook University, Townsville, QLD, Australia

Michael Henderson Monash University, Melbourne, VIC, Australia

Matthew Hill Southern Cross University, Lismore, NSW, Australia

Hui Huang Monash University, Melbourne, VIC, Australia

Lisa Jacka Southern Cross University, Lismore, NSW, Australia

Janice K. Jones University of Southern Queensland, Toowoomba, QLD, Australia

Bjørn Jæger Molde University College, Molde, Norway

Kristine Ludvigsen University of Bergen, Bergen, Norway

Colin Macgregor James Cook University, Townsville City, QLD, Australia

Timothy McDonald Curtin University, Perth, Australia

Angela Murphy University of Southern Queensland, Toowoomba, QLD, Australia

Sarah Pasfield-Neofitou Monash University, Melbourne, VIC, Australia

Torsten Reiners Curtin University, Perth, Australia

Amit Rudra Curtin University, Perth, Australia

Michael Steurer Curtin University, Perth, Australia

Hanna Teräs Murdoch University, Perth, Australia

Marko Teräs Curtin University, Perth, Australia

Marcia Thorne James Cook University, Townsville City, QLD, Australia

Alice U-Mackey Auckland University of Technology, Auckland, New Zealand

Denise Wood Central Queensland University, Rockhampton, QLD, Australia

Lincoln C. Wood University of Otago, Dunedin, New Zealand

Abbreviations

3D3C	3D world, Community, Creation and Commerce
3DVLE	Three-Dimensional Virtual Learning Environment
ALAM	Action-based Learning Assessment Method
ALAS	Action-based Learning Assessment System
BEHAVE	Basic Exploratory Human Actions in Virtual Environments
CoI	Community of Inquiry
CSCMP	Council of Supply Chain Management Professionals
D	Distinction
DIE	Describe, Interpret and Evaluate
EfSD	Education for Sustainable Development
ELT	English Language Teaching
ERP	Enterprise Resource Planning
FLA	Foreign Language Anxiety
HD	High Distinction
HUD	Heads Up Display
ICT	Information Communication Technologies
IM	Instant Message
IS	Information Systems
JCU	James Cook University
LCNAU	Languages and Cultures Network for Australian Universities
LEAP	Learning, Equity and Participation
MMO	Massively Multiplayer Online games
MUVE	3D Multiuser Virtual Environments
NAV	Norwegian Labour and Welfare Administration
nDiVE	Prototype of a framework
NPC	Non-Player Characters
NS	Native Speakers
OLT	Australian Government Office of Learning and Teaching

PLANE	Pathways for Learning, Anywhere, Anytime, a Network for Educators
POPBL	Problem-Oriented, Place-Based Learning
PRS	Perceived Restorativeness Scale
QUT	Queensland University of Technology
SME	Small and Medium Enterprise
UNDESD	Decade of Education for Sustainable Development
UN	United Nations
USQ	University of Southern Queensland
VLE	Virtual Learning Environments
VTE	Virtual Training Environments
VWWG	Australia and New Zealand Virtual Worlds Working Group

Chapter 1
The Affordances of Virtual Worlds as Authentic, Culturally Diverse Learning Environments

Denise Wood and Sue Gregory

> …our involvement with new technologies generally moves from an ambivalent relationship with augmented abilities to the 'dawning of irreversible change' (Midani cited in Marcus 1996, p. 273).

The history of the application of technologies to support learning and teaching long predates the emergence of virtual worlds as immersive platforms for engaging students in authentic, culturally diverse experiential learning activities. Yet the all too familiar pattern of technological adoption described in Gartner's Hype Cycle (2017) has persisted, with an initial trigger (often accompanied by a level of ambivalence) followed by the peak of inflated expectations, the trough of disillusionment, the slope of enlightenment and then the plateau of productivity. It is at this 'plateau of productivity' stage of the hype cycle that, in Midani's words, comes the 'dawning of irreversible change' (Midani 1986, cited in Marcus 1996, p. 273), as educators engage in emerging research, experiment with innovative applications of virtual worlds to support learning and teaching, and begin to appreciate the affordances that the technology offers to engage their students.

Such has been the pattern of engagement of teachers in the use of virtual worlds in higher education since their emergence in the 1980s and their ascendance to the peak of their popularity in 2007 (Lowendahl 2016). Now ten years later, virtual worlds are no longer at the peak of the technological hype cycle, having descended into the 'trough of disillusionment' in 2010, ascended to the 'slope of enlightenment' in 2014 and having attained the 'plateau of productivity' in 2015 (Lowendahl 2016). The potential of virtual worlds as immersive environments engaging students in authentic learning activities that can help to facilitate the development

D. Wood (✉)
Central Queensland University, Rockhampton, QLD, Australia
e-mail: d.wood@cqu.edu.au

S. Gregory
School of Education, University of New England, Armidale, NSW, Australia
e-mail: sue.gregory@une.edu.au

S. Gregory and D. Wood (eds.), *Authentic Virtual World Education*,
https://doi.org/10.1007/978-981-10-6382-4_1

of the skills required of a twenty-first-century graduate is now being realised. These skills include problem-solving, the ability to work with others, communication and appreciation of, and respect for, diversity (Denson and Zhang 2010).

There is a growing body of evidence demonstrating the centrality and importance of students having the ability to communicate effectively across cultures in increasingly globalised, multicultural and networked workplaces (Freeman et al. 2009; Leask and Wallace 2011). International research has also demonstrated the ways in which student experiences with diversity can positively affect other graduate attributes (Denson and Zhang 2010). Intercultural competence is an employability skill identified by employers as a major factor influencing graduates' performance in the workplace (CSWDF 2013) and is identified as an important generic skill in many university graduate attribute profiles (Donelavey 2011; Oliver 2011). Students also need to develop a nuanced understanding of the dynamic and fluid dimensions of culture (Guo and Jamal 2007) and engage with the contested nature of essentialist categorisations of culture and diversity (Bozalek 2011).

Deardorff (2006, pp. 247–248) defines intercultural competence as 'the understanding of others' world views' and 'the ability to communicate effectively and appropriately in intercultural situations based on one's intercultural knowledge, skills, and attitudes'. Graduates of the twenty-first century need to be able to demonstrate intercultural skills such as being able to communicate and work collaboratively across cultures, be aware and responsive to others' world views, have a deep understanding and knowledge of culture, including contexts, respect and value other cultures, be open to intercultural learning and to people from other cultures, and demonstrate the ability to tolerate ambiguity and uncertainty (Deardorff 2006).

It is now well recognised that twenty-first-century graduates need to be able to respond to complexity and uncertainty (Craft 2006; Florida 2003; McWilliam 2007). One way of equipping our graduates with these employability skills is to embed creative problem-solving within authentic tasks (Lindsay and Wood 2015) designed to 'reflect the way the knowledge will be useful in real life' (Brown et al. 1989, p. 2). Creative problem-solving involves the development of domain-relevant skills, creativity-relevant processes and task motivation (Amabile 1996). Domain-relevant skills are required for learners to understand the full range of response possibilities from which new responses are to be synthesised, and the information against which the new responses are to be judged (Csikszentmihalyi 1999). Creativity-relevant processes assist students to respond in ways that extend their response in a given domain (Dewett 2003), and learning is enhanced when tasks are intrinsically motivating (Csikszentmihalyi 1999), and authentic.

Brown et al. (1989) argue that learning is a process of enculturation, and students learn best through situated learning in which the activities are authentic, coherent, meaningful, purposeful and situated within the practices of the relevant professional culture. The principles of authentic learning are based on Brown, Collins and Duguid's theories of situated cognition and cognitive apprenticeship. Herrington, Reeves and Oliver's (2010) authentic learning framework identifies nine elements of authentic learning: (1) authentic contexts; (2) authentic tasks; (3) access to expert performances and the modelling of processes; (4) multiple roles and perspectives;

(5) collaborative construction of knowledge; (6) reflection to enable abstractions to be formed; (7) articulation to enable tacit knowledge to be made explicit; (8) coaching and scaffolding; and (9) authentic assessment of learning.

The affordances of virtual worlds make these technologically mediated environments well suited to facilitating the development of students' employability skills including the ability engage in creative problem-solving and to communicate effectively across cultures through authentic learning activities. An affordance can be defined as the perceived and actual properties of the technology that determine how that technology can be used for learning (Salomon 1997, p. 51). Dalgarno and Lee (2010) have identified five primary affordances of the virtual worlds in higher education: (1) enhancing spatial knowledge representation of the explored domain; (2) enabling experiential learning activities that would be impractical or impossible to undertake in the 'real world'; (3) facilitating intrinsically motivating learning tasks; (4) providing learning opportunities that support the transfer of knowledge and skills to 'real' situations through contextualisation of learning; and (5) facilitating rich and effective collaborative learning tasks. Similarly, Savin-Baden et al. (2010) suggest that the affordances of virtual worlds make them ideally suited for scenarios, simulations and role-plays, and activities involving teamwork or team building. Thus, virtual worlds provide an ideal medium for engaging students in collaborative, intrinsically motivating, authentic learning activities that enable them to develop graduate employability skills including creative problem-solving, and cultural understanding while facilitating the transfer of knowledge to 'real' situations.

In 2009, virtual world academics and researchers from Australian and New Zealand decided to join forces to form the Australian and New Zealand Virtual Worlds Working Group (VWWG). The VWWG began with ten members and has since grown to approximately 200, with most educational institutions represented in the group. Members have come and gone but the numbers remain steady. The members range from a vast variety of disciplines with academics involved in teaching and research: Higher Degree Research candidates, project managers, virtual world builders and developers, and educators in the VET sector. The academics and researchers collaborate to identify research gaps and providing best practices in the use of virtual worlds for teaching and learning. Members were invited to contribute to this book, of which there are ten chapters from esteemed authors from across the two countries. They share their experiences of engaging students in authentic learning activities designed to facilitate the development of their technical and employability skills by utilising the affordances of the virtual world platform.

In the first chapter, Marcia Thorne and Colin MacGregor describe the use of virtual worlds in a blended learning approach to provide their students with authentic learning activities designed to facilitate students' ability to apply real-world critical thinking and problem-solving relating to environmental, social and economic challenges facing humanity in the twenty-first century. Applying a communal constructivist learning approach, the authors found that the authentic learning activities undertaken in the virtual world supported knowledge sharing between students, and enhanced their creative and problem-solving abilities as they engaged with virtual spaces that provide an online representation of real-world sustainability projects, and provided teachers and students with access to professional global sustainability networks.

In Chap. 2, Debbie Corder and Alice U-Mackey discuss their use of the virtual world for facilitating the development of students' intercultural competence in a first-year module. The authors explore the symbiotic synergies between the affordances of virtual worlds for intercultural competence development, and the need for intercultural competence for effective engagement in virtual worlds. The authors describe the pedagogical approach adopted, including introducing students to intercultural competence theory and tools for intercultural competence development, followed by an introduction to sociocultural and sociolinguistic theoretical concepts. Students were introduced to the virtual world as an example of a different culture, and the affordances of the platform for developing intercultural competence were explained. Using a case study approach, the authors describe the complex interplay between intercultural competence attributes and intercultural encounters in the virtual world.

The use of virtual worlds as restorative environments is the focus of the third chapter by Janice Jones, Helen Farley and Angela Murphy. The authors describe the final stage of a three-year study of future educators' well-being, awareness of natural environments and sustainability, and creativity. This third stage of the study involved an investigation into impact of engaging students in natural-seeming environments through an immersive virtual world experience on restorative effects such as reduced attentional fatigue and affective states.

In Chap. 4, Torsten Reiners and colleagues demonstrate a prototype of a framework (nDiVE), which combines authentic education, gamification, emerging technology and design-principles used in the game industry to create an engaging learning space for students and workers in the context of Health and Safety within Logistics Infrastructures. They describe the nDiVE framework as a potentially effective approach to providing students with authentic unrestricted and unsupervised exploration of virtual world spaces while also providing them with scripted guidance and formative feedback; in a sense, the technology provides the expert guidance that would be available to apprentices in a real-world context.

Chapter 5 focuses on an innovative approach to conducting formative assessment of action-based learning scenarios conducted in the virtual world. The authors, Ali Fardinpour, Torsten Reiners and Lincoln C. Wood, describe features of the Action-based Learning Assessment Method (ALAM), which provides formative assessment of students' performed goal-oriented actions in a simulated virtual world environment. Their research aims to provide an automated assessment solution to the provision of high-level formative feedback in virtual worlds.

In Chap. 6, Scott Grant, Hui Huang and Sarah Pasfield-Neofitou discuss the potential of virtual worlds for providing authentic study abroad experiences by engaging students in activities that enable them to develop their language and communicative competence. The authors explore the impact on students' level of foreign language anxiety (FLA) through task-based learning activities in a virtual world environment that simulates an authentic study abroad experience.

Cognitive engagement in language learning through authentic virtual world activities is the focus of Chap. 7. In this chapter, Michael Henderson, Lyn Henderson, Scott Grant and Hui Huang describe eight key affordances of virtual worlds for teaching and learning of second languages and intercultural awareness. They suggest that undertaking such activities in virtual worlds can promote deeper-level thinking processes, providing there is appropriate alignment of the sequence of tasks and clarity of instructional design to enable students to focus on thinking about the content rather than instructions.

In Chap. 8, Lisa Jacka and Matthew Hill explore pre-service teachers' perceptions of virtual worlds as having potential for use in their future classrooms. The authors posit that by increasing future educators' knowledge about virtual worlds as both users and to design meaningful learning experiences for their future students, a higher level of engagement will be achieved.

In Chap. 9, Des Butler describes the use of Second Life machinima facilitated narratives to support cognitive and imaginative engagement across the undergraduate law curriculum. He suggests that machinima provides an authentic learning experience that is a cost-effective means of promoting the imaginative engagement of students, while assisting cognition, provoking active thinking and providing contextual clues that aid later recall. He concludes that machinima has the potential to create authentic learning experiences that can enable students to take an active and practical role in their learning, while also helping them to appreciate the relevance to their future professional careers.

The use of virtual worlds to facilitate students' business decision-making skills is the focus of Chap. 10 written by Amit Rudra, Bjørn Jæger and Kristine Ludvigsen. Using a case study approach, the authors discuss the affordances of virtual worlds for supporting the mediation of tacit knowledge to support decision-making in a simulated global and distributed business environment.

These examples of the innovative use of virtual worlds to facilitate employability skills in an authentic learning environment provide evidence that virtual worlds have indeed now reached the 'plateau of productivity' and suggest that their impact, for at least the authors of this collection, has led to a 'dawning of irreversible change' (Midani 1986). The hype and overinflated expectations of virtual worlds have now passed, and the experiences that the authors of the following ten chapters share demonstrate the pedagogical approaches that educators are now employing to maximise the affordances of virtual worlds in ways that provide an authentic and engaging learning experience for their students as future professionals.

References

Amabile, T. M. (1996). *Creativity in context: Update to the social psychology of creativity*. Boulder, CO: Westview Press.

Bozalek, V. (2011). Acknowledging privilege through encounters with difference: Participatory Learning and Action techniques for decolonizing methodologies in Southern contexts. *International Journal of Social Research Methodology, 4*(6), 465–480.

Brown, J. S., Collins, A., & Duguid, P. (1989). Situated cognition and the culture of learning. *Educational Researcher, 18*(1), 32–42.

Czikszentmihalyi, M. (1999). Implications of a systems perspective for the study of creativity. In R. Sternberg (Ed.), *Handbook of creativity*. Cambridge: Cambridge University Press.

Core Skills for Work Developmental Framework (CSDWF). (2013). Retrieved from http://www.innovation.gov.au/SKILLS/CORESKILLSFORWORKFRAMEWORK

Craft, A. (2006). Creativity in schools. In N. Jackson et al. (Eds.), *Developing creativity in higher education: An imaginative curriculum* (pp. 19–28). London: Routledge.

Dalgarno, B., & Lee, M. J. W. (2010). What are the learning affordances of 3-D virtual environments? *British Journal of Educational Technology, 41*(1), 10–32.

Deardorff, D. K. (2006). The identification and assessment of intercultural competence as a student outcome of internationalization at institutions of higher education in the United States. *Journal of Studies in International Education, 10,* 241–266.

Denson, N., & Zhang, S. (2010). The impact of student experiences with diversity on developing graduate attributes. *Studies in Higher Education, 35*(5), 529–543.

Dewett T. (2003). Understanding the relationship between information technology and creativity in organizations. *Creativity Research Journal, 15*(2–3). doi:10.1080/10400419.2003.9651410.

Donleavy, G. (2012). Proclaimed graduate attributes of Australian universities: patterns, problems and prospects. *Quality Assurance in Education, 20*(4), 341–356. doi:10.1108/09684881211263984.

Freeman, M., Treleavan, L., Ramburuth, P., Leask, B., Caulfield, N., Simpson, L., Ridings, S., et al. (2009). *Embedding the development of intercultural competence in business education. Final report*. Australian Learning and Teaching Council. Retrieved from http://www.olt.gov.au/system/files/resources/CG6-37_Sydney_Freeman_Final%20Report_July09.pdf.

Gartner Hype Cycle. (2017). Retrieved from http://www.gartner.com/technology/research/methodologies/hype-cycle.jsp.

Guo, S., & Jamal, Z. (2007). Nurturing cultural diversity in higher education: A critical review of selected models. *The Canadian Journal of Higher Education, 37*(3), 27–49.

Herrington, J., Reeves, T., & Oliver, R. (2010). *A guide to authentic e-learning*. New York and London: Routledge.

Leask, B., & Wallace, J. (2011). *Good practice report: Learning and teaching across cultures*. Office for Learning & Teaching. Retrieved from http://www.olt.gov.au/system/files/resources/GPR_Learning_and_Teaching_Across_Cultures_Leask_2011.pdf.

Lindsay, N. & Wood, D. (2015). Facilitating creative problem solving (CPS) in the entrepreneurship curriculum through authentic learning activities. In V. Bozalek, D. Ng'ambi, D. Wood, J. Herrington, J. Hardmann, & A. Amory (Eds.), *Activity theory, authentic learning, and emerging technologies: Towards a transformative higher education Pedagogy*. London and New York: Routledge.

Lowendahl, J.-M. (2016). Gartner 2016 Hype Cycle. In J. Gary (2016). *Hype Cycle of Education IT*. Retrieved from http://moka.emporia.edu/uploads/moka_presentations/2016_Hype_Cycle_Education_IT.pdf.

Marcus, S. (1993). Multimedia, hypermedia and the teaching of language. In M. Monteith (Ed.), *Computers and language* (pp. 21–43). Oxford: Intellect Books.

Midani, A. (1986). A matter of perception. Featured address—EDUCOM '86, Pittsburgh, Pennsylvania.

McWilliam, E. (2007). *Developing pedagogical models for building creative workforce capacities in undergraduate students. Final Fellowship Report*. Retrieved from http://www.olt.gov.au/system/files/resources/McWilliamWebsite.zip.

Oliver, B. (2011). *Good practice report: Assuring graduate outcomes*. Australian Learning and Teaching Council. Retrieved from http://www.olt.gov.au/system/files/resources/Assuring%20graduate%20outcomes.%20ALTC%20Good%20practice%20report.%20Oliver%2C%20B%202011.pdf.

Savin-Baden, M., Gourlay, L., Steils, N., Tombs, G., & Mawer, M. (2010). Situating pedagogies, positions and practices in immersive virtual worlds. *Educational Research, 52*(2), 123–133.
Salomon, G. (Ed.). (1997). *Distributed cognitions—Psychological and educational considerations*. Cambridge: Cambridge University Press.

Author Biographies

Denise Wood is a Professor, Engaged Research Chair and Director of the Centre for Regional Advancement of Learning, Equity, and Participation (LEAP) at Central Queensland University, Australia. She had led over AU$6 million in national-funded research projects focusing on learning and teaching, and the innovative use of information and communication technologies, including virtual worlds, to enhance learning outcomes and the social and educational participation of people from under-represented groups in Australia and South Africa. One of these projects, which is of particular interest to this publication, was an Australian Learning and Teaching-funded national project, 'facilitating flexible, enquiry-based experiential learning through an accessible, three-dimensional virtual learning environment (3DVLE)', the outputs of which included guidelines for academics teaching in virtual worlds about the affordances and features virtual worlds for learning and teaching in higher education, case studies across a range of disciplinary fields and the development of an accessible virtual world viewer.

Sue Gregory is an Associate Professor, Chair of Research and a member of the ICT education team in the School of Education at the University of New England, Australia, where she is responsible for leading and driving research within the school and training pre-service and postgraduate education students on how to incorporate technology into their teaching. She is a long-term adult educator and, since 2008, has been teaching in Second Life, in which she has created and manages several in world spaces including classrooms and a playground for students. Sue's research focus is on adult learning, authenticity, engagement, immersion, impact, and the efficacy of virtual worlds for education; in particular, she has been examining student perceptions of their learning in a virtual world. Sue is chair of the Australian and New Zealand Virtual Worlds Working Group (VWWG) and recently led an Australian Government Office of Learning and Teaching (OLT)-funded project entitled 'VirtualPREX: Innovative Assessment using a 3D Virtual World with Pre-Service Teachers'.

Chapter 2
Pedagogy and Learning for Sustainability in a Virtual World Scaffold

Marcia Thorne and Colin Macgregor

Introduction

The United Nations (UN) proclaimed the years 2005 to 2014 the Decade of Education for Sustainable Development (UNDESD), and in response many universities are encouraging education for sustainable development (EfSD) within their curricula. In 2012, James Cook University (JCU) in Cairns, Australia, introduced the *Bachelor of Sustainability*, a cross disciplinary undergraduate degree offering majors in business, science, and social science. A key strategic intention of JCU is to better meet sustainable education and lifestyle outcomes, while also responding to an expanding green job sector looking for sustainability professionals.

This chapter presents a case study of the use of Second Life, a virtual world, to augment sustainability learning in *EV2011 The Case for Sustainability*, a core second year subject in the *Bachelor of Sustainability,* presented at JCU for the first time in 2013. Second Life was created by and is hosted by Linden Lab, a private company established in 1999 to provide shared 3D entertainment and learning opportunities. Second Life was made available to the public in 2003 (Linden Research Inc 2016). In this learning activity, exploratory learning in Second Life was free for the university and for students.

Sustainability learning typically involves practical application of real-world critical thinking and problem-solving experiences (Orr 1996; Sipos et al. 2008). Cortese and McDonough (2001) contend that real-world problems provide a solid foundation for EfSD learning experiences. These authors also emphasise, 'we must

M. Thorne (✉) · C. Macgregor
James Cook University, Townsville City, QLD, Australia
e-mail: marcia.thorne@jcu.edu.au

C. Macgregor
e-mail: colin.macgregor@jcu.edu.au

S. Gregory and D. Wood (eds.), *Authentic Virtual World Education*,
https://doi.org/10.1007/978-981-10-6382-4_2

increase group work learning so students may be able to effectively collaborate as managers and leaders on complex problems' (Cortese and McDonough 2001, p. 3).

Being a virtual world, Second Life can simulate real-world situations and can provide opportunities for students to deal with challenges (albeit virtual challenges) in a collaborative manner. In effect, virtual world sustainability-related sites provide a platform to experience sustainability initiatives and as such they facilitate problem-oriented, place-based learning (POPBL) (Sipos et al. 2008). Some virtual worlds within Second Life are a virtual presence for a real-world place or activity (e.g. part of a university campus). These offer students tangible real-world connections. Others exist only as a virtual world. However, real-world linkages were not important in achieving the subject learning outcomes.

The capacity and affordances of virtual worlds and Second Life in higher education learning is subject to robust exploration as increased use of virtual world pedagogy in tertiary education is encouraged (Ahmad et al. 2011; Jarmon et al. 2009; Siragusa et al. 2007). Virtual worlds are well suited to project-based experiential learning (Jarmon et al. 2009; Yalcinalp et al. 2012), and Second Life is the most popular tertiary virtual world learning platform in the UK (Warburton 2009). In Australia, the Virtual Worlds Working Group (VWWG) was formed in 2009 to support teaching and learning in virtual worlds, and the group has members from over 54 higher education institutions in Australia and New Zealand (www.vwwg.info).

This subject departed from solely positioning sustainability learning in a real-world context and extended student learning experiences to enhance learner engagement to better meet subject learning outcomes and develop graduate attributes (Ahmad et al. 2011; Dawley 2009; Garrison and Kanuka 2004; Jarmon et al. 2009; Raes et al. 2012; Siragusa et al. 2007; Warburton 2009). The specific subject learning outcomes and graduate attributes of *EV2011* are explored in the methodology section of this chapter and are listed in Fig. 1.1.

Working in pairs, students undertook a review and comparison of *Etopia Island Community*, a virtual world in Second Life dedicated to advancing sustainability, by comparing it with one other sustainability focused virtual world in Second Life identified by the class tutor. The review framework was constructed by teaching staff to meet subject learning outcomes and graduate attributes and resembled an explore, review, compare, evaluate and disseminate process (see theoretical framework in Table 2.1). The review process involved students in: developing familiarity with Second Life in-world protocols, conceptual understandings of the sustainability issues presented in Second Life, appraisal of the effectiveness of the sustainability messages presented, and evaluation and comparison of the two sustainability focused virtual worlds as tools to support education for sustainability. After discussion and evaluation, students presented team findings in real-world assessable written and oral formats. A real-world assessment format was chosen to authenticate learning tasks, as virtual world assessment rubrics require further development (Reiners et al. 2011).

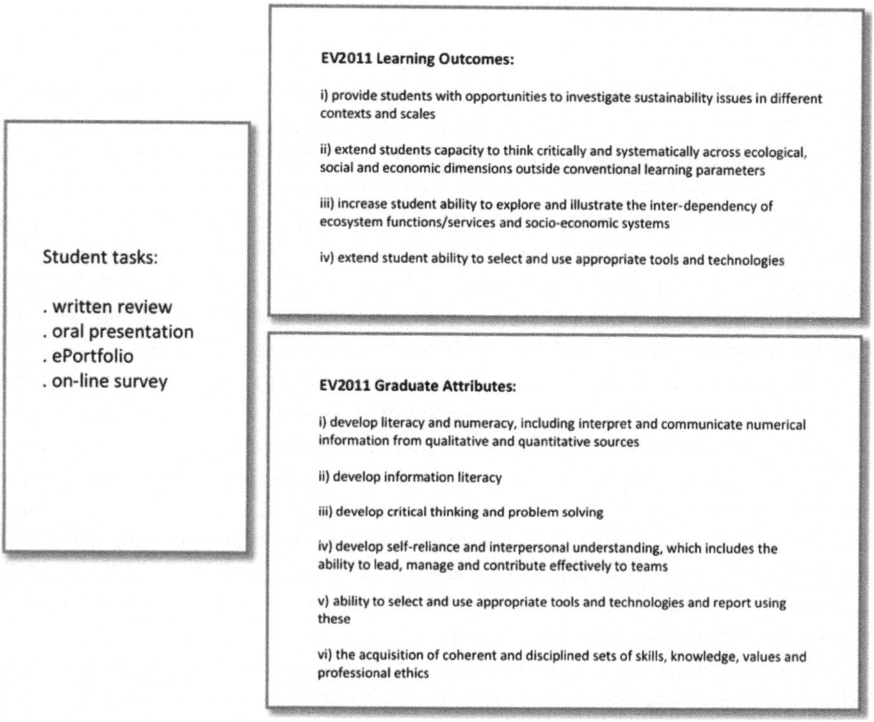

Fig. 2.1 Student tasks and EV2011 learning outcomes and graduate attributes

Table 2.1 Theoretical framework for blended learning in Second Life

Theoretical Framework for Blended Learning for Sustainability in a virtual world		
Recognise the importance of:	*To develop a:*	*To achieve:*
Considerations for virtual world teaching and learning Technical infrastructure, immersion and socialisation (Warburton 2009)	Community of Inquiry (CoI) Cognitive, social and teaching presences (Dawley 2009; Garrison and Kanuda 2004)	Communal Constructivist Learning Interact with the environment, collaborate, dynamic knowledge construction, publish (Girvan and Savage 2010)
Desired competency:	*Desired competency:*	*Desired competency:*
Engagement with Second Life space	Interaction with Second Life, peers and learning activity	Collate and present findings

Theoretical Framework

A blended learning environment supported the theoretical framework of *EV2011s* virtual world learning activity (Garrison and Kanuka 2004). Identifying and adopting theoretically appropriate pedagogy to match the student cohort was important (Dawley 2009; Girvan and Savage 2010; Lorenzo et al. 2012). Pedagogy was informed by a number of theoretical frameworks, as depicted in Table 2.1. This 'assemblage' of virtual world pedagogical theories afforded development of a structured praxis inclusive of critical and reflective thinking suitable for the diverse needs of a multi-age student cohort with varied computer skills (Garrison and Kanuka 2004; Kozan and Richardson 2014; Traphagan et al. 2010).

All 28 students in EV2011 were new to Second Life, and most were not regular computer game players. A third of the cohort expressed concern about the relevance of situating sustainability learning in a virtual world. Therefore, when introducing the learning task, Warburton's considerations for teaching and learning were adopted. The aim was to allow time and provide support to students as they became familiar with the technical infrastructure, immersion in the Second Life space, and the in-world socialisation protocols (2009). Time spent gaining familiarity with navigating and communicating in Second Life proved to be an essential foundation to learning in this particular virtual world.

A Community of Inquiry (CoI) learning space was established to support cognitive, social and teaching presences (Dawley 2009; Garrison and Kanuka 2004; Lorenzo et al. 2012). The CoI supports interactive oral and written communication in a blended learning environment and fosters higher order learning through critical discourse and reflective thinking (Garrison and Kanuka 2004). The desired teaching outcome was competent interaction with Second Life, peers and the learning activity. This occurred through in-world communications as students attended in-world talks and events and communicated with their study pair and with peers. A CoI learning space also existed in the real world as students interacted with each other, tutors and reference materials.

A communal constructivist learning space (Girvan and Savage 2010) was established to complement the CoI. In communal constructivist learning, students interact with the environment (in this case, Second Life) and actively collaborate and engage in: knowledge construction, publishing that knowledge and transferring that knowledge between groups within a dynamic and adaptive learning environment (Girvan and Savage 2010). In *EV2011,* it was found that students recognised the support this learning space provided and were generally very motivated to engage.

Context

JCU's Bachelor of Sustainability is a multidisciplinary degree offering science, business and social science majors. In 2013, the degree sat within the Faculty of Science and Engineering with collaborative delivery involving five schools: Earth and Environmental Sciences, Education, Marine and Tropical Biology, Business, Arts and Social Sciences. *EV2011* builds on understanding and knowledge gained in the first year subject, *EV1011 Introduction to Sustainability*. Therefore, *EV2011* students have a rudimentary understanding of the considerable environmental, social and economic challenges facing humanity in the twenty-first century and are developing an appreciation for the philosophy and ethics foundational to a sustainability vision. *EV2011* also provides students with the opportunity to explore, compare and contrast a variety of sustainability case studies such as: natural resource management, energy generation and distribution, forest management, community development and planning, sustainable towns and cities, sustainable design and use of technology, climate change adaptation, sustainable decision-making, and policy development. Teaching and learning in *EV2011* involves guest lecturers and tutorial and workshop activities employing a variety of engagement techniques and media, for example, fieldwork, student presentations, creation of an ePortfolio, as well as the Second Life virtual world exploratory learning activity.

Methods

The Second Life virtual world learning activity took place over two, 2-h class tutorials in a computer laboratory. The 2013 student cohort of 28 was divided into two groups of equal size, necessitating a repeat of each tutorial. In the first virtual world tutorial, students were introduced to *Etopia Island Community*, a virtual world in Second Life dedicated to advancing sustainability, and students learnt the in-world protocols. In the second tutorial, students continued with exploratory learning, addressing learning tasks that were designed to allow students to fulfil the subject's learning outcomes (see Fig. 1.1). Specific activities in these tutorials are discussed more fully in the following paragraphs. Note that tutor support was available throughout the learning process to assist students gain familiarity with the medium and to assist them in understanding the requirements of the learning tasks. Note also that the Second Life client had previously been installed in the computer laboratory by university IT personnel.

In tutorial one, students were introduced to Second Life via an in-world demonstration with a live application of Second Life projected onto a screen to assist students to familiarise themselves with the Second Life space. This direct and demonstrated instruction session was foundational to creating a collaborative learning process (Dawley 2009) and instrumental in establishing a CoI (Garrison and Kanuka 2004). Students met the 'avatars' (in-world identities) of the class tutors and learnt rudimentary navigation procedures. Students created an account by joining Second Life (free of charge), whereupon they created their own avatar. Approximately thirty minutes of guided instruction about the specifics of Second Life prepared students for individual and team exploratory learning. This included rudimentary instructions about 'teleporting', navigating, communicating (including instant messaging—IM), avatar animation, menu locations and changing avatar appearance. Several URLs for tutorial videos were provided. These offered instructions on how to: connect with Second Life communities, find interesting places and how to approach and chat with other 'residents' (virtual world users). As Second Life is an open community, students were briefed about 'griefers' (virtual world bullies) and the correct response protocol. Students were also shown how to: a) install the Second Life client software on personal computers for out of laboratory access to Second Life; b) take in-world photographs and copy and paste these into *Paint* and *Word*, as a basis for the review tasks; and c) co-ordinate the local time zone within Second Life time in order to attend in-world events.

After gaining familiarity with *Etopia Island Community* (approximately halfway through the first tutorial), students self-selected into teams of two and were provided with the learning tasks. Class tutors randomly nominated each team their comparative sustainability focused virtual world from the following list: *CNDG Virtual Campus, The Frontier Project HUB, Four Bridges Innovation Centre South, Loving the Rainforest* and the *Giving Circles Network,* all separate 'islands' (virtual worlds) within Second Life. Students assessed each of their virtual worlds by examining their contribution to sustainability learning from a triple-bottom-line perspective (environment, economic and equity). Class tutors provided one-to-one assistance as required but it was evident that peer-to-peer learning was also taking place during tutorials.

Team reviews of findings were presented in a 600-800 word report and a five-minute oral presentation using *PowerPoint*, with each contributing 10% of the total assessment for *EV2011*. Both of these documents were saved in PDF format, and they made important contributions to the students' ePortfolios. It is notable that for ePortfolio assessment, students were required to comment on their impressions of how all the learning experiences in *EV2011* contributed to development of the subject's learning outcomes and graduate attributes.

Assessment of student review papers and oral presentations revealed a depth of penetration and understanding of the sustainability issues presented by the virtual worlds and a high level of student engagement with the Second Life platform. Figure 1.1 outlines student tasks and summarises *EV2011* subject outcomes and graduate attributes relevant to this virtual world pedagogy.

The formal assessment criteria for the written review and the oral presentation of the Second Life learning activity are summarised in Table 2.2. Each assessment piece involved students taking a unique perspective when evaluating and presenting the sustainability content found. Learner engagement was formally and informally

Table 2.2 Formal assessment criteria for the Second Life learning activity in EV2011

Formal assessment criteria		
Written review	70%	Methods of inquiry, relating findings, quality of discussion
	30%	Review style and technique
Oral presentation	40%	Evaluation of triple bottom line of sustainability
	60%	Presentation style and technique

assessed through: (a) tutor in-class observations; (b) self-assessments presented by students in ePortfolio submissions; and, (c) responses in a voluntary, confidential online student survey.

Findings

The findings from this project are organised around four student engagement processes, which are:

(1) assessable tasks:

  (a) written review;
  (b) oral presentation; and
  (c) comments provided in ePortfolios;

(2) data from survey results;
(3) tutor in class observations;
(4) tutor conversations with students.

Assessable Written Review and Oral Presentation

More than one-third of *EV2011* students achieved either a high distinction (HD) or distinction (D) grade for the assessments associated with the Second Life virtual world learning activity. Responses in the written reviews indicate multi-level learning and higher order thinking. Assessment of the virtual world tasks demonstrated learning in four of the five learning outcomes for the subject (Table 2.3).

The distribution is slightly above what was found with the other assessment tasks in *EV2011*. Indeed, these grades are higher than has been typically found with most other assessment tasks in other subjects in the *Bachelor of Sustainability*. This may imply students were better able to demonstrate progress in meeting the specified learning outcomes in the virtual world learning activity compared with

Table 2.3 Formal assessment grades awarded for the Second Life learning activity in EV2011

Grade awarded	Virtual world written review (No. of students)	Virtual world oral presentation (No. of students)
HD	2	2
D	8	10
C	15	12
P	3	4

Note HD-High Distinction, D-Distinction, C-Credit, P-Pass

other more traditional learning activities. As this was the first delivery of *EV2011*, there were no comparative data for sustainability learning in a virtual world.

Assessable EPortfolio Submissions

In ePortfolios, students self-assessed how the virtual world learning activity assisted them in achieving the learning outcomes and graduate attributes identified for *EV2011*. The ePortfolio task contributed 15% to the overall assessment of EV2011 so the Second Life activity was just one aspect of the students' ePortfolio. Table 2.4 summarises students' comments about the Second Life activity that are relevant to graduate attributes. Students expressed overall improvements in: sustainability knowledge, the benefit of teamwork to address sustainability issues, critical thinking to analyse and evaluate data, and improved communication and reporting skills. Students' comments on average were 77% positive about outcomes achieved

Table 2.4 Students' ePortfolio comments about graduate attributes from EV2011

Graduate attribute	Supportive comments (n = 51)	Non-supportive comments (n = 12)
Literacy and numeracy	Has enhanced my knowledge of useful links	
	Dynamic way of collecting and analysing data related to sustainability and sustainability education	
Information literacy	Good to see the different applications a virtual world can provide, and the future potential (×2)	Found it difficult to connect with the worlds in such a short period of time but can understand their potential benefits (×2)
	Useful links	True potential might be hindered by technological issues and the lack of knowledge of computer systems by some individuals
Critical thinking and problem-solving	Thinking critically to analyse and evaluate data, to reason a response clearly and logically, to think systematically (×8)	Provides a somewhat superficial representation of sustainability —not realistic (×2)
	Possible strategies for increasing a globalised understanding of sustainability.	There are better ways to teach about sustainability
Self-reliance and interpersonal understanding	Benefit of teamwork for sustainability problems, for self-improvement (×10)	Experience was hindered by a lack of commitment and enthusiasm from partner students (×2)
	Collaborative effort so we were able to overcome the difficulties	

(continued)

Table 2.4 (continued)

Graduate attribute	Supportive comments (n = 51)	Non-supportive comments (n = 12)
Using tools and technologies	Gaining a broad knowledge of how to use appropriate tools for interpreting and assessing sustainability (×3)	Searching around to find something useful was a waste of time
	Enhanced my ability in public speaking (×5)	There are better tools and programs available when looking for sustainable education
	Enhanced my computer skills (×7)	
Learning achievement	Extremely useful for examining how sustainable design and planning principles in relation to the three pillars of sustainability can be incorporated and adapted to reality	Found the delivery of the content for the task to be ineffective
	Overall the virtual world was a useful experience in modern-day education techniques (×2).	
	Provided the opportunity to view sustainable education and learning from an entirely new point of view (×2)	
	Enhanced communication skills (×4)	I didn't really understand the exercise and I don't feel that this is a skill I need
	Use a more open mind in future for learning in a different way	
	A flexible and creative way to deliver messages about sustainability	

Note ×2, ×3, ×4, etc., indicates the number of similar comments

from this learning experience and 23% were either negative or they questioned the value of this virtual world pedagogy. These findings are based on the 51 supportive comments and 12 non-supportive comments as listed in Table 2.4.

Online Survey

At semester end, students were offered the opportunity to comment about this virtual world learning experience in a confidential, non-assessable survey. Students were emailed a *Survey Monkey* URL providing access to a 15-min online questionnaire. The eight, five-point Likert scale questions were framed to understand student engagement with the virtual world learning experience. Answer options were: Not Sure, Very Little, OK, Quite Helpful and Excellent. An open comment field was attached to each question to receive any further comments. Of the class cohort of 28, five surveys were completed (response rate = 18%).

Table 2.5 summarises the survey questions and responses. The first two questions are concerned about whether or not students found the Second Life activity helpful

Table 2.5 Summary of online survey questions and responses in EV2011 s Life learning activity

Question	Positive comments	Negative comments
How did you find the Second Life activity?	Helpful—3 respondents	Not helpful—2 respondents
What do you feel you learnt from the Second Life activity?	Learnt about sustainability—4 respondents	Learnt very little about sustainability—1 respondent
How well did the Second Life activity assist in achieving subject learning outcomes?	Met in a small way —3 respondents Met quite well—2 respondents	
How well did the Second Life activity assist in achieving graduate attributes?	Met in a small way —2 respondents Met quite well—2 respondents	Not met—1 respondent

for sustainability learning. Seventy per cent indicated it was helpful and 30% unhelpful. However, in questions seven and eight of the survey, students were asked about how well the activity assisted them achieve the subject's learning outcomes and graduate attributes. Ninety per cent felt the activity was helpful, and 10% felt it was not. In summary, students evidently found this to be a positive learning experience and data from student ePortfolios and the online survey indicate the activity assisted students meet the subject's learning outcomes and graduate attributes.

Observed Learner Engagement

The degree of learner engagement with Second Life in *EV2011* was primarily gauged through tutor in-class observations and conversations with students. Most students were open to the new platform and ready to engage. Within the first half hour of the first tutorial, over 90% of students were positive about exploring and learning in Second Life and actively engaged. As the classes progressed, however, interacting with Second Life became challenging for some students, particularly mature age students with limited IT skills. Approximately 40% expressed annoyance and frustration about sustainability learning in a virtual world platform. One-to-one tutor support and peer-to-peer learning had alleviated most frustrations by the end of the first tutorial. Ten per cent of the student cohort expressed annoyance at having to engage with Second Life and questioned the validity of learning about sustainability in a virtual world.

Discussion

This section will focus on the profile of the student cohort, choice of pedagogical design, student responses, learning outcomes achieved, the challenge of developing virtual world pedagogy using Second Life, possible future improvements to this pedagogy and JCU's research alignment.

The student cohort was challenged by this pedagogy. Students were asked to view sustainability learning from a new perspective, that of reviewer in an unfamiliar context. Learning comfort zones were stretched. The virtual world learning format was completely foreign to all students as 100% of the cohort were new to Second Life and most were not computer 'gamers'. Students were from disparate backgrounds and had wide ranging computer skills. Student ages and life experiences in the *EV2011* cohort were diverse, ranging from direct high school graduates (20%), young mature age students with ages ranging from early 20s to 35 (30%), mature midlife students aged from 35 to 60 (40%), to retiree aged students over 60 (10%). All students were passionate about sustainability and keen to learn and communicate sustainability to the wider community.

To facilitate learning ease, pedagogy utilising a blended learning environment proved effective. The theoretical framework was a combination of Warburton's considerations for teaching and learning in a virtual world, which established a CoI learning space and encouraged communal constructivist learning. Pedagogy involved stepped introduction of content, one-to-one support and peer-to-peer learning. Class time focused on developing effective in-world communication skills and formalising work teams to assist students' in-world socialisation and collaboration.

In the first tutorial demonstration and instruction segment, just under half the students displayed varying levels of apprehension about the usefulness of this learning activity and some were concerned about their ability to engage with Second Life as a learning platform. This was revealed in students' questions, comments and even body language. Prior discussion about the benefits and discomforts of the learning activity could perhaps have eased this learning transition from real world to a virtual world. As the first tutorial progressed, students became familiar with the virtual world medium and the exploratory learning mode and most were impressed with the depth of sustainability information and the global connectivity provided by Second Life. We believe the establishment of a CoI assisted this process. Frustrations visibly lessened as tutorials progressed, mainly as a result of the one-to-one in class assistance provided by the tutors and because of peer-to-peer communication. However, some resistance and a lack of resonance to learning in a virtual world were evident. Approximately 10% of the cohort continued to express frustration as they engaged with content. As noted above, this was also expressed in some negative survey comments.

Assessable learning tasks focused students' exploratory learning and provided data about student engagement with the learning activity. Students benefited from knowledge sharing as each group prepared their written review and delivered an oral presentation using *PowerPoint*. Students compared two virtual worlds for their ability to support EforSD. Both these assessments demonstrated that students had achieved a high level of engagement with the sustainability issues presented in Second Life. In future *EV2011* learning, the oral presentation—knowledge sharing with the whole cohort—will precede the written review to facilitate greater peer-to-peer learning. The written review may also be set as an individual task to consolidate reflective and critical thinking.

Online survey responses provided rather ambiguous feedback perhaps in part because of the low number of respondents. Nevertheless, it was valuable to solicit non-assessable student feedback about feelings and thoughts, benefits gained, motivation to engage and satisfaction derived (López-Pérez et al. 2011). The honest confidential student feedback about the quality of learning engagement in Second Life has assisted the subject coordinator in making pedagogical adjustments to ensure successful learning transactions (Warbuton 2009). The low response rate to the online survey was disappointing but not surprising. Nevertheless, the limited data from the survey impacted on the adaptive management capacity (learning by doing) of the subject (Domask 2007), where the intention is to review and adapt the subject partly in response to student feedback. In future *EV2011* delivery, the online survey will be a compulsory component of the virtual world assessment task and will be included in a later tutorial.

Using Second Life as a teaching and learning platform was new to both authors. Initial low-level resistance to engaging with Second Life to develop pedagogy had to be overcome by the first author (a non-gamer). Second Life is an Internet-based immersive environment suitable for education, and while it is not a game (Dawley 2009), it can be viewed from a gamer's perspective. Interestingly, White's 2007 manual Second Life—*A Guide to Your Virtual World*—supported the first author's transition to thinking and working within a virtual world to develop the virtual world pedagogy. Familiarity with Second Life led to excitement about the potential offered by Second Life for learning about sustainability. The teaching and learning experience was rewarding, and additional improvements for future delivery of this virtual world pedagogy are an on-going conversation.

Development of this virtual world pedagogy and learning aligns with one of James Cook University's learning and teaching priorities, that is, to support EfSD. This learning activity also aligns with the JCU's Strategic Intent, 'A brighter future for life in the tropics, world-wide', and through use of technology in a blended learning environment to develop critical thinking and problem-solving skills. This blended learning format is also consistent with global higher education teaching and learning values (Garrison and Kanuka 2004). An added value of learning in a virtual world is that continued and lifelong learning is supported through access to the Second Life platform by students' post course work (Gregory 2011).

Conclusion

This virtual world blended learning environment created team-based exploratory learning through review and comparison of sustainability centric virtual worlds to enhance critical thinking and problem-solving for real-world sustainability. The pedagogy followed Warburton's (2009) virtual world teaching and learning considerations to develop a Community of Inquiry learning space (Garrison and Kanuka 2004), and it resembled Girvan and Savage's (2010) communal constructivism learning. Student grades for the virtual world learning activity, feedback on learning and teaching in *EV2011*, and in-class conversations between tutors and students confirmed that learning in a virtual world platform supports knowledge sharing between students and enhances creative thinking and problem-solving. Students were introduced to the power of networking in a virtual world and to global connections of sustainability advocates. Overall, the authors contend that this learning activity enhanced students' capacity for sustainability, and they acknowledge and value the contribution this virtual world pedagogy has made in achieving *EV2011's* subject learning outcomes and graduate attributes.

The major factor contributing to a successful student learning experience within this virtual world blended learning study was the stepped introduction of content to better engage the diverse class cohort and to create a Community of Inquiry learning space. To enhance future delivery of *EV2011,* it will be important to put more emphasis on promoting the learning activity to students through discussion of the benefits of participation, addressing any discomforts students may have, and in carrying out further research as to how to maximise learning in this format. The suggested minor changes to assessment tasks should improve student engagement with learning outcomes and graduate attributes.

This blended learning project has been very valuable professionally, from a teacher and a researcher perspective, and we believe from a student perspective. An innovative sustainability discourse that incorporates an online teaching–learning platform is readily available through a virtual world. Some of these spaces are an online representation of real-world sustainability projects, linking the virtual and physical. In addition, this virtual world pedagogy provided ready access to professional global sustainability networks and valuable new ideas for sustainability pedagogy.

Acknowledgements The authors would like to thank the 2013 students in EV2011 The Case for Sustainability at James Cook University, Cairns, Australia, for their willingness to participate in an experiment of innovative learning for sustainability.

References

Ahmad, N. S. H. N., Wan, T. R., & Jiang, P. (2011). Immersive environment courseware evaluation. *Procedia—Social and Behavioral Sciences, 15,* 1667–1676. doi:10.1016/j.sbspro.2011.03.350.

Cortese, A. D., & McDonough, W. (2001). Accelerating the transition to sustainability through higher education. Retrieved from http://www.mma.gov.br/port/sdi/ea/deds/arqs/antcort_wilmcdon.pdf.

Dawley, L. (2009). Social network knowledge construction: Emerging virtual world pedagogy. *On the Horizon, 17*(2), 109–121.

Domask, J. J. (2007). Achieving goals in higher education: An experiential approach to sustainability studies. *International Journal of Sustainability in Higher Education, 8*(1), 53–68.

Garrison, D. R., & Kanuka, H. (2004). Blended learning: Uncovering its transformative potential in higher education. *The Internet and Higher Education, 7*(2), 95–105. doi:10.1016/j.iheduc.2004.02.001.

Girvan, C., & Savage, T. (2010). Identifying an appropriate pedagogy for virtual worlds: A communal constructivism case study. *Computers & Education, 55*(1), 342–349.

Gregory, S. (2011). Teaching higher education students with diverse learning outcomes in the virtual world of Second Life. In R. Hinrichs & C. Wankel (Eds.), *Transforming virtual world learning, cutting-edge technologies in higher education* (Vol. 4, pp. 333–362). Teynampet India: Emerald Group Publishing Limited.

Jarmon, L., Traphagan, T., Mayrath, M., & Trivedi, A. (2009). Virtual world teaching, experiential learning, and assessment: An interdisciplinary communication course in Second Life. *Computers & Education, 53*(1), 169–182.

Kozan, K., & Richardson, J. C. (2014). Interrelationships between and among social, teaching, and cognitive presence. *The Internet and Higher Education, 21,* 68–73. doi:10.1016/j.iheduc.2013.10.007.

Linden Reserach Inc. (2016). Start Your Second Life in June 2003. Retrieved from http://www.lindenlab.com/releases/start-your-second-life-in-june-2003.

López-Pérez, M. V., Pérez-López, M. C., & Rodríguez-Ariza, L. (2011). Blended learning in higher education: Students' perceptions and their relation to outcomes. *Computers & Education, 56*(3), 818–826. doi:10.1016/j.compedu.2010.10.023.

Lorenzo, C.-M., Ángel Sicilia, M., & Sánchez, S. (2012). Studying the effectiveness of multi-user immersive environments for collaborative evaluation tasks. *Computers & Education*.

Orr, D. W. (1996). Educating for the environment: Higher education's challenge of the next century. *The Journal of Environmental Education, 27*(3), 7–10.

Raes, A., Schellens, T., De Wever, B., & Vanderhoven, E. (2012). Scaffolding information problem solving in web-based collaborative inquiry learning. *Computers & Education, 59*(1), 82–94.

Reiners, T., Gregory, S., & Dreher, H. (2011). Educational assessment in virtual world environments. In J.D. Yorke (Ed.), *ATN Assessment Conference 2011: Meeting the Challenges* (pp. 132–140). Perth, Western Australia: Curtin University. Retrieved from http://otl.curtin.edu.au/atna2011/files/ATNA_2011_Proceedings.pdf.

Sipos, Y., Battisti, B., & Grimm, K. (2008). Achieving transformative sustainability learning: Engaging head, hands and heart. *International Journal of Sustainability in Higher Education, 9* (1), 68–86.

Siragusa, L., Dixon, K. C., & Dixon, R. (2007). Designing quality e-learning environments in higher education. *Proceedings Ascilite Singapore* (pp. 923–935).

Traphagan, T. W., Chiang, Y.-H. V., Chang, H. M., Wattanawaha, B., Lee, H., Mayrath, M. C., et al. (2010). Cognitive, social and teaching presence in a virtual world and a text chat. *Computers & Education, 55*(3), 923–936.

Warburton, S. (2009). Second Life in higher education: Assessing the potential for and the barriers to deploying virtual worlds in learning and teaching. *British Journal of Educational Technology, 40*(3), 414–426. doi:10.1111/j.1467-8535.2009.00952.x.
White, B. (2007). *Second life: A guide to your virtual world.* Indiana, USA: Que Publishing.
Yalcinalp, S., Sen, N., Kocer, G., & Koroglu, F. (2012). Higher education student's behaviors as avatars in a web based course in second life. *Procedia-Social and Behavioral Sciences, 46,* 4534–4538.

Author Biographies

Marcia Thorne is a PhD student in the School of Education at James Cook University in Cairns, Australia, and is employed as a research officer and tutor in the Bachelor of Sustainability. Marcia returned to university studies in 2008 to complete a Bachelor of Education (Professional Development) and a Master of Education (Sustainability) after a career in teaching and as an IT business owner and company director. Marcia's PhD research mirrors her lifelong commitment to conservation and preservation of the natural environment and looks to understand what ethic of care for the environment is developed in today's adolescents through formal education.

Colin Macgregor has worked as a sustainability practitioner and researcher in government agencies, as well as the corporate sector, for almost 20 years. He completed his PhD at James Cook University (JCU) in Sustainable Development in 2002 before joining the University of St Andrews where he established an undergraduate degree program in Sustainable Development. Colin returned to Australia and the University of Western Australia in 2006 but rejoined JCU as a Senior Lecturer in 2012 to establish and coordinate JCU's Bachelor of Sustainability. Colin also chairs JCU's Sustainability Action Group and is a member of the University's Sustainability Advisory Committee.

Chapter 3
Intercultural Competence and Virtual Worlds

Debbie Corder and Alice U-Mackey

Introduction

The wide use of virtual worlds, such as Second Life, in education reflects their effectiveness for experiential activities and discovery learning. Studies show, however, that despite growing evidence of their efficacy for engaging and promoting learning, there are issues with students' negative perceptions, anxiety and resistance (Childs and Peachey 2013; Dalgarno et al. 2011; Warburton 2009), which indicate that it cannot be assumed that all students will adapt to these virtual environments. Second Life, for example, has its own culture and subcultures, identities, language and social practices, as well as the culture inherent in the application of the technology itself. Interacting in the culturally diverse Second Life environment involves a process of cross-cultural adaptation, requiring attributes of intercultural competence such as flexibility, resilience, respect for different perspectives and communication styles, and critical awareness of one's values and beliefs Corder and U-Mackey 2015.

However, research shows that these attributes of intercultural competence will not automatically develop by merely encountering a different cultural environment; they need to be intentionally developed (Deardorff 2011; Stier 2006). Studies such as the one by Salt et al. (2008) show that the demands of Second Life technology could impact on motivation and engagement, and attention is paid to preparing students for the technological challenges. It would seem, therefore, that there is an

Alice U-Mackey, retired

D. Corder (✉) · A. U-Mackey
Auckland University of Technology, Auckland, New Zealand
e-mail: dcorder@aut.ac.nz

A. U-Mackey
e-mail: alice.sawu@gmail.com

S. Gregory and D. Wood (eds.), *Authentic Virtual World Education*,
https://doi.org/10.1007/978-981-10-6382-4_3

equal need to prepare students for the emotional and behavioural challenges of an environment that is, perceptually and conceptually, so culturally different from what many are used to.

This chapter explores the symbiotic synergies between the affordances of virtual worlds for intercultural competence development and the need for intercultural competence for effective engagement in virtual worlds. It is based on action research on the efficacies of using Second Life to develop intercultural competence in an undergraduate intercultural competence module at a New Zealand university. Case studies of student experiences in Second Life are used to gain a deeper understanding of the challenges faced by students, different ways in which they might manage their emotional and behavioural reactions to the challenges, and what is needed in addition to technical preparation and support, in order for them to engage more effectively in the virtual environment for the required learning to take place.

Characteristics of Intercultural Competence

As outlined by Spitzberg and Changnon (2009), there are many models and frameworks for intercultural competence, and the construct is debated and challenged from various theoretical stances. This can present problems for the research practitioner who needs to apply the construct for learning and teaching. However, according to an extensive study by Spitzberg and Changnon (2009), a good model should include common intercultural competence elements such as motivation (attitude, values, beliefs), knowledge (cultural, theoretical), skills (flexibility, openness), context (relational/conflict management, environment) and outcomes (critical self-assessment, awareness of identity, maintaining relationships). They also identify the common goal as being "the appropriate and effective management of interaction between people who, to some degree or another, represent different or divergent affective, cognitive, and behavioural orientations to the world" (Spitzberg and Changnon 2009, p. 7).

Models developed for teaching by Byram (2008) and Deardorff (2011) have been influential, particularly in language learning and teaching. Both models contain the common intercultural competence elements identified by Spitzberg and Changnon (2009). According to these models, the characteristics of the interculturally competent person include flexibility, adaptability, being able to move out of one's comfort zone and cope with uncertainty. A fundamental element in both these models is critical cultural self-awareness of one's own culture, and how culture, underpinned by values, beliefs and norms, influences one's identity, worldviews, behaviour and use of language. Without this ability to question and analyse one's own cultural framework, it is not possible to understand and respect personal and cultural differences, be open to multiple perspectives and develop the necessary behavioural characteristics or outcomes. However, Witte (2011) believes that for critical cultural self-awareness to develop, the assumptions underlying one's values and beliefs must be challenged.

Intercultural Competence Pedagogy

A number of researchers, such as Kohonen (2005) and Witte (2011), recommend an experiential, explorative and holistic pedagogical approach for intercultural competence teaching, learning and assessment. This approach encompasses socio-constructivist and sociocultural theories in order to address affect, attitudes and construction of identity and knowledge, and allow for the differing worldviews of students. Intercultural interactions and experiences need to be relevant, and there should be opportunities for discussion and critical reflection (Deardorff 2011; Kohonen 2005; Witte 2011). Witte (2011) maintains that collaborative and explorative activities facilitate construction of knowledge, challenge learners to analyse and interpret, find connections, discover cultural patterns and evaluate the new knowledge in relation to their own cultural frameworks. Collaborative and explorative activities are reliant on rich learning experiences such as group work, tandem work, critical incidents and virtual classrooms. Such activities enable the development of awareness of differences, similarities of cultural constructs and underlying values, beliefs and norms.

Intercultural Competence and the Affordances of Second Life

In view of the characteristics of intercultural competence and the recommended pedagogical approach, Second Life offers a rich authentic experiential and explorative environment for developing intercultural competence. There is a wide range of cultural environments for social interaction, language practice, cultural exploration and exposure to diverse cultural perspectives (Corder and U 2010; Corder and U-Mackey 2015; Diehl and Prins 2008; Warburton 2009; Ward 2010). Research shows that the creation and use of an avatar can be a powerful catalyst for self-awareness and self-assessment by highlighting the role of verbal and non-verbal communication, cultural variations in proxemics, and raising awareness of self and identity through exploration and evaluation of presentation of self (Corder and U-Mackey 2015; Diehl and Prins 2008; Twining 2009; Yee and Bailenson 2007).

According to Warburton (2009), the nature of the Second Life environment with its own codes, norms, language and social etiquette when establishing relationships, and the fluidity of identities and relatively no boundaries on behaviour, simulates the dynamic nature of cross-cultural encounters and can create symptoms of culture shock. Ward (2010, p. 4) found that as "newbies", students can have positive experiences of integration and assimilation, and negative ones of segregation and marginalisation. Learning to manage what can be intense emotions, and even psychological stress associated with culture shock, is invaluable intercultural competence preparation for encountering different cultures in both virtual worlds and the real world. However, for some students, it can prove too destabilising and lead to resistance and even non-participation. This could explain various negative student reactions, ranging from disapproval and suspicion to even fear that Childs and Peachey (2013) describe from various studies. If, as research indicates, intercultural competence does not develop automatically when encountering difference, knowing how students can be supported to engage with Second Life for learning to take place is a critical factor for educators.

The Intercultural Competence Module

The intercultural competence module on which this research is based was developed because of the increasing recognition of the need for intercultural competence to be a graduate attribute. The module ran for three hours a week over 12 weeks. Two hours were in class for experiential activities and theory and one in the computer room for online activities such as guided blog reflections and then for group work when it was introduced. It was offered in the BA International Studies major as a compulsory module for International Studies major students and as an elective for other majors across the university. The pedagogical approach in the module combined Kolb's (1984) experiential learning model and a hybrid of intercultural competence models largely influenced by the Byram (1997; 2008) and Deardorff (2011) models that were developed for teaching intercultural competence. Concepts from other models, such as Bennett's (1993) Developmental Model of Intercultural Sensitivity (DMIS), were used. The DMIS has a useful concept of stages of managing difference, ranging from ethnocentrism through to ethnorelativism.

In the first six weeks of the semester, students were introduced to intercultural competence theory and tools for intercultural competence development through experiential learning activities. Sociocultural and sociolinguistic theoretical concepts were introduced following the experiential activities. Reflection skills, situated in guided weekly blogs with lecturer and peer feedback, were developed using the Describe, Interpret and Evaluate (DIE) framework (Kohls 1996). Second Life was introduced to all the students as an example of a different culture, to illustrate concepts such as stereotyping and ethnocentrism. Students were also shown examples of Second Life as a medium for discovery learning in a number of disciplines ranging from sciences to language and culture learning. Some affordances for developing intercultural competence were explained.

In the last six weeks of the semester, group work was introduced as an experiential learning and assessment tool, supported by the usual learning and teaching classroom activities. Reflection on the group work process as well as evidence of research and interaction were recorded weekly in guided wikis, again with feedback from lecturers and peers. Students explored and reflected on their own and their group members' worldviews in the context of themes or sociocultural issues structured around four questions that they were helped to develop. They also evaluated their ability to establish and maintain relationships with their groups. Each group could choose a medium, such as film, print or Second Life, to explore their themes. Second Life was typically chosen for its affordances to explore and research concepts such as identity and presentation of self in real life compared to Second Life, or meeting people and making friends. Suggested readings on Second Life were provided. Because of the nature of Second Life, it involved more experiential engagement than with mediums such as film or print used by other groups. However, the technological demands were kept to a minimum, and the students only had to master the basic skills of walking, flying, teleporting, friendship offers, searching and communicating through voice, local text chat and instant messages. They could access Second Life in the time-tabled computer hour and also had an extra two-hour tutorial with a teaching assistant as required. Usually, only one group per semester has chosen to use Second Life.

Students' intercultural competence learning and development from the module were assessed through a mid-semester reflective essay based on their blogs and a reflective essay and group presentation at the end of the semester. In both the reflective essay and group presentation, students had to evaluate their own intercultural competence learning and development from their research, and how they managed the challenges and opportunities of group interaction. This evaluation had to be supported by evidence of learning recorded in their weekly wiki reflections on their group work. The Second Life groups were assessed in the same way; they were not assessed on their technological skills in Second Life.

Case Studies

Intercultural competence development is very individual and involves content and processual competencies (Stier 2006). The rationale for using a case study approach to evaluate intercultural competence development is that it provides "richness of description and detailed contextualisation" (Duff 2008, p. 59). This, as Merriam (2009, p. 46) notes, can give insights into information "to which we would not otherwise have access". The case studies in this chapter are based on two groups of students who chose to use Second Life for their group work. Data for the case studies are both qualitative, including student introspection and evidence of achieving the learning outcomes, (blogs and wikis) and quantitative (frequency of posts in blogs and wikis).

The students in the case studies (Table 3.1) were culturally diverse and represented a range of ethnicities, gender, majors and experiences in virtual worlds. As can be seen, Group 1 included two international students. It is unusual to have international students using Second Life; international students tend to prefer interacting in the physical or real world with New Zealand people and culture rather than spend time in a virtual world. No student had prior experience of Second Life. The names of the students are pseudonyms.

Both groups of students chose the theme "Identity and presentation of self in Second Life". The students explored how they portrayed themselves in Second Life through their choices and adaptations of their avatars, their behaviour in interactions

Table 3.1 Student profiles

	Ethnicity	Domestic/International	Experience of virtual worlds	Major
Group 1				
Charles	Fijian/New Zealander	Domestic	World of Warcraft and others	Languages
Yvonne	Japanese	International	None	English
Zoe	Chinese	International	None	English
Group 2				
Rachel	Maori & Pasifika	Domestic	None	Social Sciences
Felix	Eastern European	Domestic	Experienced	Social Sciences
Stacey	New Zealander	Domestic	None	Business
Kevin	New Zealander	Domestic	Limited	Languages

with others and their response to the Second Life environment itself. They met other avatars by visiting various cultural sites that had been suggested to them and a range of sites that they had searched for themselves, including bars and shops.

Each student case study described below starts with some background intercultural competence information on the student, from two blog reflections in the first half of the semester. Each student's reaction to a class culture shock experience (week 1) is briefly described, as well as their understanding of their values and cultural identity as a result of a number of experiential class activities (week 4). The class culture shock experience involved a ten-minute lecture in a language other than English. One group experienced Burmese and the other Dutch. The lecturers both looked Asian and used a PowerPoint presentation with illustrations and captions. The intention was for students to experience the unexpected and manage their reactions. They were not given any warning or explanation of what they were about to experience. After the ten-minute lecture, they were given guide questions and time to discuss the experience and their reactions. The experiential class activities in week 4 included ranking a selection of values and explaining the ranking to their classmates. The blog reflections showed that each student was at a different stage of intercultural competence development. This information provided useful insights for both the student and the lecturer, into subsequent reflections by each student on their Second Life experiences.

Group 1

Charles

It seemed that not understanding language and feeling out of place was the most significant emotion for Charles in the class culture shock situation. Family, friends and relationships were important to him, as was respect for authority, and his values were self-direction, achievement and security. His cultural identity was a mix of Fijian and European New Zealander. He came to New Zealand during his high school years, and he missed Fiji more than he had realised before using Second Life. His connections with Fiji together with his extensive experience in gaming strongly affected his perceptions of Second Life and consequent reactions.

Charles did not know what to expect from Second Life, but was curious as he was experienced in online games, and initially spent hours exploring it. However, he became very negative because he considered the graphics outdated and lacked visual appeal to him, and he was thrown because Second Life was completely different from what he was used to in virtual worlds. He realised that he needed to reserve judgement until he had learned more about Second Life, but his negativity was reinforced when he received a hostile reception when visiting a site that had been created to represent aspects of culture and society that someone had associated with "Fiji". Charles had searched for something that was familiar and which he could connect with his identity in real life, but what he found in the Second Life "Fiji" was the antithesis of the friendly, welcoming family orientation that he had associated and identified with Fijian culture.

Charles stalled in his intercultural competence development because he could not manage the challenges of the technological and cultural differences both in Second Life and in the real-life group dynamics. He could see that he stuck firmly to his values and beliefs and that his expectations could be "unrealistic and out of sync with that of my surroundings. Even in an artificial world created by humans for humans I cling to these wrongly and expect them to hold up". Additionally, he did not like group work and found establishing relationships problematic; he even named his avatar "Troublesome". He also found communicating with his group members, who were second language speakers of English, difficult and stressful. He perceived his experience in Second Life and with his real-life group as a threat to achieving academically. He acknowledged that he hated making mistakes, which would result in not making decisions or taking action. This might explain why he stalled in his intercultural competence development and never attempted to develop or apply any strategies to manage his negative emotions. Instead, he withdrew from Second Life, stopped regular self-reflection, stayed in his comfort zone and focused on working with the other two group members in real life.

Yvonne

Yvonne was confused and concerned during the class culture shock situation. Usually, she tried to fit in with new cultures and learn some of the languages, even if only greetings. Because the class culture shock situation had been totally unexpected, she had not been able to use her usual strategies. She was very aware of the effect of her body language in communication, and this, together with her values of tradition and security, were reflected in her choice of avatar, her respectful behaviour in Second Life and her choice of sites to visit. She chose to keep a default female avatar with black hair and wearing a simple dress, and made very few subsequent changes to clothing and appearance. An early foray in Second Life to a site representing "Tokyo" felt so familiar and safe that she just wanted to stay there. At the same time, she valued self-direction and, realising that she was being ethnocentric, pushed herself to explore because she was curious to see more and engage with difference.

She had initially thought that people in Second Life were dissatisfied with real life, but then believed there were similarities with the reason for the popularity of manga (Japanese cartoon books) and anime (Japanese movie or TV animations for both adults and children) in Japanese society. She continued to visit other sites that had been created to represent Japanese culture and society, and even though she thought some were not authentic enough and lacked reality, she enjoyed chatting to people there. This shift to more assertive behaviour in Second Life translated to uncharacteristic low context, direct behaviour in real life. For example, she summoned up the courage to ask Zoe what she thought of the Japanese in view of the tense relationships between China and Japan over World War II.

Zoe

Zoe attached great importance to being able to make cultural connections when faced with difference. Initially, she was comfortable in the class culture shock situation when the lecturer walked in, because she thought the lecturer looked Chinese. However, Zoe then felt confused and frightened when the language (Burmese) was incomprehensible, and she tried to make sense of the situation by looking at the lecturer's body language and visuals. Being from the Han province in China, to which Confucius belonged, Zoe's personal values of respect and conformity were influenced by Confucian values of morality, justice, harmony and sincerity. The simplified characters used in the writing system in mainland China were very meaningful for her cultural identity, conveying not just language but the values and beliefs of Chinese culture and tradition. Her need to be able to communicate effectively in interactions with others and her cultural identity strongly influenced her responses in Second Life.

Zoe thought Second Life was a time-wasting game, did not trust it and was impatient with the whole experience because it did not match her beliefs about academic study. She tried to hide her uncomfortable feelings about Second Life and was hurt when ignored by other avatars because she did not know how to initiate a conversation. At the same time, she had communication issues during discussions with her real-life group members. An early experience when she visited Second Life "China" was negative: she was shocked by what she thought was an inadequate portrayal of her country and felt that her culture was being marginalised because it was not possible to use simplified Chinese characters when chatting. This made her defensive and prevented her from identifying with anything in Second Life, and her visits to Second Life became infrequent.

However, through a process of honest reflection, she developed critical cultural awareness of her attitude and behaviour, emotions and values and beliefs. She realised that back in China, she had been uncertainty averse and would not do anything unless guaranteed success. Her choice of avatar could have reflected her fear of not achieving and in turn further prevented her from being able to engage with Second Life. Her avatar had not represented her own cultural identity, but what she believed represented western beauty. She was able to identify the influence of her values of harmony and respect. She could see that she had been trying very hard to manage her negative emotions for the good of the group and had not been wanting to burden the group members by discussing her experiences with them. As a result, she had not been going into Second Life enough. Following her increased awareness, she developed strategies to be more open and curious to face difference. She became more prepared to take risks and started to go into Second Life more frequently. Zoe came to realise that this new behaviour in fact reflected common characteristics in modern China because of recent social and cultural changes. This is something she had not realised yet by being in New Zealand and might not ever have realised had she not experienced Second Life. She resumed visits to Second Life and contributed more actively in real-life discussions.

Group 2

Rachel

Rachel's reaction to the class culture shock situation was annoyance and impatience, and a similar reaction was seen in her Second Life behaviour. Establishing relationships was very important to her. Not understanding Burmese prevented her from establishing a relationship with the lecturer, and the unexpected experience was a threat to her success in the module. She believed that her values were influenced by what she identified as her subcultures of being a parent, sister and Christian. However, unrestrained by her normal socially appropriate behaviour and appearance that she believed were necessary in order to be respected in real life, her persona and behaviour in Second Life were initially the complete opposite of her real-life self.

Rachel initially perceived Second Life as a community of "losers" who could not face reality and she thought it was acceptable to behave badly towards everyone. When she experienced repeated rejection, she changed her avatar from male to a robot and then a female. However, the female was overly provocative and resulted in amorous responses from other avatars that she had not intended to encourage. She took longer to change her provocative behaviour and offensive communication style, despite going from being irritated by being ignored, to feeling sorry for her avatar as it was always alone. Finally, overcome by feelings of rejection by the very community she had pre-judged so negatively, she realised she needed to change her behaviour if she was to interact and have fun like her group members: "I wanted to feel included. I changed my behaviour and the way I approached residents".

She learned the need to assess her behaviour to suit the context and be more accepting of difference as can be seen from her comment that "people won't necessarily behave or react in the way I assume". She also learnt that she had to adapt her behaviour and communication style from being "rude, conceited and condescending, to what would be acceptable to Second Life culture" in order to form relationships in Second Life. It took several weeks for this learning to take place. This delay might be attributed to her infrequent reflection on her Second Life experiences, which prevented her from processing them effectively, as well as not wanting to ask group members for help in both real life and Second Life. By the end of the group work, however, it could be seen that through her Second Life experience, she was able to see the implications, in both real life and Second Life, of not adapting behaviour to the context.

Felix

From the class culture shock situation, Felix noticed that he did not cope well in an environment in which he did not understand what was going on. He felt uncomfortable and confused and began to lose interest. As an immigrant to New Zealand, he was aware of the need to adapt behaviour according to the various subcultures he belonged to and had known that there was more than one way of doing things and not just the way he had been used to. He identified with the culture of his birth, which he still referred to as "back home". His values were influenced by his Christian faith and family came first. All these factors could be seen to influence his eventual adaptation to Second Life.

Felix was an experienced user of virtual worlds, but his experiences in Second Life were not what he had expected them to be. These experiences were both positive and negative, and some surprised him. His experiences with Second Life residents were mostly positive: he found them friendlier than he had found people in real life and was impressed that they were non-judgemental towards his rabbit and then unicorn avatar. To his great surprise, he felt a strong connection with the culture of his birth when he visited his "home country" and wanted to see if there were more sites representing his cultural values and norms. Nevertheless, he still thought Second Life was silly compared to virtual worlds he was used to, so pushed the boundaries with unacceptable behaviour to see what reactions he would get. When asked to behave in a more acceptable way by Second Life residents, he realised that even though it was a virtual world, there were still norms and social expectations, many of which were similar to those in the real world, as well as the potential to be affected by others' attitude and behaviour. He was unexpectedly very hurt when laughed at for mixing up Italian words when trying to communicate with French speaking avatars, and consequently judged all French people as being rude in both real life and Second Life. He grew increasingly negative because he had thought he would have no difficulties in Second Life but actually, he could not apply all his understanding and beliefs from his gaming experience. This negativity affected his further forays into Second Life and his participation in the real-life group work.

Following discussion with his lecturer on his reflections in his wiki on his experiences, Felix began to question his attitude and behaviour. He realised he needed to overcome his interpretation of Second Life to truly understand what it was all about. In fact, he recognised that Second Life "was a truly unique learning curve not just about the people playing it but about myself as well". He saw himself as avoiding the unfamiliar if it compromised his achievements and not being open to new things. He realised that he could be very prejudiced and quick to make value judgements. He finally changed his avatar to a "proper person" and adapted his behaviour so he could develop relationships with the Second Life community and also began to collaborate more in his real-life group work.

Stacey

Stacey joined the course late and missed the class culture shock situation. She was an example of a student who did not appear to have experienced huge challenges from the Second Life environment. She expected Second Life would be different but had an open mind because she had had prior experience in an underdeveloped country and had encountered extreme cultural difference. She did not fully identify with her New Zealand national culture but more with her religion, which represented strength, perseverance and a higher power. This influenced her values and beliefs. She valued family very strongly, along with achievement because of family expectations.

However, achievement was not positively valenced as she hated studying and valued personal growth and development more. She could see the value of engaging in Second Life for intercultural competence development even though she found it cliquey. She felt shyer approaching people in Second Life than in real life and had been ignored. However, she persisted and finally "cracked the norms" of communication: "usually it would start with making a comment on something that was happening in your surroundings", which she realised was actually similar to what she would do in real life. She had assumed it would be different. Her avatar represented her ideal body, and changing her appearance in Second Life seemed no different from what she did in real life by adding hair extensions, wearing makeup and different clothes. She said she had learnt a lot about herself from exploring Second Life that she intended to transfer to interaction in real life, particularly managing her responses to variations in behaviour. However, changes in her behaviour were not as evident as they were with the other students in real-life group interactions.

Kevin

Kevin, a mature student with a degree and in a mixed-race relationship, was comfortable interacting with people from other cultures, so did not feel too uncomfortable when faced with the culture shock situation. In his personal life, he had been facing internal conflict in terms of his values and norms, which had been influenced by his following of heavy metal and the culture of nonconformity in the past. Now, he was in a relationship that required new values of conformity and family responsibilities. He had been having difficulty identifying with a national New Zealand culture, and once in Second Life, he realised that he had multiple cultural identities and was switching between them. This could explain why he moved relatively easily to a Second Life identity.

Kevin provided an excellent example of cultural adaptation and integration. He was able to effectively draw on his prior experiences of different cultures and applied the intercultural theory and tools from the module to further his intercultural competence. He tried to understand the Second Life culture and adapt by making friends, realising that body language in Second Life, like folding arms, was not necessarily intended standoffishness as it is seen to be in real life, but possibly technology-related. He observed his surroundings closely and gradually changed his avatar to be more acceptable: "As I learn more about the cultural norms of Second Life, my avatar will undoubtably (sic) change allowing me to express my own self within the culture". He developed a greater understanding of the connection between cultural assumption and language in communication, even through the choice of a name for his avatar. A number of Second Life users he met had rejected him because of his avatar's name, which was a mixture of numbers and letters in the name. Kevin had chosen the name because, for him, it was a reference to a Japanese art house film that he had liked. When he had been a member of a cyberpunk forum, names like this were normal, but in Second Life, it had the meaning of "griefer" or someone who harasses other avatars.

Because his new values of conformity and responsibility emphasised academic success, he was very motivated and quickly became the group leader. He led by being a role model, engaging in Second Life and posting frequent wiki reflections. He overcame prejudice to establish relationships with Second Life residents because it enabled him to meet the aims of the group work. Critically reflecting on this process of needing to understand and respect different perspectives in Second Life more also benefited his relationship with real-life group members. He came to understand that his frustration with his group members was the result of his own expectations of what was required for group work. He had considered that they were not contributing sufficiently and needed to engage more.

Summary of Student Intercultural Competence Development

Each student experienced respective shifts in their intercultural competence. They all developed a deeper understanding of their own identities and underlying values and beliefs that influenced their behaviour. However, they varied in the extent to which they applied their understanding to develop strategies and adapt their behaviour, both in Second Life and in real life. It would seem that there is a complex interplay between the extent of engagement in the group work process: forays into Second Life, frequent reflections and willingness to develop strategies to apply learning in Second Life and in real life. Although it is beyond the scope of this chapter to compare results with non-Second Life users, it is worth noting that the depth of critical awareness achieved by these Second Life users was more significant and dramatic than that achieved by non-Second Life users.

Bennett's (1993) DMIS concept provides a useful tool to plot the students' intercultural competence development. The initial stages in the DMIS are ethnocentric stages of denial, defence and minimisation of difference. In these stages, an individual's own worldview determines interpretation of reality, and behaviour can include stereotyping and denigration. The final stages are ethnorelative stages of acceptance, adaptation and integration. The acceptance to adaptation stages are achieved when one is able to add different worldviews to one's own, and adaptation

Table 3.2 DMIS stages and student intercultural competence development

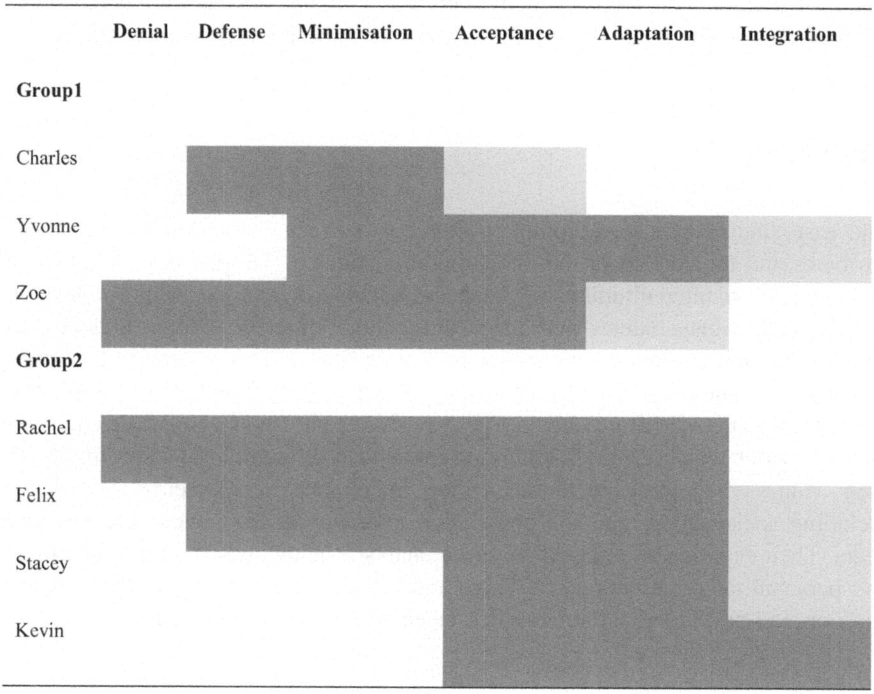

to integration occurs when one is able to move comfortably between different worldviews. In these stages, there is recognition of other interpretations of reality and understanding of one's own values and beliefs. These stages are used in Table 3.2 to provide a visual summary of the students' intercultural competence development. Light grey indicates threshold achievement and dark grey, achievement.

Charles started with defence, progressed to minimisation but stalled at the threshold of acceptance. He identified his intercultural competence weaknesses but was not willing yet to develop strategies to change, and remained in his comfort zone in both Second Life and real life. Yvonne and Zoe, both international students, could be perceived as having a high level of intercultural competence because they chose to come to New Zealand to study in a different cultural and linguistic environment. However, both reacted and managed differences differently. Yvonne started with minimisation of differences in Second Life and demonstrated adaptation and threshold integration. She used skills learnt in Second Life to interact more effectively in real life. This could be seen in her using a more confident low context, communication style usual in New Zealand, with group members. Zoe started with denial and progressed through acceptance to adaptation. Adaptation was more evident in her real-life interaction with group members than in Second Life.

Rachel started with denial and achieved adaptation, while Felix went from the defence stage to threshold integration. It took them longer to reach the ethnorelative stages in Second Life and also in real-life group interaction than the other group members. Stacey and Kevin both entered at the acceptance stage and moved quickly to adaptation. However, Kevin engaged much more in Second Life and critical reflection and demonstrated more depth in his intercultural competence learning and development in Second Life and real-life interaction than Stacey.

Discussion

The case studies indicate a complex interplay between intercultural competence attributes and the context of the intercultural encounters. Despite prior knowledge and preparation, intercultural competence did not always manifest itself nor develop automatically when students were faced with cultural difference. Some students had positive experiences, but there were many negative ones. Their reactions echo many of those in studies described by Childs and Peachey (2013) and Ward (2010) and are symptomatic of culture shock. These reactions and management of emotions and behaviour were very individual and influenced by complex factors involving their values, beliefs, expectations, prior intercultural competence experience including socialisation, and the preparation and support from their lecturers and peers. Their experiences and responses are analysed below, based on the situational and personal factors identified by Paige and Goode (2009) that can cause intense emotion and psychological stress when faced with cultural differences.

Cultural Difference and Ethnocentrism

The more negatively one evaluates cultural differences, the greater the stress (Paige and Goode 2009). All the students had preconceptions based on value judgements, some more negative than others. Experienced gamers, Felix and Charles, felt very negative towards the Second Life environment because of what they were used to in other virtual worlds, and this made it more difficult for them to adapt to Second Life. They felt disdain for what they judged to be outdated graphics compared to what they were used to in other virtual worlds, and were disconcerted by the absence of clear rules. Yvonne and Zoe searched for sites that represented their culture during their initial experiences of Second Life. Yvonne found it very comforting when she found cultural similarities with her own culture. When she later found some sites that she judged to be non-authentic, she did not seem to suffer any negative emotions. This was possible because her initial experiences in Second Life had been very positive, so she had become sufficiently relaxed in the environment and was able to engage. In contrast, Zoe judged the portrayal of her culture very negatively and she experienced strong negative emotions towards the environment. This seemed to reinforce her initial perceptions of Second Life, which had been negative, and she then found trying to interact in Second Life extremely stressful.

Being able to identify and reflect critically on both positive and negative value judgements is a key intercultural competence tool to manage responses to cultural difference (Byram 1997, 2008).

Reflecting in their wikis helped students to process their behaviour and attitudes and to identify ethnocentric value judgements that had caused denial and defensiveness and had made the experiences threatening. Each student sooner or later worked on strategies to shift to being more open and accepting of different perspectives and behaviour in Second Life, and significantly, also used them to make their interactions in real life more effective. The exception was Charles who stalled at the point of realising the implications of his value judgements of Second Life. He needed more time to overcome his natural averseness to making mistakes and get to the stage where he was able or willing to work on strategies to deal with his emotions.

Cultural Immersion, Isolation and Language

All interaction involves interpretation and negotiation of meaning, verbally and non-verbally. In the Second Life environment, many of the usual body language cues are not possible, so the implications of how much body language is relied on in real life for communication of meaning seem to be intensified. Interaction required persistence and resilience, and students found it demanding and often confusing. Drawing on their knowledge of linguistic principles of interaction, Kevin and Stacey persisted in engaging with Second Life right from the start and kept trying to establish relationships to be accepted as in-group members. Others like Rachel ignored linguistic cues and experienced isolation until almost the end of the group work.

Visibility and Invisibility, and Status

Finding something or somewhere that they could identify with and connect to their real-life identity, values and beliefs seemed an important catalyst for the students to engage constructively in Second Life. There was a need to feel part of an in-group and have shared experiences. When there was mismatch or clashes with their expectations, some were deeply affected emotionally. Managing identity issues they had not experienced in real life was challenging. Zoe could not believe that aspects of Chinese culture that she strongly identified with had been ignored. She felt discriminated against and became very emotional. Rachel, who did not think there was anything she could identify with in Second Life, created identities that did not represent her real-life identity. Consequently, she was faced with responses that she was inexperienced to manage, and ran away in fright when her excessively provocative female avatar was attacked.

Expectations, Power and Control

A different culture can cause feelings of loss of personal efficacy and can be problematic for those who value academic achievement or fear making mistakes. Charles and Felix did not seem to have very much advantage in Second Life from their extensive experience of gaming and like Zoe, had to manage their fear of making mistakes as they were faced with an unfamiliar culture. Anxiety over not being able to achieve well academically using Second Life motivated Kevin right from the start to find strategies to manage his anxiety and engage. It took longer for others to find strategies to manage their anxiety, and Charles disengaged from Second Life completely after a few weeks.

Prior Intercultural Experience

Prior intercultural experience can help reduce the stress when having to manage cultural difference. All the students had varying prior intercultural experiences and had been provided with intercultural theory and tools from the module. However, some students who appeared to effectively manage intercultural experiences in the classroom were challenged by those in Second Life. Their responses varied because each student was at a different stage of intercultural competence development, and because intercultural competence, being a contextual life-long learning process, is variable. International student Zoe had been demonstrating intercultural competence attributes of curiosity, openness, flexibility and resilience in real life. She was shocked by her emotional stress in Second Life and initially withdrew. However, through critical reflection, she developed greater awareness of her values and beliefs, and their impact on her attitude, emotions and behaviour not just in Second Life but also in real life.

Conclusion

The case studies show that the affordances of Second Life were very effective for the students to explore their group work theme of identity and presentation of self, and also provided valuable authentic formative intercultural competence experiences. The students demonstrated very individual intercultural competence development, and the shift in their perspectives was reflected in both Second Life and real-life interactions. In fact, the shift in critical cultural awareness was much more apparent and dramatic in these students than for the non-Second Life users.

Interacting in Second Life provided the challenge to the students' values and beliefs that research indicates is necessary for intercultural development to occur, and even those with prior experience as gamers had to manage emotional and often uncharacteristic behavioural responses as a consequence. The impact of the need to adapt to the different culture in Second Life was reflected in the varied nature and extent of each student's engagement in Second Life and with group members in real life, frequency of critical reflection and willingness to develop strategies for interaction in Second Life and in real life. Even with prior intercultural experiences and equipped with intercultural theoretical knowledge and tools from the intercultural competence module, they all showed symptoms of culture shock to varying degrees, and their negative reactions echoed those of other studies such as reported by Childs and Peachey (2013), and Ward (2010). This would indicate that interacting in Second Life involves a process of cross-cultural adaptation.

Cross-cultural adaptation is an emotional process, requiring intercultural attributes such as flexibility, resilience and respect for difference in perspectives and communication styles. However, intercultural competence is contextual, and individuals, whatever their level of intercultural competence, can be affected unexpectedly by culture shock. Recent study abroad research into effective student engagement in a different cultural environment, and for transformative learning to occur, indicates the importance of having theoretical intercultural knowledge, including an understanding of culture shock, regular critical reflection on experiences and the interventions of a mentor to guide the process (Hemming Lou et al. 2012). Transformative learning is considered to have taken place when a student is able to identify what triggers emotional responses, and the psychological adjustments made as a consequence of shifts in perspectives. Similarly, a combination of prior intercultural experiences, theoretical knowledge and tools, and lecturer interventions proved essential for the Second Life students to persevere and engage in the virtual environment, and allow critical cultural awareness to develop and for their formative learning experiences to be optimised so effectively.

The findings from the case studies indicate that there are symbiotic synergies between the affordances of virtual worlds such as Second Life, for intercultural competence development, and the need to already be interculturally competent to some extent, for effective engagement and learning to take place. However, they also echo findings of intercultural research such as by Deardorff (2011), Hemming Lou et al. (2012) and Stier (2006) that effective engagement and learning is not guaranteed by students going into a culturally different environment, and that ongoing intercultural support in the environment is an important factor. In other words, students should be prepared and supported not only for the technological challenges, but also for the emotional and behavioural challenges of virtual cross-cultural interaction. This has implications for the role of education and educators when considering graduate attributes. Childs and Peachey (2013) maintain that digital literacies will include being able to interact in virtual worlds in the future. If this is the case, then it would seem that intercultural competence is an essential graduate attribute for successful interaction in virtual worlds as well as in the real world.

References

Bennett, M. J. (1993). Towards ethnorelativism: A developmental model of intercultural sensitivity (revised). In R. M. Paige (Ed.), *Education for the intercultural experience*. Yarmouth, ME: Intercultural Press.

Byram, M. (1997). *Teaching and assessing intercultural communicative competence*. Clevedon, UK: Multilingual Matters.

Byram, M. (2008). *From foreign language education to education for intercultural citizenship: Essays and reflection*. Clevedon, UK: Multilingual Matters.

Childs, M., & Peachey, A. (2013). Love it or hate it: Students' responses to the experience of virtual worlds. In M. Childs & G. Withnail (Eds.), *Experiential learning in virtual worlds* (pp. 27–45). Freeland, Oxfordshire, UK: Inter-Disciplinary Press.

Corder, D. & U, A. (2010). Student cultural exchanges in Second Life. In J. Impagliazzo (Editor-in-chief), *ACM Inroads, Special Section on Global Intercultural Collaboration, 1*(3), 43–50.

Corder, D. M., & U-Mackey, A. (2015). Encountering and dealing with difference: Second Life and intercultural competence. *Intercultural Education, 26*(5), 409–424. doi:10.1080/14675986.2015.1091213.

Dalgarno, B., Lee, M. J. W., Carlson, L., Gregory, S., & Tynan, B. (2011). An Australian and New Zealand scoping study on the use of 3D immersive virtual worlds in higher education. *Australasian Journal of Educational Technology, 27*(1). Retrieved from http://www.ascilite.org.au/ajet/ajet27/dalgarno.html.

Deardorff, D. (2011). Intercultural competence in foreign language classrooms: A framework and implications for educators. In A. Witte & T. Harden (Eds.), *Intercultural Competence: Concepts, challenges, evaluations* (Vol. 10, pp. 37–54). Bern, Switzerland: Peter Lang AG, International Academic Publishers.

Diehl, W.C., & Prins, E. (2008). Unintended outcomes in Second Life: Intercultural literacy and cultural identity in a virtual world. *Language and Intercultural Communication, 8*(2), 101–118. doi:10.1080/14708470802139619.

Duff, P. (2008). *Case study research in applied linguistics*. New York, NY: Routledge.

Hemming Lou, K., Vande Berg, M., & Paige, R. M. (2012). In M. Vande Berg, R. M. Paige, & K. Hemming Lou (Eds.), *Student learning abroad: What our students are learning, what they're not, and what we can do about it* (pp. 411–419). Sterling, Virginia: Stylus Publishing, LLC.

Kohls, R. L. (1996). *Survival kit for living and working abroad*. Yarmouth, ME: Intercultural Press.

Kohonen, V. (2005). Experiential learning, intercultural learning and teacher development in foreign language education. In J. Smeds, K. Sarmavuori, E. Laakkonen, & R. de Cillia (Eds.), *Multicultural communities, multilingual practice* (pp. 123–135). Turku: Annales Universitatis Turkuensis B 285.

Kolb, D. (1984). *Experiential learning: Experience as the source of learning and development*. Englewood Cliffs, NJ: Prentice Hall.

Merriam, S. B. (2009). *Qualitative research: A guide to design and implementation*. San Francisco, CA: Wiley.

Paige, R. M., & Goode, M. L. (2009). ICC in international education administration. In D. K. Deardorff (Ed.), *The SAGE handbook of intercultural competence* (pp. 333–349). Thousand Oaks, CA: SAGE Publications Inc.

Salt, B., Atkins, C. & Blackall, L. (2008). Engaging with Second Life: Real education in a virtual world. *SLENZ project*. Retrieved from http://slenz.files.wordpress.com/2008/12/slliteraturereviewa1.pdf.

Spitzberg, B. H., & Changnon, G. (2009). Conceptualizing intercultural competence. In D. K. Deardorff (Ed.), *The SAGE handbook of intercultural competence* (pp. 2–52). Thousand Oaks, CA: SAGE Publications Inc.

Stier, J. (2006). Internationalisation, intercultural communication and intercultural competence. *Journal of Intercultural Communication, 11,* 1–12.

Twining, P. (2009). Exploring the educational potential of virtual worlds—some reflections from the SPP. *British Journal of Educational Technology, 40*(3), 496–514. doi:10.1111/j.1467-8535.2009.00963.x.

Warburton, S. (2009). Second Life in higher education: Assessing the potential for and the barriers to deploying virtual worlds in learning and teaching. *British Journal of Educational Technology, 40*(3), 414–426. doi:10.1111/j.1467-8535.2009.00952.x.

Ward, M. (2010). Avatars and sojourners: Explaining the acculturation of newcomers to multiplayer online games as cross-cultural adaptations. *Journal of Intercultural Communication, 23*. Retrieved from http://www.immi.se/intercultural/nr23/ward.htm.

Witte, A. (2011). On the teachability and learnability of intercultural competence: Developing facets of the 'Inter'. In A. Witte & T. Harden (Eds.), *Intercultural competence: Concepts, challenges, evaluations* (Vol. 10, pp. 89–108). Bern, Switzerland: Peter Lang AG, International Academic Publishers.

Yee, N., & Bailenson, J. (2007). The proteus effect: The effect of transformed self-representation on behaviour. *Human Communication Research, 33,* 271–290.

Author Biographies

Deborah (Debbie) Corder is Associate Head of the School of Language and Culture at the Auckland University of Technology. She has taught Japanese at secondary and tertiary levels, but her focus now is teaching intercultural competence courses with colleague, Alice U-Mackey, and curriculum design and development. Her research interests include learner autonomy, ICT, intercultural competence and study abroad.

Alice U-Mackey is Senior Lecturer in the School of Language and Culture at the Auckland University of Technology. She has extensive tertiary level teaching experience in English Language Teaching (ELT). She now mainly teaches intercultural competence courses with colleague, Deborah Corder, and courses in general and applied linguistics. Her research interests include intercultural competence, group assessments and academic literacies.

Chapter 4
Virtual Worlds as Restorative Environments

Janice K. Jones, Helen Farley and Angela Murphy

Introduction

This chapter draws data gathered from a study conducted in Queensland, Australia. However, the concerns that gave rise to that study are pertinent to governments and nations globally, and the study's findings will have relevance for contexts beyond the physical location in which the research took place. Sustainability, creativity and resilience for individuals and communities have been presented as priorities for Australia in a globalised economy (MCEETYA 2008). A research team, funded by the University of Southern Queensland (USQ), undertook a three-part study focusing upon how far pre-service teachers' self-perceptions of creativity, engagement and their sense of well-being were impacted by immersive experiences in natural and natural-seeming virtual world environments. The three phases extended over a two-year period and included pre-service teachers studying on campus or online as participants. The team of four researchers included a teacher educator and senior lecturer in the arts, two technology experts with substantial experience in research in education and virtual worlds in particular, and an Indigenous artist, educator and cultural advisor. The focus of phase three of the study was to add to an emerging body of knowledge relating to the restorative qualities of virtual world environments. It focused specifically upon the benefits of immersion in a natural-seeming virtual world environment upon undergraduate pre-service teachers' self-perceptions of creativity and well-being.

J.K. Jones (✉) · H. Farley · A. Murphy
University of Southern Queensland, Toowoomba, QLD, Australia
e-mail: jonesja@usq.edu.au

H. Farley
e-mail: helen.farley@usq.edu.au

A. Murphy
e-mail: angela.murphy@usq.edu.au

S. Gregory and D. Wood (eds.), *Authentic Virtual World Education*,
https://doi.org/10.1007/978-981-10-6382-4_4

A Disease of Modern Times

While there is ample evidence of the economic benefits of globalisation, industrialisation and urbanisation for many nations (Corvalan et al. 2005, p. 7), negative impacts have also been recognised. Rapid population growth and pressure for resources have forced a shift from rural to urban environments, and greater health benefits from improved medical treatments have resulted in rapid increases in the world's population and consequently, competition for natural resources. In this global context, a neoliberal shift over the last two decades has re-positioned education as a means for the production of a skilled and adaptable labour force (Lipman 2013), with a concomitant emphasis upon competition between individuals and education providers. Patrick (2013) contends that this change in thinking about the purposes of life-long education has informed the commodification of the self as an economic consumable so that pressures to achieve through years of schooling and higher education have intensified, with a trend towards 'zero tolerance' (Korner 2011) and with negative impacts upon the personal and social health and well-being of students reported in the USA (Greeson et al. 2014), Europe (Woolcock 2010), Australia (Cranston et al. 2011) and Asia (Hou et al. 2012). The trend for large-scale schools (Cotton 1996) and the closure of small and rural schools (Australian Bureau of Statistics 2010; Carbonell 2004; Skelton 2006) have informed the urbanisation of education and impacted upon students' disrupted sense of connectedness between home, community and school (Mitchell 2000).

Against this shifting socio-economic background, Greeson and colleagues (2014) document findings that more than one-half of college students in their USA study exhibit symptoms of depression and sleep disturbance. Research studies into the impact of urbanisation upon children's well-being (Kellert 2004; Kirkby 1989; Louv 2008), and of academic pressures upon the psychological well-being and risk of suicide in young people (Hou et al. 2012), have been paralleled by a growth of multinational research into the benefits for young people and their families of engagement in natural environments (Browning et al. 2013; Collado et al. 2013; Laaksoharju et al. 2012; Maller et al. 2008). The work of Chawla (2014) is representative of a new dynamic in education that focuses upon enhancing well-being through experience in natural environments, building upon Lynch and Banerjee's (1977) 'Growing up in Cities' project and extending this across eight countries. At the same time, there has been a growth in research into the potential benefits of immersion in natural-seeming virtual environments (Valtchanov 2010; Valtchanov et al. 2010; Depledge et al. 2011).

Researching Educators' Well-being

There is a lack of research into future educators' well-being, awareness of natural environments and sustainability, and creativity. The research team who undertook this study focusing upon those aspects of pre-service educator experience did so over three stages, and three years. This chapter focuses upon the third stage of the study. In the study's preliminary stage, data were captured in a survey of 114 commencing pre-service teachers across three campuses of an Australian university in 2009. The data indicated that undergraduates lacked confidence in fine arts skills and knowledge, with participants reporting perceptions that they lacked personal creativity. The majority of respondents reported limited experience of recreational and natural environments over the last decade (i.e. since their years of primary schooling). The findings of that data analysis have been reported in conference proceedings (Jones 2012a; Jones and Moodie 2012). The second stage of the study commenced the following year, focusing upon the impact of immersive experiences in natural environments upon participants' sense of well-being and creativity, with a group of 88 first-year on-campus pre-service teacher's students spending two hours per week over six weeks working in self-selected partnerships or groups during which they experienced immersion in a Japanese garden. At the end of their immersion experience, they presented visual, dance and dramatic works to peers. Data captured included student reflections upon their experience on each visit and responses to an anonymous online survey at the conclusion of their six-week experience. Findings suggested that students felt more creative and able to enter into 'flow' experiences, more in tune with nature, and less constrained by peer expectations in a natural environment. Flow is a term that was first coined by Mihaly Csikszentmihalyi (1990) and refers to a mental state that athletes equate with 'being in the zone' (Aldrich 2009, p. 5). The findings from this stage of the study have been reported in a journal article (Jones 2012b). A smaller group of students experienced a visit to a site of cultural significance for the Indigenous peoples of Queensland, with a painting used as a tool for intercultural meaning-making. The day included visits to an outdoor education centre in a bushland environment and to a museum. Findings have been reported in conference papers, journal articles and a book chapter (see Jones and Moodie 2014).

In stage 3, which is the central focus of this chapter, a group of final-year pre-service teachers participated in a short study over a period of two weeks in 2012. During a two-hour period, measures of pre-and-post affective (moods, feelings and attitudes) and behavioural perceptions of attentional fatigue and perceived attention restoration were taken, following participants' immersive experience in an environment resembling a natural setting in the virtual world of Second Life.

Literature Review

A growing international body of research points to the importance of engagement in natural environments for human health and well-being. This research has focused upon several areas: how proximity to natural environments may have restorative effects for human health and recovery from psychological, physical and spiritual distress (Hartig et al. 1996; Hartig and Statts 2006); how physical engagement in natural environments may benefit children's learning and psychosocial adjustment (Corraliza et al. 2012;

Laaksoharju et al. 2012; Wagner et al. 2010); how human-created views of seeming natural environments in the form of real or created windows onto greens spaces may bring the same benefits (Ulrich 1999); how immersion in virtual worlds where participants may engage in 3D virtual experiences may impact upon restoration of attention from stress or fatigue; or how it may support psychosocial well-being (Depledge et al. 2011; Valtchanov et al. 2010). While the impact of experiences in virtual worlds is represented through a limited and relatively recent body of international research, early findings suggest that immersion in virtual worlds may also bring psychological and physical benefits.

Hartig and colleagues (1997a) identified four requirements for an environment to have the potential to provide a successful restorative experience. A feeling of *being away* requires the ability to escape from unwanted distractions and removal from usual work demands. *Fascination* is considered to be a process of pleasant and effortless engagement and exploration of the environment. A third component, *coherence*, refers to the connectedness or relatedness of the environmental components to each other. This construct is seen as a representation of the ease with which a scene can be organised or structured within the imagination of the viewer. The final component is *compatibility,* which refers to an alignment between the demands of the environment and the goals and needs of the individual. The extent to which each of these characteristics is present in an environment is related to the potential of the environment to be restorative. Hartig and colleagues (1996) recognised that psychological distancing from an environment is more impactful than geographical distancing. Virtual environments that simulate these characteristics should therefore be able to provide a similar restorative experience to an equivalent natural environment. Natural environments have been found to be significantly more restorative than built environments (Hartig et al. 2001); however, natural environments may not always be easily accessible when restorative moments are most needed.

The findings of Canadian researchers Valtchanov et al. (2010) suggest that virtual worlds may offer an alternative to natural environments as restorative environments. While their research drew upon data from a relatively small sample (21 participants), respondents signalled that they found that experiential immersion in virtual environments, rather than viewing a slideshow of the same environment, reduced perceptions of stress and enhanced recovery time from stressful experiences. Similarly, in their study into the impact of a virtual environment, *Emma's world,* on the psychological recovery of participants with post-traumatic stress disorder, Banos and colleagues (2011) found that virtual immersion was as effective as other more traditional approaches, such as cognitive therapy.

Method

The aim of the third stage of the study was to determine whether immersion in a natural-seeming virtual world environment could be considered effective in promoting restorative effects such as reduced attentional fatigue and improved affective states. Two short survey instruments were used to measure changes in attentional fatigue and affective states: Staats et al. (2003) affective and behavioural measures of attentional fatigue and Hartig et al. (1997a) perceived restorativeness scale.

The Virtual World

A Second Life island, named RejuveNation, was purchased and terraformed (landscaped) with advice from the research team. It included natural-seeming environments designed to represent Australian grasses, trees and wildlife. Sounds included cicadas (insect sounds), water (rivers and a sea-cove) and a bird song. The environment included grasslands with kangaroos, rock formations, desert areas, rainforest and eucalyptus woodland. The river took the form of a serpent, representing the land-emergent knowledge and narratives of the first peoples of Queensland. There were many references to Queensland Indigenous culture on the Second Life island as an understanding and appreciation of cultural diversity, and an embedding of Indigenous perspectives was one of the aims of the programme from which the participants were derived but also reflected the vision of the university more broadly.

Participants

Participation was open to both online and on-campus students in a four-year Bachelor of Education course. Students were recruited to the study through participation requests during class time and through electronic email invitations. As the university has a limited number of courses that use virtual worlds, on-campus access to Second Life was available only through an on-campus computer laboratory. As a result of these challenges, only six on-campus students participated in the study. The data from that on-campus group were excluded from the results presented in this chapter due to the small sample size. However, a total of 49 online students participated in the study, and all participants who successfully completed the study were entered into a prize draw to win a gift voucher. Eight participants' provided incomplete responses. These were removed from the data so that a final sample of 41 was retained.

Research Instruments

Staats et al. (2003) postulated that based on attention restoration theory, a person's ability to ward off distractions was diminished, resulting in difficulties concentrating, increased irritability and an increased probability of making errors on cognitive tasks. To measure attentional fatigue, the research team developed four items to assess affective state (feeling irritated, tired, worn out and mentally exhausted) and four items to measure diminished attentional behaviour (would you be able to make a well-balanced decision? concentrate? foresee the implications of a complex situation? or pay attention to a long lecture?). These self-report items were scored by participants using a seven-point Likert scale ranging from 1 (not at all) to 7 (very much for affective items; very well for behavioural items). The scale was found to have a Cronbach's alpha score of 0.97, and a total attentional fatigue score was calculated by reversing scores on the behavioural items and obtaining a mean score for all eight items.

The perceived restorativeness scale (PRS) (Hartig et al. 1997a) was based on the attention restoration theory of Kaplan and Kaplan (1989), Kaplan (1995). It consisted of 26 items that were designed to measure the perceived restoration potential of natural or other environments that could be used to restore attentional capacity. The original scale consisted of only 16 items; however, an additional 10 items were added to the scale in 2001 to strengthen the constructs (Hartig et al. 2001). The scale was then divided into four subscales designed to measure psychological constructs that are considered to work together in restorative experiences: (1) being away, (2) fascination, (3) coherence and (4) compatibility (Hartig et al. 1996). In this study, participants selected from a seven-point scale from 0 (not at all) to 6 (completely) to indicate the extent to which each statement described their experiences in a given setting. Six of the items were reverse scored when compiling the subscale scores, and an overall score was calculated by obtaining an average of each of the four subscale means. Cronbach's alpha for the subscales ranges from 0.71 to 0.90 (Korpela et al. 2001). An overall PRS score was calculated as the average for each of the four subscales.

Data Collection Procedure

Students who agreed to participate in the study were sent an email outlining the aim of the study and were provided with a link to an online form which contained staged, detailed instructions on how to access the virtual environment and the research instruments. The first page of the online form provided detailed instructions on how to download and install the virtual world, Second Life, register as a new user, choose an avatar, move around and interact with objects. Participants were also provided with additional links to videos which demonstrated how to download, install and setup Second Life for the first time, and were provided with contact details for the research team for further assistance if required. As soon as registration was completed, the student's avatar appeared on a purpose-developed private island, RejuveNation. Once they had installed Second Life, the students were instructed to return to the survey and answer the eight affective and behavioural measures of attentional fatigue to obtain a base measure of fatigue for each participant.

To effectively measure the impact of RejuveNation as a restorative environment, participants were instructed to spend 30 min of quality time (undistracted time focused only on the island) in the virtual environment walking around and exploring or sitting quietly in a favourite place. Participants were requested not to spend less than 30 min on the island and not to break the time into shorter periods. Once they completed the 30-min immersion, participants were instructed to return to the survey to complete Hartig and colleagues' (1997a) perceived restorativeness scale and to repeat the attentional fatigue items. Respondents were also asked open questions about their experiences on the virtual island. The results of the study were compared to scores obtained for these instruments with those from participants who engaged in natural environments during stage two of this study, and as reported in the literature (Hartig et al. 1997b).

Findings

A reliability analysis, using Cronbach's alpha, was performed for the overall attentional fatigue scale, and each of the four PRS subscales and reliability was found to be high (see Table 4.1). As shown by the results of the attentional fatigue scales in Fig. 4.1, it is evident that the virtual environment was not effective at reducing attentional fatigue among student participants ($t(40) = -1.99$, $p = 0.052$). On the contrary, although the result was not significant, attentional fatigue at a total level appeared to be marginally worse ($M = 3.71$, $SD = 1.26$) after compared to before ($M = 3.37$, $SD = 1.31$) exposure to the virtual island. Further analysis of the subscales also revealed that students experienced a significant increase in irritation ($M = 3.44$, $SD = 1.96$; $t(40) = -3.16$, $p < 0.05$) and felt significantly less able to make a well-balanced decision ($M = 4.39$, $SD = 1.66$; $t(40) = 3.19$, $p < 0.05$), concentrate ($M = 4.12$, $SD = 1.72$; $t(40) = 2.42$, $p < 0.05$) or foresee implications of a complex situation ($M = 4.12$, $SD = 1.82$; $t(40) = 2.77$, $p < 0.05$) after spending time on the island. Although scores on the feelings of being tired ($M = 3.46$, $SD = 1.57$; $t(40) = 1.46$, $p = 0.63$), worn out ($M = 3.29$, $SD = 1.72$; $t(40) = 0.49$, $p = 0.63$) and mentally exhausted items ($M = 3.15$, $SD = 1.90$; $t(40) = -0.48$, $p = 0.64$) were reduced after immersion, these changes were not statistically significant.

Table 4.1 Internal consistencies (Cronbach's alpha) for the attentional fatigue scale and the perceived restorativeness subscales

Attentional fatigue	Cronbach's α
Attentional fatigue pre	0.87
Attentional fatigue post	0.86
Perceived restorativeness subscales:	Cronbach's α
Being away	0.87
Fascination	0.92
Coherence	0.70
Compatibility	0.90

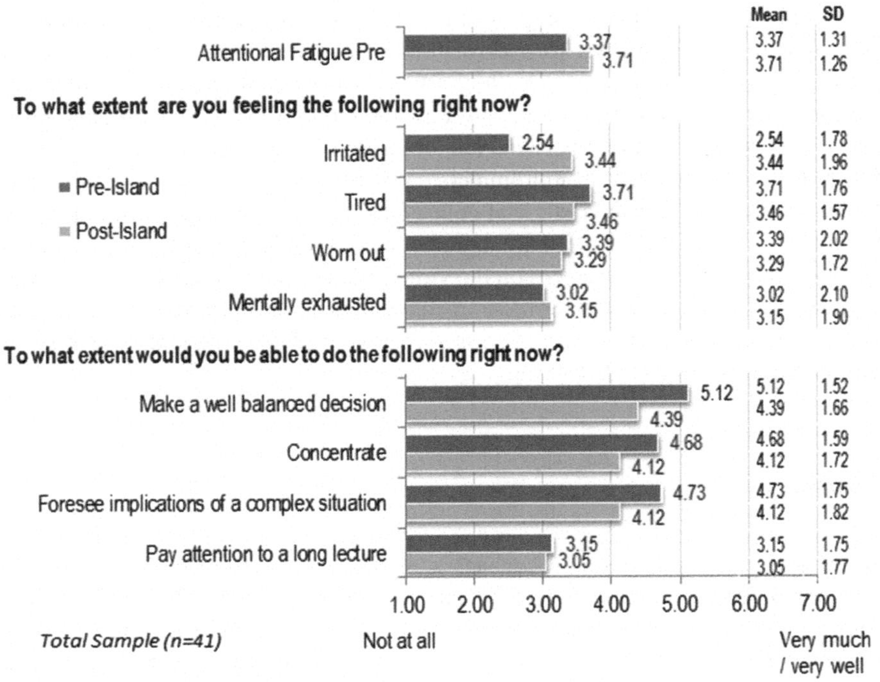

Fig. 4.1 Attentional fatigue scores prior to and after immersion in the virtual island

The team hypothesised that these findings, which were contrary to the expected outcomes, were possibly the result of lack of familiarity with virtual world environment. Although all courses used for the survey sample included a virtual world environment as a component of the learning experience, 88% of the students who participated in the study (n = 36) indicated that they had never spent time in a virtual world such as Second Life before. This suggests that even though the virtual world option is available for students in these courses, many students are not actively spending time in such environments.

Students were also requested to state exactly how much time they spent in the virtual environment prior to completing the second set of surveys. Seven students spent less time on the virtual island than requested in the research instructions, with 4 of these spending under 15 min; 22 students spent between 30 and 40 min; and 12 spent between 45 min and 2 h. Using Spearman's rho, however, the results indicated no significant relationship between overall attentional fatigue after immersion ($r = 0.19$, $p = 0.27$) and time spent on the island.

To determine the potential of the virtual world island to result in attention restoration, despite the apparent negative impact on attention fatigue, results on the PRS subscales were compared to existing scores identified for natural environments in the literature. In the first study, Hartig et al. (1997b) used the PRS scale to compare the restoration potential of four broad environment groups: natural outdoor, built outdoor, natural indoor and natural outdoor. A sample of undergraduate university students were randomly assigned to field-based ($n = 43$) and simulated ($n = 52$) study settings. Although the sample sizes for these two groups are similar to the present study, only the mean values for the overall PRS scale and the coherence subscale were presented. Korpela and colleagues (2001) compared mean scores on the four PRS subscales between imagined favourite and unpleasant places identified by a sample of 160 undergraduate university students. They found that students imagined natural environments as favourite places with greater frequency than any other types of environment. Restoration was also found to be significantly greater for these natural favourite places, particularly for the being away and compatibility subscales.

The overall PRS score for RejuveNation was found to be 2.74 ($SD = 1.07$) (see Fig. 3.2). Of the four environments examined by Hartig et al. (1997b), the mean overall score is identical to the field-based natural indoor environment ($M = 2.74$, $SD = 1.10$) and similar to the simulated natural indoor environment ($M = 2.53$, $SD = 1.12$), which was actual experience with, or video footage of, a study room with fixed seating, large planters and large windows facing onto adjacent trees. The score was significantly less than the general score identified for the both the simulated built ($M = 4.48$, $SD = 1.13$; t(40) = -10.40, $p < 0.001$) and natural outdoor environments ($M = 5.13$, $SD = 1.09$; t(40) = −14.28, $p < 0.001$) which were a large outdoor shopping mall with a fountain and potted plants and a rock garden in the centre of a large park. RejuveNation did, however, perform significantly better as a restorative environment than both the simulated ($M = 1.79$, $SD = 0.98$; t (40) = 5.67, $p < 0.001$) and the built ($M = 1.61$, $SD = 1.04$; $t(40) = 6.74$, $p < 0.001$) indoor environments, a large concrete parking structure.

The scores on each of the PRS subscales were compared to the mean values identified by Korpela and colleagues (2001) when examining the favourite and unpleasant spaces identified by students (see Table 4.2). Using an independent sample t-test, all the scores on each of the subscales for virtual island were found to be significantly less than the scores for the favourite places, yet significantly more than the unpleasant places. While the experience on the virtual island was not considered by students to be highly restorative for any of the four components, compatibility was found to be the subscale which performed most poorly. This suggests that the possible reason for the low restorative potential of the environment was due to a lack of familiarity and fit with the virtual environment as shown in Table 4.2.

Discussion

The research team considers that respondents' written and statistical responses signal that a lack of familiarity with the environment may have been the cause for findings of a lack of perceived restorativeness of student experiences in the virtual world environment. In order for the virtual world environment to be restorative, it needs to engender 'immersion' in participants. Immersion can be described as 'the

Table 4.2 Scores on the Perceived Restorativeness subscales for the virtual island compared to the pleasant and unpleasant places identified by Korpela et al. (2001)

	Mean	SD
Total PRS	2.74	1.07
Being Away	2.88	1.39
1. Being here is an escape experience. *	1.95	1.64
2. Spending time here gives me a break from my day-to-day routine. †	2.07	1.72
3. It is a place to get away from it all.	2.07	2.02
4. Being here helps me to relax my focus on getting things done.	1.51	1.55
5. Coming here helps me to get relief from unwanted demands on my attention.	1.78	1.59
Fascination	2.78	1.54
6. This place has fascinating qualities. *	2.49	2.00
7. My attention is drawn to many interesting things. *	2.56	2.01
8. I want to get to know this place better. †	2.34	1.80
9. There is much to explore and discover here. *	3.27	1.55
10. I want to spend more time looking at the surroundings. †	2.22	1.88
11. This place is boring. (-)	2.95	2.16
12. The setting is fascinating.	2.83	1.88
13. There is nothing worth looking at here. (-)	2.49	2.06
Coherence	3.30	1.25
14. There is too much going on. (-) *	2.20	1.79
15. It is a confusing place. (-) *	3.66	1.78
16. There is a great deal of distraction. (-) *	2.56	1.55
17. It is chaotic here. (-) *	2.39	1.74
Compatibility	1.99	1.26
18. Being here suits my personality. *	1.73	1.69
19. I can do things I like here. *	1.73	1.72
20. I have a sense that I belong here. *	1.37	1.68
21. I can find ways to enjoy myself here. †	2.32	2.01
22. I have a sense of oneness with this setting. *	1.37	1.62
23. There are landmarks to help me get around. ‡	2.71	1.55
24. I could easily form a mental map of this place. ‡	2.17	1.83
25. It is easy to find my way around here. ‡	2.44	1.63
26. It is easy to see how things are organized. ‡	2.12	1.52

Notes: (-) an item for which the value must be reversed in coding; (*) the item is from the earlier PRS and is in its original form; (†) the item is from the earlier PRS but is in a revised form; (‡) the item was designed to represent legibility.

PRS Subscales:	Virtual Island		Korpela et al., (2001)							
			Favourite place				Unpleasant place			
	M	SD	M	SD	t value	sig	M	SD	t value	sig
Being Away	2.88	1.39	4.80	0.98	-8.859	0.000	0.73	0.96	9.901	0.000
Fascination	2.78	1.54	4.62	1.27	-7.653	0.000	1.85	1.28	3.890	0.000
Coherence	3.30	1.25	4.73	1.22	-7.345	0.000	2.45	1.69	4.356	0.000
Compatibility	1.99	1.26	4.86	0.97	-14.561	0.000	0.87	1.13	5.715	0.000

Note Values fall on a scale from 0 to 6 where lower values indicate, for example, lower fascination. Scores for the virtual island to the favourite and unpleasant places identified by Korpela et al. (2001) ($p < 0.001$)

subjective impression that one is participating in a comprehensive realistic experience' (Dede 2009, p. 66). Immersion happens when an individual perceives him or herself to be part of the virtual environment and is able to interact with that environment. This is compromised when the environment is difficult or unfamiliar or when the hardware used to access the environment performs poorly (Farley 2013). It is thought to be these factors which have negatively impacted on the participants' sense of immersion and hence on the restorativeness of the environment. This is supported by comments from the participants who expressed frustration with the unfamiliar interface.

> I found it frustrating and very unrelaxing. For students who are familiar with this type of experience it may be restorative.

However, some written responses strongly suggest a positive association between participants' experience of the virtual environment and feelings of relaxation, pleasure and well-being.

> The beach and waves were really calming.

> The experience allowed an escape from the stresses of real life. Had a calming influence and I forgot about day-to-day worries while in the virtual world.

Fear of the unknown emerged in one respondent's observation that she felt 'alone' in 'a strange place'. In this participant's response was a strong affective connection between being alone in a realistic natural environment, which gave rise to a sense of pleasure and wonder. This was swiftly followed (within 10 min) by a sense that real-world dangers may attend to her immersion in a virtual environment. She felt a need to escape to the safety of the known.

These findings suggest that it would be productive to conduct further studies with participants who have had some prior experience in immersive virtual worlds or in gaming environments so that the physical challenges of navigating with unfamiliar tools, and perceived fears that an unfamiliar world may present dangers, do not counter the potentially restorative qualities of the engagement. Participants' written comments provide a second layer of information pointing to their more nuanced and pleasurable experience of virtual natural environments as places of pleasure and relaxation. For a future where our overcrowded planet may require that we restrict travel to natural and wild places, and where urbanisation makes such places inaccessible for many, virtual experiences of natural environments may bring rich possibilities for relaxation, restoration and learning about the natural world.

Conclusion

In a world increasingly characterised by globalisation, urbanisation and alienation from the natural environment, it seems prudent to look for ways to maximise the well-being of individuals. It is especially important to nurture an awareness of the impact environments upon well-being in pre-service teachers whose personal and professional practice influences the next generation of workers, parents and citizens. This chapter has considered whether virtual environments may have a role to play in supporting well-being against the broader context of megatrends impacting upon human well-being and feelings of connectedness. The investigation considered the immersive potential of natural and virtual world environments as part of a broader study. It responded to earlier findings, from phase 1 of the study, that revealed a lack of arts skills and knowledge in pre-service teachers, a perceived lack of personal creativity, and limited experience of recreational and natural environments since their years in primary school. Potential antidotes to the problems described in the first part of the investigation were examined through immersive experiences in a formal Japanese garden and during a visit to a place of cultural significance for local Indigenous peoples during phase 2 of the study.

The focus of this third phase of the study has been to examine the restorative potential of virtual worlds upon pre-service teachers. Because these environments are potentially available from the desktop, irrespective of time or geographical location, virtual world environments, if they can be shown to be restorative, hold potential for alleviating the stresses and strains of everyday living and the impacts those tensions have on well-being. However, the results of this preliminary investigation are inconclusive. While natural-seeming virtual world environments do score better as restorative environments than those environments deemed to be unpleasant, such as undercover car parks, they were scored by participants as being significantly less effective than pleasant natural places in promoting feelings of well-being. However, contradictory evidence, in the written responses of participants who reported pleasurable and calming experiences in virtual worlds, suggests that virtual environments' lack of restorativeness in this study may be due to the unfamiliarity of the environment and interface to participants. These factors undermine the sense of immersion in the virtual world environment which is a necessary pre-condition for restorativeness. The study findings indicate that further research needs to be undertaken with participants who have overcome the novelty factor of virtual environments, and for whom navigating and engaging with the environment are familiar processes, before testing the restorational benefits of their immersive experiences in virtual environments.

Acknowledgements The authors wish to thank the University of Southern Queensland for its support and funding of the study that informed this chapter and the peer reviewers whose anonymous feedback informed enhancements in the final work.

References

Aldrich, C. (2009). *Learning online with games, simulations, and virtual worlds: Strategies for online instruction*. San Francisco: Jossey-Bass.

Australian Bureau of Statistics. (2010). *4221.0 - Schools, Australia, 2010* Retrieved from http://www.abs.gov.au/ausstats/abs@.nsf/lookup/4221.0.

Banos, R. M., Guillen, V., Quero, S., Garcia-Palacios, A., Alcaniz, M., & Botella, C. (2011). A virtual reality system for the treatment of stress related disorders: A preliminary analysis of efficacy compared to a standard cognitive behavioural program. *International Journal of Human-Computer Studies, 69*(June), 602–613.

Browning, M., Marion, J. L., & Gregoire, T. G. (2013). Sustainably connecting children with nature – An exploratory study of nature play area visitor impacts and their management. *Landscape and Urban Planning, 119,* 104–112. doi:10.1016/j.landurbplan.2013.07.004.

Carbonell, R. (2004). Rural schools closing a sign of the times *AM* [Radio Interview Transcript]: Australian Broadcasting Corporation Online.

Chawla, L. (2014). Children's engagement with the natural world as a ground for healing. *Greening in the Red Zone* (pp. 111–124). Dordrecht, The Netherlands: Springer.

Collado, S., Staats, H., & Corraliza, J. A. (2013). Experiencing nature in children's summer camps: Affective, cognitive and behavioural consequences. *Journal of Environmental Psychology, 33,* 37–44. doi:10.1016/j.jenvp.2012.08.002.

Corraliza, J. A., Collado, S., & Bethelmy, L. (2012). Nature as a moderator of stress in urban children. *Procedia - Social and Behavioral Sciences, 38,* 253–263. doi:10.1016/j.sbspro.2012.03.347.

Corvalan, C., Hales, S, & McMichael, A. (2005). *Ecosystems and human well-being: Health synthesis A Report of the Millennium Ecosystem Assessment* (M. E. A. Board Ed. Vol. 5). Washington, DC: Island Press.

Cotton, K. (1996). School size, school climate, and student performance. *School Improvement Research Series: Northwest Regional Educational Laboratory,* (20). http://www.nwrel.org/scpd/sirs/10/c020.html

Cranston, N., Reid, A., Keating, J., & Mulford, B. (2011). *The forces and dynamics shaping education* (Vol. 4). Retrieved from http://www.agppa.asn.au/content/view/11/15/.

Csikszentmihalyi, M. (1990). *Flow: The psychology of optimal experience*. New York: Harper Perennial.

Dede, C. (2009). Immersive interfaces for engagement and learning. *Science, 323*(66), 66–69.

Depledge, M. H., Stone, R. J., & Bird, W. J. (2011). Can natural and virtual environments be used to promote improved human health and wellbeing? *Environmental Science and Technology, 45,* 4660–4665. doi:10.1021/es103907m.

Farley, H. (2013). Facilitating immersion in virtual worlds: An examination of the physical, virtual, social and pedagogical factors leading to engagement and flow. In B. Tynan, J. Willems, & R. James (Eds.), *Outlooks and opportunities in blended and distance learning* (pp. 189–203). Hershey, PA: IGI Global.

Greeson, J. M., Juberg, M. K., Maytan, M., James, K., & Rogers, H. (2014). A randomized controlled trial of Koru: A mindfulness program for college students and other emerging adults. *Journal of American College Health, 62*(4), 222–223. doi:10.1080/07448481.2014.887571.

Hartig, T., Kaiser, F. G., & Bowler, P. A. (1997a). Further development of a measure of perceived environmental restorativeness. *Institute of Housing Research, Working paper*, (5).

Hartig, T., Kaiser, F. G., & Bowler, P. A. (2001). A measure of restorative quality in environments. *Environment and Behavior, 33*(4), 590–607.

Hartig, T., Korpela, K., Evans, G. W., & Gärling, T. (1996). Validation of a measure of perceived environmental restorativeness. *Goteborg Psychological Reports, 26*.

Hartig, T., Korpela, K., Evans, G. W., & Gärling, T. (1997b). A measure of restorative quality in environments. *Scandinavian Housing and Planning Research, 14*(4), 175–194.

Hartig, T., & Staats, H. (2005). Linking preference for environments with their restorative quality. In B. Tress, G. Tress, G. Fry, & P. Opdam (Eds.), *From landscape research to landscape planning: Aspects of integration education and application* (pp. 279–292). Dordrecht, The Netherlands: Springer.

Hartig, T., & Statts, H. (2006). Linking preference for environments with their restorative quality. In B. Tress, G. Tress, G. Fry & P. Opdam (Eds.), *From landscape research to landscape planning: Aspects of integration, education and application* (pp. 279–292). Dordrecht, The Netherlands: Springer.

Hou, X., Sun, J., & Dunne, M. P. (2012). Academic stress among adolescents in China. *Australasian Epidemiologist, 19*(1), 9–12.

Jones, J.K. (2012a). *Pre-service teachers' experiences of creativity and enhanced appreciation of natural environments.* Paper presented at the Canada International Conference on Education, University of Guelph, Ontario.

Jones, J. K. (2012b). Re-discovering the arts: The impact of engagement in a natural environment upon pre-service teacher perceptions of creativity. *Thinking Skills and Creativity*. doi:10.1016/j.tsc.2012.08.001.

Jones, J. K., & Moodie, D. (2012). *Dinawan dreaming: Pre-service teachers seeing the world with fresh eyes.* Paper presented at The 9th Engagement Australia International Conference: Next Steps Community Engaged Learning, Queensland University of Technology, Brisbane, Australia.

Jones, J. K., & Moodie, D. (2014). Dinawan dreaming: Seeing the darkness or the stars. In J. K. Jones (Ed.), *Weaving words: Personal and professional transformation through writing as research* (pp. 92–114). Newcastle upon Tyne, UK. IS: Cambridge Scholars Publishing.

Kaplan, R., & Kaplan, S. (1989). *The experience of nature.* A Psychological Perspective. New York, USA: Cambridge.

Kaplan, S. (1995). The restorative benefits of nature: Toward an integrative framework. *Journal of Environmental Psychology, 15,* 169–182.

Kellert, S. (2004). *Ordinary nature: The value of exploring and restoring nature in everyday life.* Paper presented at the Proceedings 4th International Symposium on Urban Wildlife Conservation, University of Arizona, Tucson.

Kirkby, M. (1989). Nature as refuge in children's environments. *Children's Environments Quarterly, 6*(1), 7–12.

Korner, A. (2011). It's zero tolerance at schools, Online *The Queensland Times*. Retrieved from http://www.qt.com.au/story/2011/04/18/its-zero-tolerance-at-schools/

Korpela, K. M., Hartig, T., Kaiser, F. G., & Fuhrer, U. (2001). Restorative experience and self-regulation in favorite places. *Environment and Behavior, 33*(4), 572–589.

Laaksoharju, T., Rappe, E., & Kaivola, T. (2012). Garden affordances for social learning, play, and for building nature–child relationship. *Urban Forestry & Urban Greening, 11*(2), 195–203. doi:10.1016/j.ufug.2012.01.003.

Lipman, P. (2013). *The new political economy of urban education: Neoliberalism, race, and the right to the city.* London, U.K.: Routledge.

Louv, R. (2008). *Last Child in The Woods-Revised: Saving our children from nature-deficit disorder* (2nd ed.). New York: Algonquin Books of Chapel Hill.

Lynch, K., & Banerjee, T. (1977). Growing up in cities: Studies of the spatial environment of adolescence in Cracow, Melbourne, Mexico City, Salta, Toluca, and Warszawa (Vol. (1977). *Cambridge*. MA.: MIT Press.

Maller, C., Townsend, M., St Leger, L., Henderson-Wilson, C., Pryor, A., Prosser, L., & Moore, M. (2008). *Healthy parks, healthy people: The health benefits of contact with nature in a park context: A review of relevant literature.* Paper presented at the Healthy Parks, Healthy People Conference, Melbourne. http://www.healthyparkshealthypeoplecongress.org/images/stories/documents/hphp.pdf.pdf

MCEETYA. (2008). *Melbourne declaration on educational goals for young Australians.* Melbourne: Curriculum Corporation. Retrieved from http://www.curriculum.edu.au/verve/_resources/National_Declaration_on_the_Educational_Goals_for_Young_Australians.pdf.

Mitchell, S. (2000, Summer). Jack and the Giant School. *The new rules: Exploring community, mobility, scale and trade* (pp. 12–18). Retrieved from https://ilsr.org/new-rules-journal-summer-2000/.

Patrick, F. (2013). Neoliberalism, the knowledge economy, and the learner: Challenging the inevitability of the commodified self as an outcome of education. *International Scholarly Research Network: Education, 2013,* 8. doi:10.1155/2013/108705.

Skelton, G. (2006). Six new super schools. *Adelaide Now...* [News article]. Adelaide: The Advertiser.

Staats, H., Kieviet, A., & Hartig, T. (2003). Where to recover from attentional fatigue: An expectancy value analysis of environmental preference. *Journal of Environmental Psychology, 23,* 147–157.

Ulrich, R. S. (1999). Effects of gardens on health outcomes: Theory and research. In C. C. Marcus & M. Barnes (Eds.), *Healing gardens: Therapeutic benefits and design recommendations* (pp. 27–86). New York: Wiley.

Valtchanov, D. (2010). *Physiological and affective responses to immersion in virtual reality: Effects of nature and urban settings (Unpublished doctoral dissertation).* Ontario, Canada: University of Waterloo.

Valtchanov, D., Barton, K. R., & Ellard, C. (2010). Restorative effects of virtual nature settings. *Cyberpsychology, Behavior, and Social Networking, 13*(5), 503–512. doi:10.1089/cyber.2009.0308.

Wagner, C., Gordon, D., & Aia, H. (2010). *Planning School Grounds for Outdoor Learning.* Washington, DC: National Clearinghouse for Educational Facilities. Retrieved from http://citeseerx.ist.psu.edu/viewdoc/download?doi=10.1.1.204.7883&rep=rep1&type=pdf.

Woolcock, N. (2010). Thousands of key stage tests cancelled after teachers boycott exams Online, *The Times.* Retrieved from http://www.timesonline.co.uk/tol/life_and_style/education/article7122207.ece.

Author Biographies

Janice K. Jones has 30 years' international teaching and management experience in schools and universities and 15 years' experience of technology systems implementation. Janice's teaching and research bring together emerging technologies, creativity and arts-informed leadership and practice in intercultural contexts. A Senior Lecturer in Arts Education at the University of Southern Queensland, Australia, Janice's publications include an edited book, co-authored books and numerous book chapters, refereed journal articles and conference proceedings.

Helen Farley is an Associate Professor (Digital Life Lab Administration) at the University of Southern Queensland, working there since 2010. Prior to that, she was a Research Fellow at the Centre for Educational Innovation and Technology and a Lecturer (Learning Technologies) at the Teaching and Educational Development Institute at the University of Queensland. Helen has published extensively on educational technologies, particularly immersion and presence in virtual worlds, authentic movement in 3D virtual environments and the use of gaming consoles for learning. Her current research is focused on improving digital literacies in incarcerated students through the use of digital technologies for learning.

Angela Murphy is Manager, Learning Analytics in the Office for Advancement of Learning and Teaching at the University of Southern Queensland, having been a Research Fellow with the university since 2011. During this time, she has collaborated on the development and evaluation of a number of research projects around the use of digital learning technologies, most notably in the field of mobile learning and sustainable innovation. Angela is a research psychologist with a PhD from the University of South Africa (UNISA) and has over ten years research experience in the corporate, government and academic sectors. She is skilled at project management, research design, evaluation and complex data analysis.

Chapter 5
Self-guided Exploration of Virtual Learning Spaces

Torsten Reiners, Lincoln C. Wood, Marko Teräs, Hanna Teräs, Sue Gregory, Vanessa Chang, Michael Steurer, Timothy McDonald and Ali Fardinpour

Introduction

The moment of truth for a learner occurs when the acquired knowledge and trained skill set has to be recalled, practised and performed outside of the safe environment we find in the classroom. Reality does not provide the range of experimental set-ups where the experiment serves the demonstration of learnt theory but includes all the

T. Reiners (✉) · M. Teräs · V. Chang · M. Steurer · T. McDonald
Curtin University, Perth, Australia
e-mail: t.reiners@curtin.edu.au

M. Teräs
e-mail: imperfectus@gmail.com

V. Chang
e-mail: Vanessa.Chang@cbs.curtin.edu.au

M. Steurer
e-mail: msteurer@iicm.edu

T. McDonald
e-mail: timothym632@gmail.com

L.C. Wood
University of Otago, Dunedin, New Zealand
e-mail: Lincoln.wood@otago.ac.nz

H. Teräs
Murdoch University, Perth, Australia
e-mail: hanna.teras@gmail.com

S. Gregory
University of New England, Armidale, Australia
e-mail: sue.gregory@une.edu.au

A. Fardinpour
Wise Realities, Curtin University, Perth, Australia
e-mail: Ali.fardinpour@curtin.edu.au

S. Gregory and D. Wood (eds.), *Authentic Virtual World Education*,
https://doi.org/10.1007/978-981-10-6382-4_5

side effects that influence the outcome. The guidelines in textbooks, or instructions in the classroom, are replaced with an unsupervised environment where decisions include the selection of tools and methods as well as further attributes like sequences, colleagues, safety, resources, effectiveness or efficiency. In a real-world setting, failures can result in serious consequences; there is no reset button or option to go back in time for another run.

While the existing skill gap between the qualification of graduates from educational institutions and industry expectation has many dimensions, we focus on two factors in this chapter: mass vs. individualised education and the lack of authenticity. First, the classroom is not a homogenous group of equal learners; instead, we are faced with classes of students from diverse backgrounds and sometimes with dissimilar needs (Wood and Reefke 2010). It is safe to say that each individual learner has unique needs in processing information and acquiring the knowledge that is needed to make sophisticated decisions in known and, especially unknown, situations. We have to acknowledge the individuality to help create an effective and efficient learning process, a condition that is generally not achievable in classrooms or on-the-job training with respect to available resources, such as time and staff. Second, learning from a book or video does not necessarily prepare a student for the tasks and challenges they are likely to experience in their professional life. Instead, many students struggle to go from the 'academic' understanding of theory to understanding of practice and how to use this to frame their actions in a real-life working situation.

In this chapter, we describe the development of an immersive authentic virtual learning space, depict mechanisms to increase engagement and motivation, introduce the inclusion of indirect guidance of the learner and explain how immediate formative feedback to the learner can be achieved. This project (known as nDiVE) is ongoing; however, preliminary results and a resulting framework to create future learning units will be demonstrated and outlined in this chapter.

Stories as the Canvas for Individualisation

Storytelling is an ancient profession that creates an illusion to immerse the audience in a fictional or non-fictional space. The storyteller orchestrates words, gestures, expressions and other stylistic means (e.g. suspense) to create a draft framework, which is padded by each listener in a (slightly) different way. The story defines the space and its objectives, the narrative, or the path to reach these objectives and should involve the individual experience and knowledge; allowing one to explore the space and use creativity to find solutions (Reiners et al. 2014a, b).

The framework addresses self-guided and motivated learning, focusing on understanding and critical thinking (Friedman 2006). The suggested virtual learning spaces are not considered to replace the traditional classroom but provide an opportunity to evaluate and validate the readiness of the acquired knowledge and skills. The story is told beforehand to 'provide relevance and meaning to the experience. It provides context' (Kapp 2012, p. 41). The virtual learning space provides the means to individualise the story, where rough milestones on the path are defined and incentives are given to either attract learners to a certain direction, to encourage them from going in the wrong direction, or passing on guidance or options on how to continue. Stories are the 'original form of teaching' (Pederson 1995, p. 2), yet we have to include state-of-art technology to reach out for learners of today and to sculpt and design the narrative to match individual learners (Reiners et al. 2014a, b).

Immersion and Virtual Learning Space

Immersion is 'the subjective impression that one is participating in a comprehensive, realistic experience' (Dede 2009, p. 66), whereas the experience does not depend on how or with what means the immersive presence was created. In our research, we further advance the perceptual immersion (Biocca and Delaney 1995), i.e. using head-mounted displays such as the Oculus Rift (Oculus 2013) or a Computer Assisted Virtual Environment (CAVE, space with projections of the environment on all walls) to submerse a user into a virtual environment.

Making research more difficult, both in common and academic language, the term 'immersion' is regularly used loosely and even imprecisely. In common language it may be acceptable to be imprecise with language, yet it creates a challenge for the researcher to capture the right phenomenon in surveys, interviews or experiments. In academic language, the definition distinguishes itself from various other human experiences related to concepts such as flow, engagement, involvement, presence and cognitive absorption (cf. Jennett et al. 2008; Slater 2003). In relation to discipline, context, scenario and experience, it can translate to anything from an affordance of a technological system (e.g. Mestre and Vercher 2011; Slater and Wilbur 1997) to a psychological concept or an experience (e.g. Witmer and Singer 1998; Brown and Cairns 2004).

Palmer (1995) suggests technology-generated immersion could be considered different from psychological immersion. This involves the depth of engagement with a given task, such as found with relatively simple games (e.g. solitaire on a PC). According to Ermi and Mäyrä (2005), to understand what a game is, we need to learn more about the act of playing and the experience of gameplay. The authors observed Finnish game-playing children and their non-playing parents, conceptualising a heuristic gameplay model covering three distinct components: sensory, challenge-based and imaginative immersion (SCI-model) (cf. Browns and Cairns 2004). The authors validated their model by analysing Finnish video game players (N = 193) with self-evaluation questionnaires addressing three different immersion dimensions, observing that many of the popular games received high scores in immersion. As the model has been developed studying only the Finnish population, with the input and output of questionnaires perhaps slightly too directly validating the model, it should be noted that more research is needed to assess the model. This is similar with the case involving a small study by Brown and Cairns (2004) who used Grounded Theory to study seven gamers through open-ended questions to understand and define immersion. They report that players use immersion as a term to describe their involvement with games. Three levels of involvement were found: engagement, engrossment and total immersion. System or human barriers, such as game construction or concentration, control access to each of these engagements. They also note, that 'each level of involvement is only possible if the barriers to the level are removed' (Brown and Cairns 2004, p. 2).

Although more research in this area is still needed, such studies support the fact that well designed games, despite definitions, have the ability to 'draw people in' (Jennett et al. 2008, p. 641), and emerging frameworks and definitions can prove valuable vessels on the journey to understand how to develop and achieve similar results with immersive virtual environments and gamification in various contexts, for example education. Gamification is 'a process of enhancing a service with affordances for gameful experiences in order to support user's overall value creation' (Huotari and Hamari 2012, p. 19). The convergence of video games and immersive virtual environments, namely, game design mechanics used in immersive virtual environments mediated by a head-mounted display and other controls promoting more embodied user experience, is taking research in new directions.

Authenticity, Fidelity and Realism

Authenticity is the representation of real-world tasks. When these are recreated in virtual environments, realism (exactness in visualisation) and fidelity (exactness in functionality) become essential as authentic activities mirror the 'kind of activities people do in the real world' (Herrington and Kervin 2007, p. 223). In authentic learning activities, students find and solve problems with the 'complexity and uncertainty of the real world' (Herrington 2006, p. 3). Simulations and virtual environments provide spaces for authentic learning experiences to occur where real-life costs and consequences are avoided (Gregory 2011). The authentic simulations discussed here should be realistic and the relevant activity emerges due to the interaction between the participants, the simulator and the context (Rystedt and Sjoblom 2012, p. 785).

The 'Carrot and Stick' Framework

Many commonly used educational practices focus on implicitly coercive approaches to encouraging student compliance with educators' wishes—applying a 'stick' approach. However, the term 'carrot and stick' implies both a threat of punishment coupled or used in conjunction with something tempting, dangled in front of the student in order to motivate them. While some elements may be used as an extrinsic motivator of this sort (e.g. the use of gold stars for young children that can be redeemed for a reward when they collect enough), the use remains somewhat limited, with most practices designed to punish non-compliance (e.g. detention or loss of grades under some circumstances). Effective education may require application of sticks but there is increasingly room to include carrots.

With self-directed learning, the focus shifts further away from the use of punishments and coercive acts to ensure compliance while enabling the student to engage in their self-directed study. A self-directed study suggests design with greater reliance on intrinsic motivation and may be supported by self-determination theory as an approach to create more powerful forces that encourage instincts supportive of learning (Ryan and Deci 2000). Note that a 'carrot' by nature is a reward but we tend to think of this as a purely extrinsic motivator; where you make progress, you are rewarded.

Within a self-guided learning environment, supported in a virtual world or gamification, the use of both carrots and sticks can be easily applied. Sticks can be as simple as providing greater points for completing a task directly or more quickly; failure to comply results in fewer points or perhaps in explicit penalties where points are deducted. An extrinsic carrot may involve rewarding progress towards objectives, e.g. allocating points to specific tasks in a way that also provides feedback on overall progress in the learning scenario. Appropriate design to provide scalable challenges to learners may also include the use of artificially intelligent software agents or bots (i.e. non-player characters) that adapt to learners and continue to push them (Wood and Reiners 2013).

Intrinsic motivator carrots include many of the contemporary gamification mechanisms applied to create and support intrinsic motivation to support tasks. The use of multiple lives or save points enables experimentation and trials to take place without negative consequences for the student, encouraging a range of actions to be attempted and enabling the sating of curiosity about a particular situation. The use of leaderboards can provide a learner with an overall perspective of success and how they are fairing against others in a way that motivates them to continue as they collect points rather than becoming frustrated when being penalised for failing tests (McGonigal 2011). The use of ghost or shadow images (Hebbel-Seeger 2013) or other comparative techniques enables observation and reflection on performance with the ability to learn from others, or from oneself, or from the difference in previous attempts in comparison to the attempts of others.

Gamification processes can aid the shift away from extrinsic motivators as carrots towards developing intrinsic motivation. Application of appropriate gamification design can increase the propensity of a student to engage in self-directed learning. In this way, the 'carrot' can become a multidimensional or multi-layered approach to developing, encouraging and supporting the students' willingness to explore and engage in the learning environment. The ultimate focus is to shift the development of motivators away from extrinsic to intrinsic motivators over time while increasingly reducing the use of sticks in the environment (Landers et al. 2015); in this way, gamification can be supportive when designed to run in parallel with authentic learning (Wood et al. 2013).

The Two Faces of Technology

It is simple to equip existing learning spaces with state-of-the-art technology. But it is not a simple process to use the technology to improve the learning. The short life cycle of modern technology causes continuous changes and adaptations where the focal point risks integrating the technology while sacrificing an emphasis on the story as a justification of the investment. Efforts to demonstrate improvement of the learning and teaching quality through integration of technology are a simple strategy for the administrators and managers; yet, this neglects the content and the story, which is the key to success (Bates and Sangra 2011). Another aspect is how the story is told by the storyteller and experienced by the audience. Here, technology can also become the only means of creating the visible environment and therewith the needed context. While immersion can be achieved by imagination alone, it can be intensified when multiple sensory impressions are combined (Cummings et al. 2012). For example, the learner can look at photos of an unknown city; yet it is almost impossible to derive the general dynamics, such as the noise or the aromas from this media format. Technology enables addition of further dimensions, e.g. using a movie to add the dynamic or using sound to be immersed from all directions.

We use technology in our framework to add further dimensions to the learning space. The selection of the technology is based on our objective of an authentic skills acquisition. The skill gap implies the deficiency of theory for the later practice; forcing additional training requirements after graduation. Skills training needs authenticity and so context and functionality of the learning space should closely match real requirements. A preliminary study to select the most promising technology included traditional media, virtual worlds on traditional 2D monitors and 3D displays (similar to the 3D TV's that have become popular as part of a home entertainment system) as well as emerging technology, e.g. head-mounted displays (HMD) (Reiners et al. 2014a, b). Recent releases of HMDs have focused on providing consumer-ready equipment that promises to eliminate large investments in dedicated rooms such as CAVEs.

Figure 5.1 depicts examples of technology supporting interaction with the virtual learning space, but also allows records to be created of the activities for later analysis. The interaction is further distinguished between input and output, i.e. triggering the sensory system. Input concerns tracking the body in the real world and mapping these movements onto an avatar. This has traditionally been accomplished with a keyboard and mouse; contemporary controllers use emerging technology (e.g. head movements with sensors in the head-mounted display; walking in a harness; arm movements monitored by camera systems or wearable sensors; facial expression captured with cameras; voice using microphones and earpieces; or [the ultimate, but still speculatively] in-the-future, by-thought-controller). Output directly addresses the sensory system, i.e. vision (using displays; either head-mounted or fixed display), audio (e.g. surround sound headsets), touch (e.g. data or haptic gloves), or force (e.g. pressure vests). Further technology is needed to gather data about the learner as well as the environment. Most relevant is

Fig. 5.1 Variability of input devices and recording methods of output data: (*1*) head-mounted display; (*2*) walking platform; (*3*) game controller; (*4*) space tracking systems for hand movements; (*5*) close range hand movement traction; (*6*) person movement tracking; (*7*) visual observation of the candidate; (*8*) EEG recording; (*9*) EKG recording and (*10*) interview and surveys

data about any change in the environment (e.g. moving objects), sensor data from input and output devices related to the virtual space (e.g. viewing direction and object in focus) and the learner itself (e.g. EEG reading, video stream). The data is used to document the learning progress, but also to create formative feedback (see Reiners et al. 2014a). The set-up allows synchronisation of protocols from both the real world and the virtual environment; especially, the change in biometric data in the real world implies a feedback from the virtual environment (Gibson and Jackl 2015). This can be used to support the measurement of immersion and awareness of the virtual space. Further data is collected from the environment by protocolling every action and event in short time intervals.

Preliminary experiment in Reiners et al. (2015b) examined the intensity of immersion in 3D virtual worlds (Second Life using a traditional 2D monitor rather than the version for head-mounted displays) compared to the use of a head-mounted display. Despite the difference in user-control (third person vs. first person), participant comments and ratings unanimously indicated the outcome: the HMD experience supported the 'feeling of being there' far more than the 2D display did. In addition, the sensory feedback was experienced more intensively, including minor negative side effects such as dizziness. In addition, the experience was considered as 'more authentic' as the navigation was more aligned with the body. Note, participants may not consider 'realistic' and 'authentic' to be different concepts.

Gamification and Game Design

An early and well-known example for game design using storytelling is the game Dungeons and Dragons (Loh 2007), in which the players form a team and undergo an adventure guided by the storyteller to ensure progress. The game design provides the storyteller with god-like features enabling them to interfere and direct events at any time while still allowing players the freedom to decide on the narrative, i.e. which path to follow.

The storyteller has the most influence on the learner's decision (Bauman and Briggs 1990). However, in self-guided explorative learning spaces, it is either the learner undertaking the journey (Danilicheva et al. 2009) or the environment itself providing the guidance. This is commonly done in modern, so-called open world games, which allow the free exploration of the environment. Yet, a good game design blends the storyline with the chosen narrative of the player, such that non-player characters (NPC) or an event reminds the player of the overall game objectives, so players are 'nudged' in the desired direction (Reiners et al. 2014a, b). These reminders may be weak (e.g. an NPC talking about something while the player walks by) or compelling (e.g. all paths but one are blocked by obstacles to drag the player in one direction). The same mechanism needs to be applied in learning spaces; the scope of the narrative must be suitably broad for learners to engage a sense of curiosity and develop intrinsic motivation for learning, while being limited to enable the instructor to ensure completion of learning objectives and course outcomes. The environment has to continuously track the player against the expected narrative and ensure that milestones are achieved and key actions are performed. For example, the loading of a container on a vessel requires that: (1) it is validated that the container has to be loaded on the vessel; (2) that the goods are first deposited in the container; and, then (3) the container is transported to the container bridge to be loaded. The player must fulfil these rules to be successful; yet, there is free choice, among others, of transport vehicle, path and speed. Figure 5.4 provides the narratives of an expert, and Fig. 5.5 of an inexperienced learner, (see also the Evaluation and Formative section).

Examples for Explorative Authentic Learning Spaces

We conducted experiments to evaluate how a learner explores the virtual learning space based on a general induction of the objectives. The scenario is called 'Open Container' and is set on an active virtual container terminal. The background story is that customs inspected a container and forgot to secure it according to safety guidelines. The learner's task is to go to the container (a map where the location is provided) without getting injured, killed or simply disturbing the working process. Note that the container terminal is unrealistic as it contains an unusually high number of dangerous situations.

The learner is wearing the Oculus Rift with headphones for a high degree of immersion, while using a PlayStation controller to move and turn the avatar. The head and viewing direction is aligned with the movement of the Oculus Rift. The player starts outside of the container terminal in a room where the controls are explained and a video about the objective is shown. Figure 5.2 shows the view after leaving the container. There are three dominant points of interest: the warehouse on the left, a large building ahead and the container terminal. The given task, as well as an open gate, increases the attraction for the latter one. Experiments showed that most walked directly through this gate.

Fig. 5.2 View after leaving the starting location: *Left image* shows the view to the warehouse and parts of the building; *right image* is the container terminal with the open gate to the container terminal

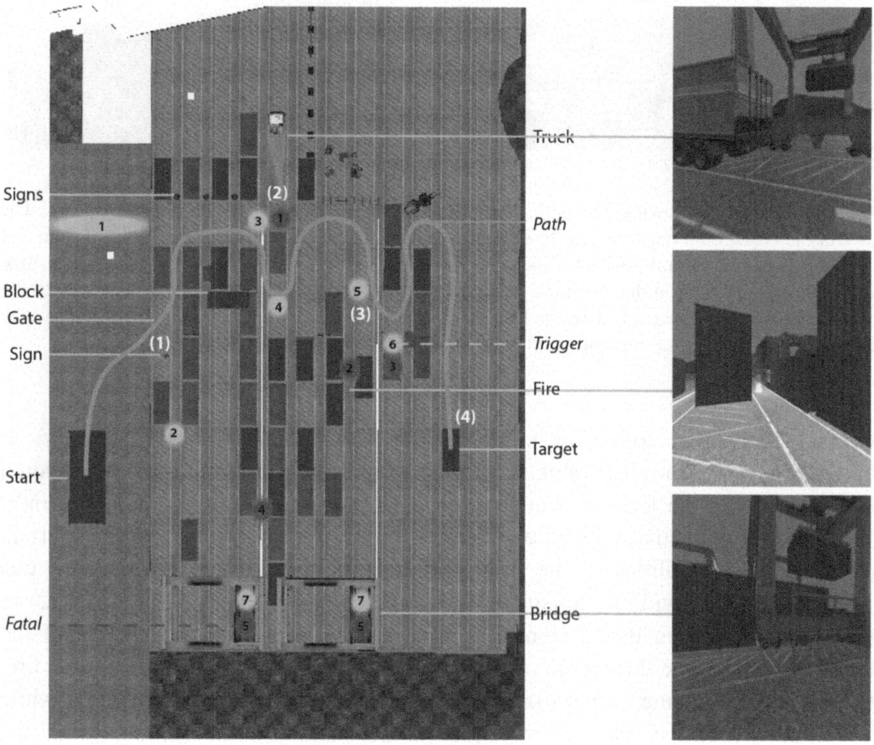

Fig. 5.3 Overview of the container terminal scenario. *Yellow markers* are triggers (*1–7*), *red* indicates an area where the learner can die (*1–5*), white numbers are milestones that the learner should reach (*1–4*), the *blue line* shows the path an expert walked while solving the task

Figure 5.3 elaborates the path and methods to indirectly guide the students. In these experiments, we left open the options to stray from the ideal so we could investigate the participants' behaviour; however, we provided visual hints (signs),

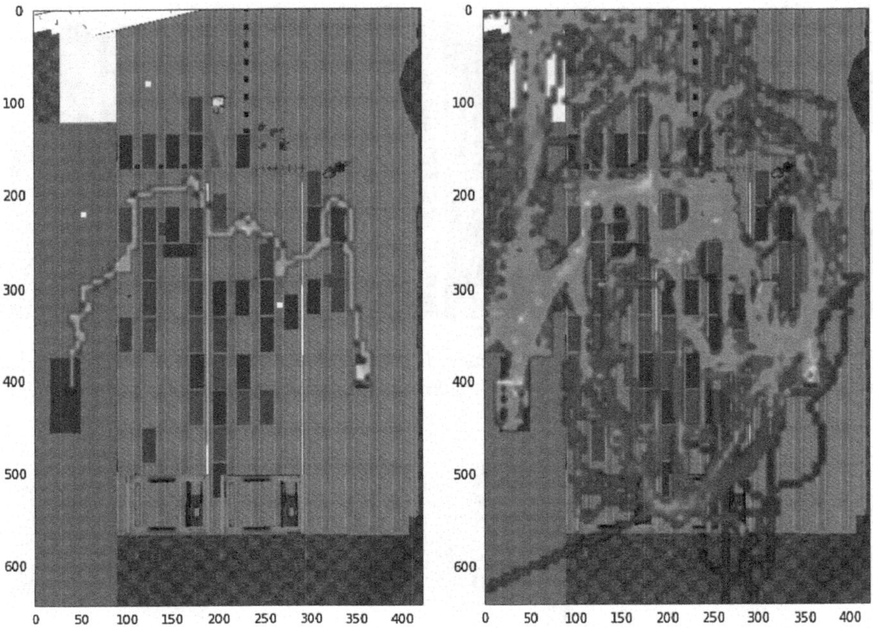

Fig. 5.4 Heatmaps showing the path of one participant (*left*) and all participants (*right*). The intensity is based on a log function (to emphasise areas of interest) over the accumulated time that an avatar was at a certain position. Note that a brighter colour (*yellow* or *red*) implies more time was spent by an avatar at this position. For example, on the left side, the *red spot* half way to the target indicates that the student reacted on the moving bridge, waited for its path to find a way without getting under the hanging container

points of attraction (open areas, gaps), blocks (container blocking a path) or dynamic actions (moving vehicles, fire) to direct the participants in the desired direction. While the learner is unable to pass through a container, signs are indicators and do not actively block exploration. Figure 5.3 shows triggers that start an activity and possibilities to die or be injured on the terminal. Triggers in this scenario are (1) providing guidance towards the container terminal by voice, (2) as in (1), but indicating that a sign said 'wrong way', (3) starts the backup of the truck, (4) starts the bridge to move towards the learner, (5) ignites the fire, (6) closes the container while the learner is in it and (7) drops the container while the learner is under it. The red areas indicate the location where a learner can die, e.g. (1) crushed by the truck, (2) burn in the fire, (3) locked in a container, (4) hit by the bridge or (5) a dropping container. The scenario is further explored in Reiners et al. (2014b).

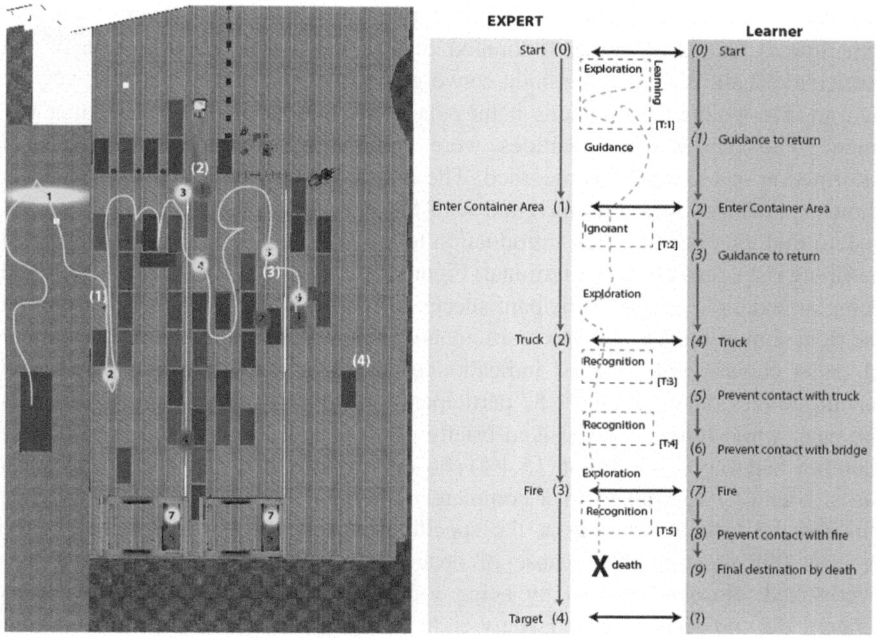

Fig. 5.5 Comparison of narratives—expert and learner

Evaluation and Formative Feedback

The evaluation in these experiments was manually conducted by analysing the log files generated during experimentation. The log file captured the coordinates, the viewing direction and the object in sight in 0.25-s intervals. For the analysis, the data was visualised using a self-developed tool to create heatmaps (colour coding to highlight the range of differences observed) and analysed by categorising the behaviour throughout the experiment. In addition, the data is used to replay the whole experiment, allowing the experimenter to gain further insight from different perspectives, including the view of the student. This step is chosen as a result of the early stage of the implementation. See below for more details on the next stage of the environment and how gamification is used to motivate replays.

The focus of the experiment was on whether the scenario design enabled participants, without detailed instruction, to acquire necessary information and complete desired tasks while understanding the inherent dangers of the scenario. The participants were involved in a public event at Curtin University (Festival of Learning; http://www.curtin.edu.au/learningfortomorrow/festival-of-learning.cfm)[1]

[1]Note that the linked website also includes a video showing the set-up of the experiment; however, the video is for marketing and not for research purposes.

and had the choice to participate in the experiment (using the container terminal experiment), use another head-mounted display for a roller coaster ride or not participate at all. We noticed a slight convergence towards the roller coaster; yet, we had no disappointed participants if they had only the option of the container terminal. The participants' identities were completely anonymous; no personal information or bio data was recorded. The introduction to the scenario included a short explanation of how to navigate with the PlayStation controller, their overall task to find the one container, introduction to the map outside the start location and outlining risks on a container terminal. Figure 5.4 shows two heatmaps; the left one being an example of one participant successfully finding the container, the one on the right shows overlay of all the participants in the experiment. It shows the variety of paths chosen, with a clear indication of the main and also anticipated path leading to the container. Of the 52 participants, 36 (69.2%) moved directly towards the gate, while four (7.7%) walked briefly past the gate, but realised immediately that they had to go back. Eight (15.4%) chose to explore the house despite the given tasks; four (7.7%) walked in a completely different direction. Only 20 (38.5%) finished the task by arriving at the specified container; 22 (42.3%) died in the process (the most frequent cause of death was the falling container as it was overlooked, closely followed by being locked in a container when participants ignored the 'no entry' sign). Twenty-eight (53.9%) explored the virtual environment before finding the goal. General feedback was that they enjoyed the opportunity to explore a space that is not accessible in the real world. Only six (11.5%) had to stop the experiment early as they felt light dizziness.[2]

This experiment is used to understand how learners address an unknown virtual environment, i.e. not their field of study. We used a container terminal; a scenario most participants know of and have a rough understanding of the processes that happen. The short introduction let them know about risks (most of them are common knowledge as they included fire, moving vehicles and other large objects) but providing them with no special training. All but a few of the participants had not experienced HMDs, which added to the novelty of the experiment. Observations supported the above-mentioned experiment regarding the usability and immediate capability to navigate in the virtual environment; an experience that we did not observe from other environments such as Second Life. We recognised physical reactions with some participants, but less intensive compared to scenarios like roller coaster and racing simulators. Feedback after the experiment suggests that this is related to the real-world relation of the scenario and the focus on the task as a subliminal distraction. The analysis of the individual heatmaps showed that most participants were following given attractors to choose their paths and also focused on getting to the final destination. The low success rate, as well as the large number

[2]Note that this could be reduced by going through a set-up process before the experiment, which takes up to 5 min. Furthermore, the next model of the HDM device will have a higher resolution and better sensors to counteract the dizziness.

of deadly accidents, demonstrated that container terminals were not safe environments and training and extensive induction should be undertaken.

We consider the immediate formative feedback as one of the most important components in a self-explorative environment. While the first stage is using visual feedback for guidance and messages in case of errors, we are also implementing two methods for an automated evaluation of given activities including various gamification mechanisms; see Reiners et al. (2014b) for more details. The first method uses defined milestones to derive this from the activities and, most importantly, the shortfalls. Figures 5.3 and 5.5 show some milestones on the container terminal that the learner should reach according to the scenario. For the example of the container terminal, milestones could be:

- Walking through gate (1): The learner enters the actual learning space; the passage of time or distance walked could provide an indication of how quickly the learner understood the task (reading maps or instructions) or found the relevant area.
- Passing the truck (2): Indication that the learner walked in the correct direction, did not follow a path that was indicated as a no-entry zone and did not get hit by the truck. The milestone is reached if the learner turns right before the truck; the alternative of passing quickly behind the truck is considered as unsafe.
- Past the second container bridge (3): The main path is past the second container bridge, yet it is important to consider movements as well as potential risks walking below the container. The milestone is reached beyond this area.
- Passing the fire (4): The next milestone is either walking the north-east loop or waiting for the fire to be extinguished and the explosion to subside.
- Finding the target container (5): Reaching and entering the container that was indicated on the map as the final destination.

Figure 5.5 shows the comparison of narratives done by the expert and learner. The first step is the alignment of matching milestones, e.g. (e1) and (l2) for entering the container area. Even up to this point in time, the expert and learner followed different narratives, e.g. the learner triggered [T:1] and walked further. This variation allows us to deduct feedback of the learner based on predefined templates associated with triggers and analytics of the collected data as described above. The milestone (l1) is created by trigger [T:1], which is associated with walking in the wrong direction. The immediate feedback is a message (voice or text) about the objective and where to go (guidance); furthermore, the analytics show larger distances than expected, which may indicate an exploration of the environment or that the learner is lost. The information with additional hints can be passed to the learner ('You walked in the wrong direction [template] and covered a distance of 250 m instead of 180 m, requiring 30% more time than expected [analytics]. Please go back and use the gate to the container area [guidance]'). The relative straight walking line shows that the guidance helped to get back on track and reach the milestone (e1). A similar strategy is used in the following steps, whereas ignorance indicates overlooked signs/restricted areas, recognition indicates the awareness of danger (not dying) and exploration indicates a longer walking distance than expected. In this example, the learner died by walking in a container that was ready to be closed and shipped. We focus in our framework on milestones and the deduction of what happened in between by using collected data and/or information from triggers and other objects. We are not detailing the behaviour or gestures of avatars in detail; see Fardinpour and Reiners (2014) for some examples on how an analysis of human behaviour can be further processed.

The training scenario is gamified in different ways. First, feedback on performance relative to previous experiences and overall outcomes is provided based on records of sectors defined by milestones and time. Second, quality of the experience is indicated by an overall score, i.e. based on time, absence of errors, and most importantly, not running into a deadly situation. Accuracy (short distance), time or recognition of danger are positive (to get a carrot), while other situations are punished (stick) by adding penalty points. Third, additional gamification elements include rewind functions allowing learners to reinspect a situation, competitive incentives and being in an authentic environment.

Conclusion

Virtual training environments have changed significantly over the last decade. Second Life created the critical mass of users demonstrating that it is time to consider real alternatives for textbooks and restricted classroom. Virtual worlds expanded the lecture by breath live into the learning material and created a new understanding of collaborative learning in distance education. However, Second Life is an open space not primarily designed for education but the smallest denominator to allow any discipline to find tools and processes without being overwhelmed. The lack of educational support became the seed of other environments; SLoodle and Vacademia are just two examples that show how to link the world to subsidiary systems for supporting the learning process.

In this chapter, we demonstrated the ongoing research project nDiVE (http://www.ndive-project.com), which focussed on an authentic and immersive learning process in the context of Health and Safety within Logistics Infrastructures. We shifted the focus from the collaboration (as done in Second Life and similar environments) to individual goal-oriented training units; supported by emerging technology to increase the feeling of being present in the learning space. The importance is set on authenticity and the unrestricted and unsupervised exploration of the space; yet supporting the learner with supportive but hidden guidance and formative feedback. The learner is challenged to find a solution, but has to pay the same caution, as it would be necessary in the real world. nDiVE provides a preliminary framework suggesting an orchestration of hardware to experience the space, software to create the context, the automated observation and feedback generation and guidelines how to create the authentic processes that define the learning experience.

The experiments showed the validity of the 'carrot and stick' approach. Scripted events, as well as, placed objects can be used to direct the learner in the right direction and provoke the anticipated behaviour expert demonstrated in similar contexts. The underlying story with various narratives offers the learner objectives without restricting possible pathways to find the target. The analytics of the learners' tracks further supported a deeper understanding for the educators in designing learning scenarios and identifying knowledge gaps.

The head-mounted display limits the collaborative learning experience as long as the environment does not allow multiple human-controlled avatars at the same time similar to Second Life. Same restrictions apply to trainers or educators; as observation and feedback is limited to a debriefing afterwards as any other communication during the learning process would reduce the immersion. Thus, we are extending the framework to log activities and changes of the environment and reproduce the whole learning experience on a 3D cylinder space (curved 3D display with a width of approx. 6 m; using glasses for the 3D view). This allows the projection of all activities similar to a movie with rewinding and forward opportunities, but also choosing the appropriate perspective such as first person or surveillance camera. The external debriefing adds another layer of evaluation to the learning experience. The enclosed learning space supports the training by allowing to redo the scenario after receiving formative feedback from the system; yet human trainers are still required to validate the final training outcome or answer in depth questions.

Acknowledgements Support for the production of this publication has been provided by the Australian Government Office for Learning and Teaching (Grant: Development of an authentic training environment to support skill acquisition in logistics and supply chain management, ID: ID12-2498). The views expressed in this publication do not necessarily reflect the views of the Australian Government Office for Learning and Teaching.

References

Bates, A. T., & Sangra, A. (2011). *Managing technology in higher education: Strategies for transforming teaching and learning*. Jossey-Bass.

Bauman, R., & Briggs, C. (1990). Poetics and performance as critical perspectives on language and social life. *Annual Review of Anthropology, 19,* 59–88.

Biocca, F., & Delaney, B. (1995). Immersive virtual reality technology. In F. Biocca & M. Levy (Eds.), *Communication in the age of virtual reality* (pp. 57–124). Hillsdale, NJ: Erlbaum.

Brown, E., & Cairns, P. (2004). A grounded investigation of game Immersion. In *CHI '04 Extended Abstracts on Human Factors in Computing Systems* (pp. 1297–1300). New York, New York, USA: ACM Press. doi:10.1145/985921.986048.

Cummings, J. J., Bailenson, J. N., & Fidler, M. J. (2012). How immersive is enough? A foundation for a meta-analysis of the effect of immersive technology on measured presence. In *Proceedings of the International Society for Presence Research Annual Conference*.

Danilicheva, P., Klimenko, S., Baturin, Y., & Serebrov, A. (2009). Education in virtual worlds: Virtual storytelling. In *International Conference on CyberWorlds* (pp. 333–338). IEEE.

Dede, C. (2009). Immersive interfaces for engagement and learning. *Science, 323*(5910), 66–69. doi:10.1126/science.1167311.
Ermi, L., & Mäyrä, F. (2005). Fundamental components of the gameplay experience: Analysing immersion. In *Proceedings of DiGRA 2005 Conference: Changing Views – Worlds in Play*. Retrieved from http://www.gamesconference.org/digra2005/viewabstract.php?id=267.
Fardinpour, A., & Reiners, T. (2014). The taxonomy of goal-oriented actions in virtual training environments. *Procedia Technology, 13,* 38–46.
Friedman, T. L. (2006). *The world is flat: The globalized world in the twenty-first century*. London: Penguin Books.
Gibson, D., & Jackl, P. (2015). Theoretical considerations for game-based e-learning analytics. In T. Reiners, & L.C. Wood (Eds.), *Gamification in education and business* (pp. 403–416). Berlin: Springer.
Gregory, S. (2011). Teaching higher education students with diverse learning outcomes in the virtual world of Second Life. In R. Hinrichs & C. Wankel (Eds.), *Transforming virtual world learning, Cutting-edge technologies in higher education* (Vol. 4, pp. 333–362). Teynampet, India: Emerald Group Publishing Limited.
Hebbel-Seeger, A. (2013). Pedagogical and psychological impacts of teaching and learning in virtual realities. In A. Hebbel-Seeger, T. Reiners, & D. Schäffer (Eds.), *Synthetic worlds: Emerging technologies in education and economics*. New York: Springer.
Herrington, J. (2006). Authentic e-learning in higher education: Design principles for authentic learning environments and tasks. In T. Reeves & S. Yamashita (Eds.), *Proceedings of World Conference on E-Learning in Corporate, Government, Healthcare, and Higher Education 2006* (pp. 3164–3173). Chesapeake, VA.
Herrington, J., & Kervin, L. (2007). Authentic learning supported by technology: 10 suggestions and cases of integration in classrooms. *Educational Media International, 44*(3), 219–236.
Huotari, K., & Hamari, J. (2012). Defining gamification - A service marketing perspective. In *MindTrek2012* (pp. 17–22). Tampere: Finland: ACM. Retrieved from http://delivery.acm.org/10.1145/2400000/2393137/p17-huotari.pdf?ip=129.180.76.61&id=2393137&acc=ACTIVE%20SERVICE&key=65D80644F295BC0D.51DB8D6762B6E365.4D4702B0C3E38B35.4D4702B0C3E38B35&CFID=466247267&CFTOKEN=34482705&__acm__=1401166669_50fc6bf23c53e28a9373422edc13ae31.
Jennett, C., Cox, A. L., Cairns, P., Dhoparee, S., Epps, A., Tijs, T., et al. (2008). Measuring and defining the experience of immersion in games. *International Journal of Human-Computer Studies, 66*(9), 641–661. doi:10.1016/j.ijhcs.2008.04.004.
Kapp, K. M. (2012). *The Gamification of learning and instruction: Game-based methods and strategies for training and education* (1st ed.). Pfeiffer.
Landers, R. N., Bauer, K. N., Callan, R. C., & Armstrong, M. B. (2015). Psychological theory and the gamification of learning. In T. Reiners, & L.C. Wood (Eds.), *Gamification in education and business* (pp. 165–168). Berlin: Springer.
Loh, C. S. (2007). Designing online games assessment as "Information Trails". In D. Gibson, C. Aldrich, & M. Prensky (Eds.), *Games and simulations in online learning: Research and development frameworks* (pp. 323–348). Hershey: Information Science Publishing.
McGonigal, J. (2011). *Reality is broken: Why games make us better and how they can change the world* (Reprint). Penguin Books.
Mestre, D., & Vercher, J. L. (2011). Immersion and Presence. In P. Fuchs, G. Moreau, & P. Guitton (Eds.), *Virtual reality: Concepts and technologies* (pp. 93–102). London, U.K.: Taylor & Francis Group.
Oculus. (2013). About Oculus VR. Retrieved from http://www.oculusvr.com/company/.
Palmer, F. (1995). Interpersonal communication and virtual reality: Mediating Interpersonal relationships. In F. Biocca & M. Levy (Eds.), *Communication in the age of virtual reality* (pp. 277–302). Hillsdale, NJ: Erlbaum.
Pederson, E. M. (1995). Storytelling and the art of teaching. *Forum, 33*(1)

Reiners, T., Wood, L. C., & Dron, J. (2014a). From chaos towards sense: A learner-centric narrative virtual learning space. In J. Bishop (Ed.), *Gamification for human factors integration: Social, education, and psychological issues* (pp. 242–258). Hershey, PA: IGI Global.
Reiners, T., Wood, L. C., & Gregory, S. (2014b). Experimental study on technology-induced authentic immersion in virtual worlds for education and vocational training. Report Curtin University.
Ryan, R. M., & Deci, E. L. (2000). Intrinsic and extrinsic motivations: Classic definitions and new directions. *Contemporary Educational Psychology, 25*(1), 54–67. doi:10.1006/ceps.1999.1020.
Rystedt, H., & Sjoblom, B. (2012). Realism, authenticity, and learning in healthcare simulations: rules of relevance and irrelevance as interactive achievements. *Instructional Science, 40*, 785–798. doi:10.1007/s11251-012-9213-x.
Slater, M. (2003). A note on presence terminology. *Presence Connect, 3*(3)
Slater, M., & Wilbur, S. (1997). A framework for immersive virtual environments (FIVE): Speculations on the role of presence in virtual environments. *Presence: Teleoperators and Virtual Environments, 6*(6), 603–616.
Witmer, B. G., & Singer, M. J. (1998). Measuring presence in virtual environments: A presence questionnaire. *Presence: Teleoperators and Virtual Environments, 7*(3), 225–240.
Wood, L. C., & Reefke, H. (2010). Working with a diverse class: Reflections on the role of team teaching, teaching tools and technological support. In H. Huai, P. Kommers, & P. Isaías (Eds.), Presented at the *IADIS international conference on international higher education* (pp. 72–79) (IHE 2010).
Wood, L. C., & Reiners, T. (2013). Game-based elements to upgrade bots to non-player characters in support of educators. In A. Hebbel-Seeger, T. Reiners, & D. Schäfer (Eds.), *Synthetic worlds: Emerging technologies in education and economics* (pp. 257–277). Berlin: Springer.
Wood, L. C., Teräs, H., Reiners, T., & Gregory, S. (2013). The role of gamification and game-based learning in authentic assessment within virtual environments. In S. Frielick, N. Buissink-Smith, P. Wyse, J. Billot, J. Hallas, & E. Whitehead (Eds.), *Research and Development in Higher Education: The Place of Learning and Teaching* (Vol. 36, pp. 514–523). Auckland, New Zealand: Higher Education Research and Development Society of Australasia, Inc. http://www.herdsa.org.au/wp-content/uploads/conference/2013/HERDSA_2013_WOOD.pdf.

Author Biographies

Torsten Reiners is Senior Lecturer in Logistics at the Curtin University, Australia. His research and teaching experiences are in the areas of operations research, but include instructional design, development of adaptive learning environments, distant collaboration and mobile learning. His PhD thesis is about adaptive learning material in the field of operations research. He has participated in multiple projects to use 3D spaces for learning support, i.e. to improve the authenticity of learning in classes about production and simulation. He is project leader on a competitive grant from the Australian Office of Learning and Teaching (www.ndive-project.com).

Lincoln C. Wood is a Senior Lecturer (operations and supply chain management) at Auckland University of Technology and an Adjunct Research Fellow at Curtin Business School (Australia). He received the Council of Supply Chain Management Professional's (CSCMP) Young Researcher Award in 2009 in the USA and earned his PhD at the University of Auckland. After developing a strong interest in effective supply chain education, Lincoln received the Outstanding Research Award at the International Higher Education Conference in 2010 and is now the Project Co-Leader on a competitive grant from the Australian Office of Learning and Teaching (www.ndive-project.com). Lincoln has published in leading international journals.

Marko Teräs has a broad international background in developing, training and researching online learning, user experience and digital technologies in the public, private and non-profit sectors. He has founded two companies in the areas of user experience design and online learning, has a Master's degree in instructional design and technology and Bachelor's in user experience design. He is currently conducting his PhD research in immersive virtual environments, gamification and authentic learning at Curtin University, and at the same time hoping to finish all Borderlands DLCs on Xbox 360.

Hanna Teräs is Professional Learning Consultant at Curtin University in Western Australia. In her role she designs, implements and coordinates professional learning programmes for faculty academics in areas such as teaching and learning in higher education, twenty-first century pedagogies and teaching and learning with innovative technological solutions. Hanna Teräs also holds a Senior Lecturer position at Tampere University of Applied Sciences in Finland where she was the leading developer of '21st Century Educators', a fully online international postgraduate certificate program for teaching in higher education. Her research interests include authentic e-learning, online teacher professional development, social technologies in education and e-learning in multicultural learning communities.

Sue Gregory is an Associate Professor, long-term adult educator, Chair of Research and member of the ICT Education team in the School of Education at the University of New England, Armidale, Australia. She teaches pre-service and postgraduate education students how to incorporate technology into their teaching. Sue, through her avatar Jass Easterman, has been using Second Life by applying her virtual world knowledge to expose her students, both on and off campus, to the learning opportunities of virtual worlds since 2007. She has been involved with many university- and Australia-wide projects on creating learning spaces in virtual worlds.

Vanessa Chang is a Professor in Information Systems at Curtin University where she also received her PhD. Her research interests and activities are focused in Information Systems (IS) and Education. In the discipline of Information Systems, her research is focused on leadership and governance in the utilisation of Information Communications Technology in organisations. In the area of Education, her research interests are in immersive learning in 3D virtual world environment, mobile learning and e-learning ecosystems. She has ongoing research collaboration with Graz University of Technology, Austria and has worked on a number of experiments in 3D virtual worlds in Second Life, OpenSim and OpenWonderland. She has published in ranked international journals and conference proceedings.

Michael Steurer holds PhD (with hons), an MSc (with hons) and a BSc in Computer Science and Telematics from Graz University of Technology, Austria. He was a Scientific Research Assistant at the Institute for Information Systems and Computer Media at Graz University of Technology, Austria and a Visiting Scholar at the Curtin University in Perth, Australia. His main research interests are Location-based Social Networks, Data Mining, Social Network Analysis, Machine Learning, Virtual Worlds and Digital Economies.

Timothy McDonald is a student at Curtin University in Mechatronics.

Ali Fardinpour holds PhD (with hons) from Curtin University. His current role is the lead research scientist in Immersive Technologies in Learning and Assessment. His current research focus is action-based learning and assessment in virtual training environments. He also is an adjunct researcher at Curtin Learning and Teaching.

Chapter 6
Action-Based Learning Assessment in Virtual Training Environments

Ali Fardinpour, Torsten Reiners and Lincoln C. Wood

Introduction

It is common to pass an induction and attend continuous training to receive and keep permission to work on a site with health and safety risks. Furthermore, it is generally not possible to perform the training on systems that are currently used for operation due to safety and business matters. A common alternative is the usage of replica in virtual training environments to simulate relevant processes and activities as well as the surroundings and scenarios. However, it requires a well-balanced orchestration of domain expert knowledge, (educational) technology and instructional designers with experience in developing virtual training units to recreate authentic, immersive and engaging learning experiences with later transferability to the real world. The suitability of virtual environments itself is justified by depicting the infeasibility of scenarios to be considered valuable in a real world setting, i.e. high costs (space simulator), high risks of injuries for learners and educators (handling of hazardous material) or near-impossibility but with a high degree of importance (natural disaster recovery); (see Hewitt et al. 2010). Advanced technology is used to detach the learner from real and potentially unsafe environments while maintaining authenticity, e.g. using aircraft mock-ups, realistic dashboards as user interfaces and simulations of movements and situations.

A. Fardinpour (✉)
Wise Realities, Curtin University, Perth, Australia
e-mail: Ali.fardinpour@curtin.edu.au

T. Reiners
Curtin University, Perth, Australia
e-mail: t.reiners@cbs.curtin.edu.au

L.C. Wood
University of Otago, Dunedin, New Zealand
e-mail: Lincoln.Wood@otago.ac.nz

S. Gregory and D. Wood (eds.), *Authentic Virtual World Education*,
https://doi.org/10.1007/978-981-10-6382-4_6

Virtual training environments are used in a manifold of situations, e.g. training for surgery, mechanical engineering or health and safety (Filigenzi et al. 2000; Gunn 2006; Hockenmeyer et al. 2009; Kizil 2003). A key aspect of these environments is to develop or advance previous inherited knowledge by immersing (presence) and engaging (motivation) for the learner to explore the scenario and to progress towards given objectives. Given the authenticity of activities, it is possible to map the acquired knowledge later to their correlated real situations counterparts (Bastiaens et al. 2014; Herrington et al. 2010). However, learning progress is related to the understanding of the nature of errors and reflection on the actions that lead to the outcome (Sadler 1989).

Assessment of learning outcomes can be classified as formative (identify the quality of the assessment and provide constructive explanations) or summative (ranking the quality of the assessment) (Scriven 1967). Summative feedback is easy to generate, yet the sole assessment of outcomes by scores and grades seems like a naïve excuse to ignore the richness of formative feedback. The limited dimension of scores ignores how the learner reacts to stimuli and applies learned knowledge to make decisions during the learning process. The assessment has to include the sequence of actions that lead to an outcome, as it is otherwise not possible to deduct the successful application of knowledge versus successfully achieving the objective by coincidence. Furthermore, the sequence of actions can be used to generate detailed formative feedback (Reiners et al. 2013, 2014).

The drawback of successful formative feedback is the high investment of resources such as the time it takes for marking assessment tasks, i.e. with intelligent assessment systems to support or even replace the human evaluator still in its early childhood (Fardinpour and Dreher 2012). Regarding activities in virtual training environments, we are facing even further unsolved challenges; among others the recognition of human performance (activities), interpretation of the human behaviour, and a commonly accepted standard to encode and communicate the actions. In this chapter, we are addressing the encoding by suggesting an adaptive taxonomy being designed to encompass the multitude of disciplines and requirements (Chodos et al. 2014; Robertson 1997, 2000; Verhulsdonck and Morie 2009). We further describe an approach to compare consecutive training sessions (i.e. the action sequences) to identify changes in the action and their impact on the overall outcome. It is further possible to assess the learners' actions against the ones from experts to generate formative feedback and provide guidance on how to improve in further training sessions. The following section covers a brief introduction to virtual environments and action-based learning. Following, we describe the used taxonomy for user actions and provide an introduction in our method to assess the action-based learning (ALAM) and how formative feedback is generated.

Learning and Assessment in Virtual Learning Environments

Virtual learning environments (VLE) are "computer-based environments that are relatively open systems, allowing interactions and encounters with other participants" (Wilson 1996, p. 8). Virtual training environments (VTE) represent a subset of VLE by setting the focus on skills training including some specialised methods like intelligent pedagogical agents (Rickel et al. 1998), game-based tutoring (Craighead 2008), gamification- or game-based structures (Wood and Reiners 2013) or educational simulation (Dede and Lewis 1995; Dede et al. 1999). VTE are used extensively in areas like surgery training (Gunn 2006), spinal anaesthesia (Hockenmeyer et al. 2009), dynamic hip screw surgery training in vitro (Ahmed et al. 2012) or oral implantology (Chen et al. 2012). Virtual environments "allow you to do things which would be difficult or impossible to do in the physical world—both literally and pragmatically" (Twinning 2009, p. 498). And despite the generally restricted functionality with focus on building scenarios and providing collaborative communication tools, virtual worlds such as second life found wide application in education, e.g. teacher education (Gregory et al. 2011; Masters et al. 2013), engineering (Bresciani et al. 2010), health sciences (Thompson and Hagstrom 2011), logistics and manufacturing (Wriedt et al. 2008) and simulation of hazardous situations for training purposes (Reiners et al. 2013; Reiners and Wood 2013).

Avatars are digital representations being used to project the learners' view in the virtual environment. The most common and the most immersive option is a positioning of the camera, the virtual eyes, at the position of the head to provide a first-person perspective. This allows a mirroring of head movements in virtual and real space. An alternative is the third-person perspective, where the camera follows the avatar. While the learner can follow gestures and interactions of the avatar from an observer perspective, it reduces the immersive perception. The control of the avatar includes various options; among others, traditional input devices (e.g. keyboard and mouse), advanced technology (e.g. Kinect or Razor Hydra) or replicas of real world control interfaces such as the dashboard of a truck to allow the real world haptic experience. The environment is often shared with other avatars; either controlled by humans or computers, so-called intelligent bots or agents (Wood and Reiners 2013).

Authentic learning has been used in different disciplines over time to increase the quality of training in education systems. Authentic learning is about engaging students in learning about, and solving, real-life problems by the means of simulation and (educational) technology (Herrington and Herrington 2006). By reviewing the research related to the use of simulations in the classroom, Smith (1987, p. 409) concluded that the "physical fidelity" of the simulation materials is not as important as the "realistic problem-solving processes" that simulation promotes, a process Smith (1987) describes as the "cognitive realism" of the task Barab et al. (2000, p. 38) also stated that authenticity occurs "not in the learner, the task, or the environment, but in the dynamic interactions among these various components

[…] authenticity is manifest in the flow itself, and is not an objective feature of any one component in isolation." In the same way, Herrington et al. (2003) argued that the cognitive authenticity is much more important than the physical authenticity in the design of authentic learning environments.

Learning by doing or action-based learning refers to orchestrate learning by the learner (Naidu and Bedgood 2012). Thus, legitimate learning actions may vary from an active participation (e.g. building, creating or drawing something) to passive observation that is later examined, reflected on or becomes a seed for a later decision-making process (Naidu and Bedgood 2012). The literature distinguishes different models of action-based learning (Fardinpour and Reiners 2014); including problem-based learning (Barrows and Tamblyn 1980), inquiry or goal-based learning (Schank 1997), scenario-based learning (Naidu 2010) and adventure learning (Doering 2006). Whilst each model has a distinguished focus or perspective, all start with a defined problem or objective (Naidu 2007). Action-based learning is characterised by a learner-centric model where the learner studies the learning material and afterwards applies the lesson learned. This learning by doing approach differentiates action-based learning from action learning, where the learning process is "using personal experience and reflection, group discussion, and analysis, trial-and-error discovery, and learning from one another" (Lasky and Tempone 2004, p. 87). For example, one group is sharing experiences in a discussion (action learning), while the other member of the other group learns by actively performing the tasks to solve a problem (action-based learning).

Summative assessment methods such as multiple-choice or closed-answer questions are useful to rank and grade the learning outcome, but lack supportive, probing or explanatory feedback. Learners require a detailed analysis to understand the reason for their actions and deduct a change in their learning behaviour (Rogers 1951; Sadler 1989). Action-based learning is about flexibility, complexity and creativity; attributes that are difficult to judge with a score (Naidu 2010). Therefore, additional flexibility is required to cope with the assessment patterns that reflect actions of the learners, particularly at more advanced levels of learning (Wood and Reiners 2013). Thus, in VTE the demonstrated actions and abilities of learners need formative feedback as an important component of the learning process.

Assessment of learners' mastery in VTE is conducted primarily by experts who observe and analyse the training. Shute, Ventura, Bauer and Zapata-Rivera (2009, p. 299) argue that the assessments should be "seamlessly woven into the fabric of the learning environment" so that it is practically indiscernible for the learner; therefore, causing no distraction. Their stealth assessment uses automated scoring and machine-based reasoning techniques to infer, for example, the "value of evidence-based competencies across a network of skills" (Shute et al. 2009, p. 299). Shute used stealth assessment formally for the first time in 2005 during an American Educational Research Association (AERA) symposium on diagnostic assessment, but it was designed and employed two decades earlier as part of a guided discovery world called Smithtown (Shute 2011; Shute and Glaser 1990). Al-Smadi et al. (2010) propose a framework using stealth assessment to assess action choices and sequences in serious games; creating formative feedback on the interpretive level of Rogers' feedback classification (Rogers 1951).

"Assessment is authentic when we directly examine student performance on worthy intellectual tasks. Traditional assessment, by contract, relies on indirect or proxy 'items', efficient, simplistic substitutes from which we think valid inferences can be made about the student's performance at those valued challenges" (Wiggins 1990, p. 2). He further explains authentic assessment by comparing it to the traditional testing of learning outcomes. See the following list for some distinction criteria:

- Instead of testing for recognising and recall, authentic assessment requires an effective application of acquired knowledge.
- Authentic assessment is holistic in the assessment tasks to represent priorities and challenges and not limited to paper-based only one specific valid answer questions.
- Authentic assessment is about testing the understanding and reasoning of answers, not plainly repeating the only solution from the textbook.
- The validity of answers in the context of authentic assessment depends on real world validity, not a match with the textbook or course material.
- Authentic assessment maps the "ill-structured" challenges and roles of real-word scenarios; not providing a clean, discrete and simplistic reflection of it.

Meyer (1992) believed that it is very important to consider "authentic to what?" and named "few facets of authenticity: stimuli, task complexity, locus of control, motivation, spontaneity, resources, conditions, criteria, standards, consequences" (p. 40). According to Meyer (1992), each assessment needs to address at least a few of these facets, if not all, to be considered as an authentic assessment.

The Taxonomy of Human Actions

One purpose of taxonomy is the ordered categorisation and unique specification of items; in our case human actions. Robertson (1997, 2000) created the taxonomy of embodied actions for the cooperative design in a distributed company "as a possible bridging structure between the field study of cooperative work in practice and the design of technology that might support that work over distance" (2000, p. 130). Robertson embedded open and flexible categories, allowing others to adapt it to their own requirements. Embodied actions were split into different classes; relating to physical objects (among others movement or use), other person (among others monitoring or pretending) and workspace (among others moving or looking); (see also Verhulsdonck and Morie 2009).

The literature review on taxonomies of human's actions, embodied actions, actions in virtual worlds and behaviour modelling showed that researchers tend towards creating their own taxonomy of actions or behaviours based on their

Fig. 6.1 BEHAVE taxonomy classifying actions in three different classes

project's needs. Examples are Fleishman (1975) who identifies six categories of human performance: identification, discrimination, sequence learning, motor skill, scanning and problem-solving; or Goldman (1970) who identifies four categories: individuation, act-type, act-token, basic- and non-basic-actions. Goldman (1970, p. 6) disagrees with the assumption that two different actions can be both recognised as basic actions based on the same identity thesis. Goldman (1970, p. 6) reminds us that, "moving my hand is a basic action, whereas checkmating my opponent and turning on the light are not basic actions. Rather, they are actions I perform by performing some basic actions."

Fardinpour and Reiners (2014) use the "Basic Exploratory Human Actions in Virtual Environments" (BEHAVE) taxonomy of human actions to classify learners' goal-oriented actions. This taxonomy further classifies learners' actions into three levels: The Goal Act, Constitutive Acts, and Functional Acts; see Fig. 6.1. To achieve the Goal Act (primary goal in the scenario), the learner must perform a sequence of Constitutive Acts, which are composed of Functional Acts. Constitutive Acts can be considered as milestones; an approach illustrated by Reiners et al. (2013) for their narratives in virtual environments. However, Functional Acts enhance the ability of an assessor to examine how these milestones are achieved.

Action-Based Learning Assessment Method

Although action-based learning scenarios have been used in virtual training environments before, there is still a lack of comprehensive assessment methods. In this section, we describe the action-based learning assessment method (ALAM), which is focusing on the formative assessment of the learners' performed, goal-oriented, actions. The core functionality of ALAM is the classification and codification of human actions according to the BEHAVE taxonomy previously described. ALAM is a part of an overall process (action-based learning assessment system, ALAS) to record actions, analyse the behaviour, assess against expert solutions and generate formative feedback for an overall compelling learning experience. ALAM uses Rogers' 5-stage feedback classification, which is still valid and commonly used in assessing the learning outcome (Al-Smadi et al. 2010; Dunwell et al. 2011). Human assessors are capable of providing feedback on all stages; however, it is more common to simplify the process by designing multiple-choice or short-answer assessments (Stage 1 and 2). This is particularly true as formative feedback at stage 4 or 5 requires experts to understand whether the student's answer is valid with respect to the scope and body of knowledge, and if not, exploring the train of thoughts that lead to the given answer. This assessment is of higher complexity as it requires understanding of the problem, the context, and often natural language as used by the student. Intelligent assessment algorithms are not yet capable of automatically assessing the learner without introducing sufficient constraints to reduce the problem and solution space (Shen et al. 2001) in a way that largely limits the value of these algorithms in practical settings.

Action Sequence

To consider a learning experience successful, learners need to achieve a predefined goal (i.e. the Goal Act) by performing actions in a given virtual training environment. Following the recording and recognition of actions, the first process comprises the identification of relevance, aggregation of atomic actions to higher level concepts as well as classification according to the BEHAVE taxonomy (Fardinpour and Reiners 2014). For example, smiling and stretching out the arm for a handshake implies a friendly welcome gesture. This sequence of actions is used to assess the learning by analysing its components against expected outcomes and the previously recorded sequences of experts. The creation of formative feedback based on the learning purposes and will support the learner in understanding his/her actions against the expected actions and will support in changing his/her behaviour. It is important to emphasise that the comparison is not requiring an exact match but integrates deviation from the expert into the feedback by visualising the differences. In case of non-mandatory steps, sequences can use alternative actions to achieve the same goal; however, it is up to the learner and experts to judge the validity against further metrics. For example, if the learner is taking extra, non-required steps, it will not impact the primary goal but divert from the expected solution in using more resources such as time or material. The feedback is showing this difference as it shows room for improvement such as working more efficient but also allows experts to gain more insight in the process itself.

Learners' action sequences are compared to the expected action sequences recorded by experts or instructional designers. A first approximation of the

<table>
<tr><th>Action sequence</th><th>Milestones</th><th>Rules</th><th>Expert action sequence</th></tr>
<tr><td>A1: Washing Potatoes</td><td></td><td></td><td></td></tr>
<tr><td>A2: Cut potatoes in fries</td><td>M1: Potatoes are in the right size</td><td>M1-M2-M3</td><td>AS1: A1-A2-A3-A4-A5-A6-A7-A8</td></tr>
<tr><td>A3: Add oil to the pot</td><td></td><td>[A3|A4]-A5</td><td>AS2: A2-A1-A3-A4-A5-A6-A7-A8</td></tr>
<tr><td>A4: Place pot on the stove</td><td></td><td></td><td></td></tr>
<tr><td>A5: Heat oil</td><td></td><td></td><td>AS3: A1-A2-A4-A3-A6-A5-A7-A8</td></tr>
<tr><td>A6: Add potatoes to the oil</td><td>M2: Potatoes in heated oil</td><td></td><td>AS4: A2-A1-A4-A3-A5-A6-A7-A8</td></tr>
<tr><td>A7: Extract potatoes from the oil</td><td></td><td></td><td></td></tr>
<tr><td>A8: Fill potatoes into bowl</td><td>M3: Potatoes are cooked and in bowl</td><td></td><td>AS5: A1-A2-A3-A4-A5-A6-A7-A8</td></tr>
</table>

Fig. 6.2 Action sequence example for a making fries. Note that, we simplified the example for this purpose, e.g. more complex steps like "remove starch" and "adding spices" have been excluded

similarity is the match of specific milestones regarding of availability and order in both sequences and not considering the actions in-between (Reiners et al. 2013). This heuristic can provide an understanding of the general correctness of the solution, yet lacks the validation if milestones are achieved correctly. Note that, the learner is encouraged to explore the space unconstrained and at their preferred speed; thus, milestones are often the only source for (formative) feedback. This approach anticipates providing immediate feedback at milestones to compare the learning success to previous experiences.

Presented is a simple example of the action sequence and requirements with the goal to prepare a bowl of fries made from fresh potatoes. On the left side of Fig. 6.2 is a simplified presentation of the action sequence for the learner to boil potatoes with predefined rules (such as may be established by an instructional designer) but allowing for some freedom. On the right side of Fig. 6.2 are the sequences recorded from experts completing this task. Defined are three milestones, which have to be gained in the order M1–M2–M3. Milestones reflect the achievements of sub-sequences of actions, representing a defined state of the environment. In case of M1, it was expected to have the potatoes in the right size; while not being specific about the pot, type of oil or temperature of oil. M2 is reached when the condition "potatoes in heated oil" is achieved; in general, after completing the second set of actions (A3–A6). However, if M1 was not fulfilled or the learner forgot some actions, the learner will be deemed to have failed to achieve the goal.

Action Recognition

All activities in the virtual training environment were recorded as a raw stream of data, consisting of information such as coordinates of the avatar, viewing direction, relation to objects, position of arms. Regarding the understanding and comparison of action sequences, it is important to analyse the data stream and map parts of the data stream to certain actions in the taxonomy (codification process). This includes the action itself, but also the relevant attributes (e.g. adjective, preposition, location, quantity, unit, object and location). The time-based sorted actions form the action sequences that are evaluated by comparing them to the experts' action sequences. The validity of the sequence is further verified against a set of rules that are either manually specified by the experts or deducted automatically from expert action sequences. For example, the occurrence of a sequence of actions in a specific order (as part of expert action sequences) can be used to derive a rule about predecessor relations. Further, rules are stated for sequences that only appear in some approved action sequences, which would specify alternative solutions. Rules can be stated on all levels of the BEHAVE taxonomy.

Constitutive Acts must be defined by the expert and represent a specific state of the environment. The recognition can be undertaken by so-called triggers (i.e. events that happen in the VTE and are recorded in addition to the actions) or specific action sequences which define the end or start of a Constitutive Act or milestone. For example, in Fig. 6.2, the M2 milestone ("potatoes in heated oil") defines the end of the Constitutive Act of heating the oil and placing the potatoes in it. The trigger is further defined by the preceding sequence of specific action, e.g. the placing of the pot on the oven, pouring the oil in the pot and turning on the heat.

The rationale behind ALAM as an authentic assessment can be summarised by what Janesick (2006) stated about learning with authentic assessment, which students learn from experience, context, learning community and responsibility for improvement. ALAM provides a detailed formative feedback based on trainees' actions, especially their goal-oriented actions, in a certain context with a clear Goal Act. It does not limit trainees to a set of predefined questions and provides them with an opportunity to use their learned knowledge and not just the memorised knowledge. Using the generated feedback under the ALAM's feedback structure and standards, trainees can learn from their mistakes, experts' solutions and also correct their performance. These features make ALAM an authentic assessment method, used to evaluate trainees' learned knowledge in simulated environments.

Action Comparison

The evaluation of the action sequences is undertaken on the level of Constitutive and Functional Acts. The comparison analysis of the action sequence is based on the rules as well as the similarity to stored sets of expert action sequences. The comparison includes, among others, the following criteria:

- Non-compliance of rules: rules are either strict (i.e. all experts have the same sequence of actions) or loose (i.e. only some experts have the same sequence of actions). Strict rules must be followed; loose rules represent alternatives, such that an exact match is not required.
- Attributes that do not match; including a weighting of the relevance of an attribute.
- Timing of the attributes, i.e. length between two actions indicating problems in deciding what to do next.

- Sequence of Constitutional Acts in comparison to the experts.
- Achievement of the Goal Act.

In a summative scored based assessment, the non-achievement of the goal would be considered a failure, yet it can be the result of only of minor failures at one action towards the end. Therefore, the comparison is looking for partial sequences (i.e. between milestones), validity of states at milestones (objects and the environment have certain attribute settings) and how these sequences match the experts' behaviour in their action sequences. For example, the five experts have a 3:2 opinion if potatoes should be washed first then cut or vice versa (order of action A1 and A2 in Fig. 6.2). For milestone 1, the learner requires either one or both would be considered to be correct. However, the assessment frequencies (matching 2 out of 5 in case of A2–A1) can be used in the feedback generation to provide alternatives. The assessment outcome is also used in later partial action sequences to check for further correlations, i.e. the likelihood to follow the action sequence that the learner had the highest match with. This is used to provide feedback, but also to validate and weight expert solutions.

Feedback Generation

The comparison generates evaluations on the similarity of the action sequences conducted by the leaner and all experts. A straightforward approach to create an automated feedback is matching sequences with a binary answer of "yes" and "no". However, this would not reflect on the variety of possible solutions and undermines the assumed inerrability of experts. The feedback should relate the learner's outcome to the aggregated expert solutions provide a feedback that shows deviation and explains the impact of these. For example, not including action A4 (place pot on stove) is essential, thus causing an overall failure. The generated similarities (i.e. matching actions and sequences for partial sequences) can be used to generate feedback, e.g. visually comparing the chosen path and the one taken by the experts. The formative feedback must distinguish between Constitutive and Functional Acts, the first one generally being the milestones. If all experts have these milestones in their action sequence, it is required and should be achieved by the learner as well. Thus, the feedback must emphasise such mismatches. The same applies for actions that all experts have taken; yet, it is important for others that are not done by all experts (e.g. wiping the table after each step), might not be mandatory and therefore need not be done by the learner. The feedback should allow aggregating and disaggregating details; it is not relevant to focus on a single, irrelevant action if the Goal Act was not even achieved. Note that, feedback should consider case-relevant templates completed by the experts that are individualised with details from the learner (e.g. where the learner is repeating the same failure).

Figure 6.3 visualises an abstraction on the feedback generation, yet spares details with respect to the focus of the chapter. The learners performed actions (2nd

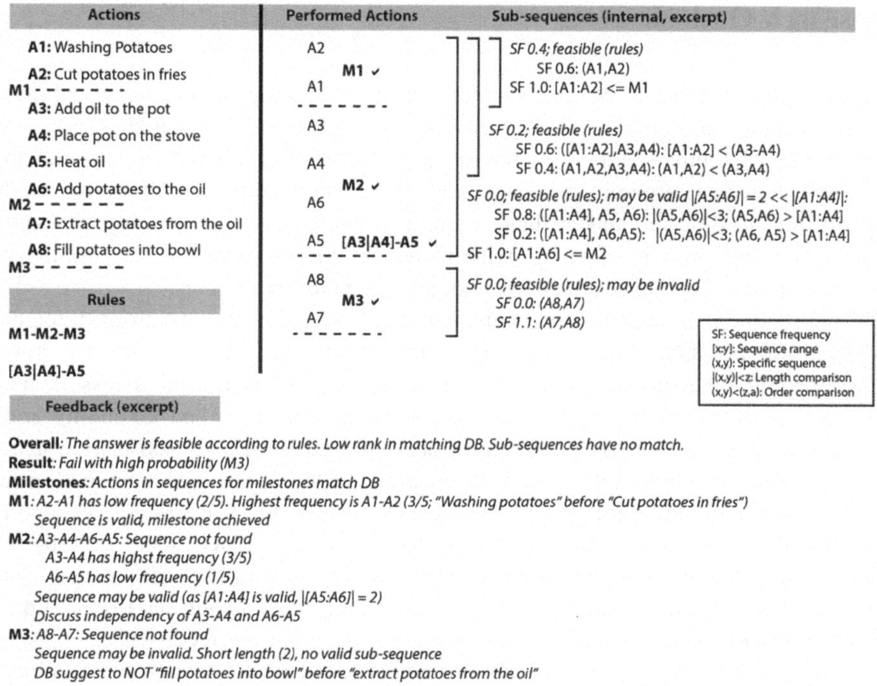

Fig. 6.3 Example of sequencing action sequences to generate automated formative feedback (excerpt)

column) are compared to the expert action sequences as shown in Fig. 6.2. The comparison is based on milestones (is a certain state achieved (environment) and corresponds with Constitutive Acts (experts)) and sub-sequences of different lengths. The feedback is based on the sequence frequency (how often is this specific sub-sequence found in the database), the feasibility according to the rules, and how likely it is to find a specific sub-sequence after previous actions. For example, the second sub-sequence covers the first four actions (A1, A2, A3, A4) and is feasible as there are no violations of the given rules. The sub-sequence is found in the database; however, has a low frequency of only 1 out of 5 cases. The low-frequency results from the order of the preceding actions (A1, A2), as a reversed order of these actions would increase the overall sub-sequence frequency to 0.4; implying a total validity of (A3, A4) with 0.6. The feedback to the learner emphasises the deviation from the expert solutions, yet shows the similarity according to frequencies that the solution is likely to be feasible.

Research Outlook

This chapter introduced the current research on evaluating performance within a virtual training environment with a focus on moving towards automated assessment using ALAM, human actions taxonomy and ALAS. The chapter is research in progress, however, preliminary experiments show the validity as well as enhanced opportunity to describe and evaluate training sessions in virtual training environments. The research is ongoing, with focus on the balancing of the similarity calculation and the improvement of automated generation of rules.

The system is intended to recognise and analyse action streams from different VTE, which are then mapped using the same taxonomy. Thus, the expert performance could be recorded in real world scenarios and later used to assess the learners' performance in a simulated environment. The described taxonomy and ALAM are part of a larger system called action-based learning assessment system (ALAS) shown in Fig. 6.4. Actions from experts (top layer) and trainee (lower layer) are identified, verified, mapped to the taxonomy and stored as action sequences. The expert sequences are further used to deduct rules; describing reoccurring patterns and dependencies that can be used during the comparison process. The reference sequences (experts) and performed sequences (trainee) are compared, and the evaluated outcome is used to generate the feedback.

Advancement in this area of automated assessment (focusing on providing formative feedback) is important to support wider adoption of the rapidly advancing use of virtual environments in education. At present, practical adoption demands formative assessment remain a small component of the system or relies on peer- or expert-provided feedback. Instead, high levels of formative feedback, as planned in the nDiVE project (ndive-project.com), require significant and effective use of formative feedback to be provided to learners to enable self-guided learning. In a nutshell, nDiVE is exploring the immersive space for health and safety training using head-mounted displays, i.e. addressing scenarios of high risk to have fatal injuries. The most prominent example in nDiVE is a container terminal simulation with tasks to solve while not risking your own or other lives.

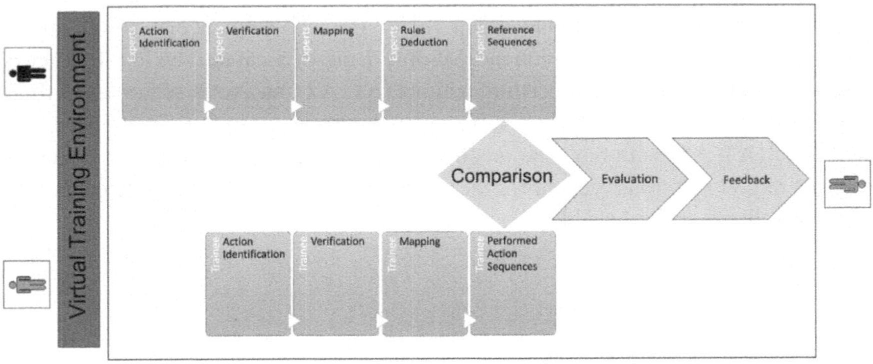

Fig. 6.4 Action-based learning assessment system; (see also Fardinpour et al. 2013)

Acknowledgements The Australian Government Office has provided support for the production of this publication for Learning and Teaching (Grant: Development of an authentic training environment to support skill acquisition in logistics and supply chain management, ID: ID12-2498). The views expressed in this publication do not necessarily reflect the views of the Australian Government Office for Learning and Teaching.

References

Ahmed, A., Maqsood, M., Saif, H., & Salman, A. (2012). Affordable interactive virtual reality system for the Dynamic Hip Screw surgery training in vitro. In *Proceedings of the IASTED International Conference on Computer Graphics and Imaging, CGIM 2012* (pp. 248–253). Crete, Greece: Acta Press.

Al-Smadi, M., Gütl, C., & Kannan, R. (2010). Modular assessment system for modern learning settings: Mass. *International Journal of Computer Applications, 1*(9), 37–43.

Barab, S. A., Squire, K. D., & Dueber, W. (2000). A co-evolutionary model for supporting the emergence of authenticity. *Educational Technology Research and Development, 48*(2), 37–62.

Barrows, H. S., & Tamblyn, R. (1980). *Problem-based learning: An approach to medical education*. Berlin: Springer.

Bastiaens, T., Wood, L. C., & Reiners, T. (2014). New landscapes and new eyes: the role of virtual world design for supply chain education. *Ubiquitous Learning: An International Journal, 6*(1), 37–49.

Bresciani, M. J., Morsi, K., Tucker, M., Siprut, M., Stewart, K., & Duncan, A. (2010). Designing and implementing an assessment plan for a virtual engineering lab. Eludamos. *Journal for Computer Game Culture, 4*(2), 277–285.

Chen, X., Lin, Y., Wang, C., Shen, G., & Wang, X. (2012). A virtual training system using a force feedback haptic device for oral implantology. In Z. Pan, A. Cheok, W. Müller, M. Chang, & M. Zhang (Eds.), *Transactions on Edutainment VIII* (Vols. 1–7220, pp. 232–240). Berlin, Heidelberg: Springer.

Chodos, D., Stroulia, E., King, S., & Carbonaro, M. (2014). A framework for monitoring instructional environments in a virtual world. *British Journal of Educational Technology, 45* (1), 24–35.

Craighead, J. (2008). Distributed, game-based, intelligent tutoring systems: The next step in computer based training? In *International Symposium on Collaborative Technologies and Systems* (pp. 247–256). Irvine, CA: IEEE.

Dede, C., & Lewis, M. (1995). *Assessment of emerging educational technologies that might assist and enhance school-to-work transitions*. Washington, DC, USA: Office of Technology Assessment, U.S. Congress.

Dede, C., Salzman, M., Loftin, R. B., & Sprague, D. (1999). Multisensory immersion as a modelling environment for learning complex scientific concepts. In W. Feurzeig & N. Roberts (Eds.), *Modelling and simulation in science and mathematics education* (pp. 282–319). New York: Springer.

Doering, A. (2006). Adventure learning: Transformative hybrid online education. *Distance Education, 27*(2), 197–215.

Dunwell, I., de Freitas, S., Jarvis, S., & de Freitas, S. (2011). Four-dimensional consideration of feedback in serious games. In S. de Freitas & P. Maharg (Eds.), *Digital games and learning* (pp. 42–62). London, UK: Bloomsbury Publishing.

Fardinpour, A., & Dreher, H. (2012). Towards developing Automated Assessment in Virtual Learning Environments. In P. Kommers, T. Issa & P. Isaías (Eds.), *Proceedings of the IADIS International Conference Internet Technologies and Society 2012* (pp. 211–216). Perth, Australia: IADIS Press.

Fardinpour, A., & Reiners, T. (2014). The taxonomy of goal-oriented actions in virtual training environments. *Procedia Technology, 1,* 38–46. doi:10.1016/j.protcy.2014.02.007.

Fardinpour, A., Reiners, T., & Dreher, H. (2013). Action-based learning assessment: Evaluating goal-oriented actions in virtual training environments. In H. Carter, M. Gosper and J. Hedberg (Eds.), *Electric Dreams. Proceedings Ascilite 2013 Sydney.* (pp. 267–277). Sydney, Australia: Macquarie University and ascilite. Retrieved from http://www.ascilite.org/conferences/sydney13/program/papers/Fardinpour.pdf.

Filigenzi, M. T., Orr, T. J., & Ruff, T. M. (2000). Virtual reality for mine safety training. *Applied Occupational and Environmental Hygiene, 15*(6), 465–469. doi:10.1080/104732200301232.

Fleishman, E. A. (1975). Toward a taxonomy of human performance. *American Psychologist, 30* (12), 1127–1149. doi:10.1037/0003-066X.30.12.1127.

Goldman, A. I. (1970). *A theory of human action.* Upper Saddle River, NJ: Prentice-Hall.

Gregory, S., Dalgarno, B., Campbell, M., Reiners, T., Knox, V., & Masters, M. (2011). Changing directions through VirtualPREX: Engaging pre-service teachers in virtual professional experience. In G. Williams, N. Brown, B. Pittard, & B. Cleland (Eds.), *Changing demands, changing directions. Proceedings Ascilite Hobart 2011* (pp. 491–501). Hobart, Australia: University of Tasmania and ascilite. Retrieved from http://www.ascilite.org/conferences/hobart11/downloads/VPREXAscilitePresentationpptx.pdf.

Gunn, C. (2006). Collaborative virtual sculpting with haptic feedback. *Virtual Reality, 10*(2), 73–83. doi:10.1007/s10055-006-0044-4.

Herrington, A., & Herrington, J. (2006). *Authentic learning environments in higher education.* Hershey, PA: IGI Global.

Herrington, J., Oliver, R., & Reeves, T. C. (2003). Patterns of engagement in authentic online learning environments. *Australian Journal of Educational Technology, 19*(1), 59–71.

Herrington, J., Reeves, T. C., & Oliver, R. (2010). *A guide to authentic e-learning.* New York, NY: Routledge.

Hewitt, A. M., Spencer, S. S., Mirliss, D., & Twal, R. (2010). Incident and disaster management training: Collaborative learning opportunities using virtual world scenarios. In E. Asimakopoulou & N. Bessis (Eds.), *Advanced ICTs for disaster management and threat detection: Collaborative and distributed frameworks* (pp. 179–200). Hershey, PA: Information Science Reference.

Hockenmeyer, C., Nussbaumer, A., Lövquist, E., Aboulafia, A., Breen, D., Shorten, G., & Albert, D. (2009). Applying a web and simulation-based system for adaptive competence assessment of spinal anaesthesia. In M. Spaniol, Q. Li, R. Klamma, & R. H. Lau (Eds.), *Advances in Web Based Learning: ICWL 2009* (Vol. 5686, pp. 182–191). Berlin: Springer. doi:10.1007/978-3-642-03426-8_23

Janesick, V. J. (2006). *Authentic assessment primer.* New York, NY, USA: Peter Lang.

Kizil, M. (2003). Virtual reality applications in the Australian minerals industry. In F. A. Camisani-Calzolari (Ed.), *Application of computers and operations research in the minerals industries* (pp. 569–574). Cape Town, South Africa: The South African Institute of Mining and Metallurgy.

Lasky, B., & Tempone, I. (2004). Practising what we teach: Vocational teachers learn to research through applying action learning techniques. *Journal of Further and Higher Education, 28*(1), 79–94.

Masters, Y., Gregory, S., Reiners, T., Knox, V., & Dalgarno, B. (2013). VirtualPREX: Developing teaching skills in second life. In C. DeCoursey & S. Garrett (Eds.), *Studies in virtual world learning and practice* (pp. 69–94). Oxford, UK: Inter-Disciplinary Press.

Meyer, C. A. (1992). What's the difference between "Authentic" and "Performance" assessment? *Educational Leadership, 49*(8), 39–40.

Naidu, S. (2007). Instructional designs for distance education. In M. G. Moore (Ed.), *Handbook of distance education* (pp. 247–258). Mahwah, NJ, USA: L. Erlbaum Associates.

Naidu, S. (2010). Using scenario-based learning to promote situated learning and develop professional knowledge. In E. P. Errington (Ed.), *Preparing graduates for the professions using scenario-based learning* (pp. 39–49). Brisbane, Australia: Post Pressed.

Naidu, S., & Bedgood, D., Jr. (2012). Action-based learning. In N. Seel (Ed.), *Encyclopaedia of the sciences of learning* (pp. 75–77). Boston, MA, USA: Springer, US.

Reiners, T., & Wood, L. C. (2013). Immersive virtual environments to facilitate authentic education in Logistics and supply chain management. In Y. Kats (Ed.), *Learning management systems and instructional design: Metrics, standards, and applications* (pp. 323–343). Hershey, PA: IGI Global.

Reiners, T., Wood, L. C., & Dron, J. (2014). From chaos towards sense: A learner-centric narrative virtual learning space. In J. Bishop (Ed.), *Gamification for human factors integration: Social, educational, and psychological issues* (pp. 242–258). Hershey, PA: IGI Global.

Reiners, T., Wood, L.C., Gregory, S., Petter, N., Teräs, H., Gütl, C., Chang, V., Herrington, J. (2013). nDiVE: The story of how Logistics and Supply Chain Management should be taught. In M. Gosper, J. Hedberg, & H. Carter (Eds.), *Electric Dreams. Proceedings ascilite 2013 Sydney* (pp. 734–744).

Rickel, J., Johnson, W. L., Way, A., & Rey, M. (1998). STEVE: A pedagogical agent for virtual reality. *The second international conference on autonomous agents* (pp. 332–333). New York, NY, USA: ACM.

Robertson, T. (1997). Cooperative work and lived cognition: a taxonomy of embodied actions. In *Proceedings of European Conferences on Computer-Supported Cooperative Work* (Vol. 97, pp. 205–220). Lancaster, UK: Springer Netherlands.

Robertson, T. (2000). Building bridges: negotiating the gap between work practice and technology design. *International Journal of Human-Computer Studies, 53*(1), 121–146. doi:10.1006/ijhc.2000.0373.

Rogers, C. R. (1951). *Client-centered therapy: its current practice, implications, and theory*. Oxford, UK: Houghton Mifflin.

Sadler, D. R. (1989). Formative assessment and the design of instructional systems. *Instructional Science, 18,* 119–144.

Schank, R. (1997). *Virtual learning: A revolutionary approach to building a highly skilled workforce*. New York: McGraw-Hill.

Scriven, M. (1967). The methodology of evaluation. In R. W. Tyler, R. M. Gagne, & M. Scriven (Eds.), *Perspectives of curriculum evaluation* (pp. 39–83). Chicago, IL: Rand-McNally.

Shen, R., Tang, Y., & Zhang, T. (2001). The intelligent assessment system in web-based distance learning education. In *31st Annual Frontiers in Education Conference,* (Vol. 1, p. TIF 7–11). Reno, NV, USA: IEEE.

Shute, V. J. (2011). Stealth assessment in computer-based games to support learning. In S. Tobias & J. D. Fletcher (Eds.), *Computer games and instruction* (pp. 503–524). Charlotte, NC: Information Age Publishers.

Shute, V. J., & Glaser, R. (1990). Large-scale evaluation of an intelligent tutoring system: Smithtown. *Interactive Learning Environments, 1*(1), 51–76.

Shute, V. J., Ventura, M., Bauer, M. I., & Zapata-Rivera, D. (2009). Melding the power of serious games and embedded assessment to monitor and foster learning: Flow and grow. In U. Ritterfeld, Cody, & P. Vorderer (Eds.), *Serious games: Mechanisms and effects* (pp. 295–321). Mahwah, NJ: Routledge, Taylor and Francis.

Smith, P. E. (1987). Simulating the classroom with media and computers past efforts. *Future Possibilities. Simulation & Gaming, 18*(3), 395–413.

Thompson, C. W. F., & Hagstrom, F. (2011). Modeling healthcare: Logistics in a virtual world. *IEEE Internet Computing, 12*(4), 100–104.

Twinning, P. (2009). Exploring the educational potential of virtual worlds: Some reflections from the SPP. *British Journal of Educational Technology, 40*(3), 496–514.

Verhulsdonck, G., & Morie, J. (2009). Virtual Chironomia: Developing Standards for Non-verbal Communication in Virtual Worlds. *Journal of Virtual Worlds Research, 2*(3). Retrieved from http://jvwr-ojs-utexas.tdl.org/jvwr/index.php/jvwr/article/view/657

Wiggins, G. (1990). *The case for authentic assessment* (pp. 1–6). Washington, DC, USA: ERIC Digest.

Wilson, B. G. (Ed.). (1996). *Constructivist learning environments: Case studies in instructional design*. Englewood Cliffs, NJ, USA: Educational Technology Publications.

Wood, L. C., & Reiners, T. (2013). Game-based elements to upgrade bots to non-player characters in support of educators. In A. Hebbel-Seeger, T. Reiners, & D. Schäfer (Eds.), *Synthetic worlds: Emerging technologies in education and economics* (pp. 257–277). Berlin, Germany: Springer.

Wriedt, S., Reiners, T., & Ebeling, M. (2008). How to teach and demonstrate topics of supply chain management in virtual worlds. In J. Luca & E. R. Weippl (Eds.), *Proceedings of ED-MEDIA 2008. World Conference on Educational Multimedia, Hypermedia & Telecommunications, Vienna, Austria* (pp. 5501–5508). Chesapeake, VA: AACE.

Author Biographies

Ali Fardinpour holds PhD (with hons) from Curtin University. His current role is the lead research scientist in Immersive Technologies in Learning and Assessment. His current research focus is action-based learning and assessment in virtual training environments. He also is an adjunct researcher at Curtin Learning and Teaching.

Torsten Reiners is Senior Lecturer in Logistics at the Curtin University, Australia. His research and teaching experiences are in the areas of operations research but include instructional design, development of adaptive learning environments, distant collaboration and mobile learning, which is also manifested in his PhD thesis (University of Hamburg, Germany) about adaptive learning material in the field of operations research. He has participated in multiple research projects using 3D spaces for learning support, i.e. to improve the authenticity of learning in classes in relation to production and simulation. His current research interests are in logistics, education technologies and emerging technologies.

Lincoln C. Wood is a Senior Lecturer (Operations and Supply Chain Management) at University of Auckland (New Zealand) and an Adjunct Research Fellow at Curtin Business School (Australia). Having received the 2009 Council of Supply Chain Management Professional's (CSCMP) Young Researcher Award (Chicago, USA) and the Outstanding Research Award at the 2010 International Higher Education Conference (Perth, Australia), Dr Wood is co-Leader on a 2012 OLT grant relating to gamified virtual environments for supply chain education. His research interests include operations and supply chain management; service operations; gamification; and educational, authentic, virtual environments.

Chapter 7
Engagement in Second Life: Language Anxiety and Motivation

Scott Grant, Hui Huang and Sarah Pasfield-Neofitou

Introduction

In recent years, virtual worlds have gained considerable attention (Blasing 2010; Dalgarno and Lee 2010; Dalgarno et al. 2011; Grant et al. 2013, 2014; Gregory 2011a, b; Gregory et al. 2010; Lee and Dalgarno 2011), in part due to advances in graphics and connections and the increasing popularity of massively multiplayer online games (MMOs) (Salisbury 2013), but also due to the increasing prevalence of internationalisation discourses in higher education. While academic mobility and student exchange remain important ways to experience the world beyond the campus and to motivate students, particularly in language learning endeavours, various practical constraints sometimes prevent students from taking up some opportunities where available. According to an *Inside Higher Ed* report, although study abroad has increased in recent years, only 9.4% of American undergraduates experience study abroad, and almost 60% of those who do are abroad for only a summer or on other short-term programs of eight weeks or less (Redden 2013). Furthermore, emerging research shows that while engagement is a key to a truly internationalised education (Kim 2009), in reality, many students who do go on exchange miss out on such opportunities in the exchange environment (Penn et al. 2013), which may be due in part to the negative impact of (foreign) language anxiety.

S. Grant (✉) · H. Huang · S. Pasfield-Neofitou
Monash University, Melbourne, VIC, Australia
e-mail: scott.grant@monash.edu

H. Huang
e-mail: hui.huang@monash.edu

S. Pasfield-Neofitou
e-mail: sarah.pasfieldneofitou@monash.edu

S. Gregory and D. Wood (eds.), *Authentic Virtual World Education*,
https://doi.org/10.1007/978-981-10-6382-4_7

For these reasons, among others, online 3D multiuser virtual environments (MUVEs) such as Second Life are being harnessed to provide a key source of motivation and learning for language students in a foreign language learning context with interactive experiences in as close to an authentic setting as possible. MUVEs like Second Life have the potential to provide learners with some degree of experiencing the world beyond the campus. One such example is the 3D MUVE 'Chinese Island' (see www.virtualhanyu.com/), where students can go shopping, eat out, visit a doctor and have a number of 'everyday' experiences in the virtual environment, complete with opportunities to develop their language and communicative competence with non-player characters (NPCs), other students and even native speakers (NSs).

Chinese Island (see Fig. 7.1) was established in 2009 to complement a formal ab initio undergraduate Chinese language and culture curriculum. It was designed to provide a 3D canvas for communicatively oriented, task-based language learning activities that represent certain cultural and physical aspects of mainland China. While the virtual township is not modelled on any specific real-world location, the restaurant, village, farmers' market, railway station, medical clinic and other locations have been designed with particular features common to real-world locations in mind. When students visit the farmers' market, they see a range of fresh fruits, vegetables and meats laid out in a style typical of many real farmers' markets in China (see Fig. 7.2), including some potentially unexpected items such as live softback turtle and eels. When they visit the virtual railway station, they see the ticket windows especially set aside for foreigners as well as the X-ray machines that form part of the security check at the entrance to the train platforms.

When students purchase ingredients at the farmers' market to make traditional Chinese dumplings, they go through the process of informing the seller what they want to buy, establishing (and even negotiating) the price, paying for the items, and

Fig. 7.1 A corner of Chinese Island

Fig. 7.2 Farmers' market

then actually using the purchased ingredients to make virtual dumplings. Moreover, when, for example, students visit the virtual medical clinic, they learn how to negotiate their way through the process of seeing a doctor and obtaining medication (which they consume to remove the symptoms of illness their virtual selves experience), communicatively interacting via text chat in Chinese with key characters (the reception nurse, the doctor, the pharmacist—see Fig. 7.3) at each stage of the process. In the lessons with live NS instructors, students work collaboratively with each other and their instructors, using spoken communication to negotiate their way through a maze of streets to find a range of everyday locations, plan out a range of suitable activities and a corresponding itinerary for a visitor coming to Chinese

Fig. 7.3 Seeing the doctor

Island, order food at a local restaurant, buy clothes in a local Chinese store, and investigate renting accommodation, among other activities.

The task-based language learning approach to lessons in the Chinese Island virtual environment provides students with opportunities to utilise linguistic knowledge learned from the set textbook *Contemporary Chinese for Beginners* (Wu 2010) and studied in the classroom to engage in purposeful communication with the Island's NPCs and live NS instructors in immersive contexts intended to simulate real-world conditions. The communicative contexts are intended to be as close to real-world interactions as possible in this type of online environment and as such some degree of performance anxiety was anticipated.

Research has established that foreign language anxiety has a negative impact on learner performance, motivation and engagement, both in the classroom context and in the real-world context (study abroad) (Allen and Herron 2003; Horwitz et al. 1986). A previous study by the authors (Grant et al. 2013) found that students experience less foreign language anxiety (FLA) when engaging in text chat communicative interaction with NPCs in the Chinese Island MUVE environment than in the face-to-face classroom setting. It appears that students' perceptions of the authenticity of conversations with the NPCs in comparison with spoken communication and conversations with human interlocutors in the 'real world' may be related to the FLA they experience, and their motivation to take advantage of the communicative opportunities provided in the 3D MUVE environment. This chapter explores the findings of a new study of students' verbal interaction in the same 3D MUVE with live NS teachers located overseas. We were particularly keen to examine to what extent students' perception of the 'realness' of this verbal interaction affected their FLA, which we believed had great implications for curricular and pedagogical development in language teaching and learning. The chapter also suggests future research directions that look at task-based learning in 3D MUVE environments.

Student in-Country Experience

Study abroad, and particularly short-term educational travel (Engle and Engle 2003; Tarrant and Lyons 2011), which has greatly grown in popularity in recent decades (Tarrant and Lyons 2011), provides opportunities to locate the language learner in the actual language and culture context. The experience of residing (and studying) in a country where a language is other than one's own is generally thought to result in the learning of many aspects of the language and culture of that country. Extensive research (e.g. Allen 2003; Carroll 1967; Kinginger 2008; Meredith 2010) has been conducted since the middle of last century to examine the effects of study abroad programs on second language (L2) language and culture learning. One frequently cited study (Carroll 1967) on the language proficiency of 2,782 college seniors majoring in French, German, Italian and Russian found that time spent abroad was one of the major predictors of overall language proficiency and that students who spent time in study abroad situations tended to acquire greater 'proficiency' in the target language than those who did not. Such studies (cf. Collentine 2004; DuFon 2006; Kinginger 2008; Meredith 2010) found that study abroad is a productive—if imperfect—environment for the development of communicative competence in foreign languages, confirming that when students participate in a study abroad program, especially when involved in a home-stay arrangement, they generally benefit linguistically (e.g. speaking with greater ease and confidence, experiencing a wider range of discourses and development in the morphosyntactic and lexical areas, Collentine 2004; Dewaele and Regan 2002; Regan 2004), socioculturally (e.g. development of intercultural comprehension: Kinginger 2008; development of interactional competence as indexed by the use of the interactionally significant particle 'ne' by English-speaking learners of Japanese, Masuda 2011; also see Dufon and Churchill 2006 for a review) and attitudinally (e.g. Isabelli-García 2006).

A number of studies have, however, suggested that negative experiences abroad, often brought about by cultural misunderstanding, can dominate a person's perspective of the new culture, and impede language acquisition and culture learning (e.g. Allen 2003; DeKeyser 1991). Allen (2003) reports two primary sources of language anxiety experienced by students in the study abroad context that negatively impact student motivation to engage linguistically with locals: lack of linguistic competence and cultural differences. Wilkinson (1998) suggests that students can sometimes arrive in the host country with cultural and linguistic assumptions that can also lead to less interaction in the foreign language and negative experiences with NSs.

It can thus be seen that although study abroad is potentially a positive part of the process of learning a foreign language, gaining a deeper understanding of the associated culture and allowing students to experience the world beyond the campus, there is no guarantee that all students will experience living and studying in the target language in the same way. Achieving positive results and minimising some of the negative experiences requires effort and engagement on the part of all concerned, including students, teachers, host families and program administrators (Kinginger 2011). Furthermore, due to a variety of economic and other practical constraints, such as family caring responsibilities, work commitments, financial constraints, not all students are able to experience study abroad. Task-based language learning in a 3D MUVE such as Chinese Island, as introduced earlier, may provide a way to partially address some of these limitations. For those intending to participate in study abroad, such lessons provide opportunities to experience close-to-authentic, purposeful communication in contexts designed to simulate some of the contexts they will encounter in-country, but with potentially reduced levels of language anxiety and the potential to build their levels of communicative confidence prior to being immersed in the real environment. For those who are unable to participate in study abroad, the opportunity to communicate in such simulated scenarios may bring some of the benefits of similar interaction in the real environment.

Opportunity and Anxiety

International exchange is often viewed as a kind of guarantee of internationalisation and the development of 'global citizenship' (Monk et al. 2015). However, as mentioned above, it is important to recognise that reported benefits such as language socialisation, intercultural competence and indeed global citizenship are not, in fact, automatic (Amit 2010; Wilkinson 1998). Rather than being entirely supported by empirical evidence, Amit claims that for the most part, belief in the benefits of student exchange are often underpinned by a longstanding belief in the educative value of travel. Due to a variety of reasons, including practical concerns, such as living in foreign-student only dormitories, or attending special classes, students may have few opportunities to communicate with NSs, as being in a temporary sojourning position itself can make it difficult to integrate (Penn et al. 2013). Even when there is the opportunity for relatively close integration, Bochner et al. (1985) show that simply living in proximity to one another does not necessarily result in the development of relationships.

Similar misconceptions exist in the domain of online intercultural exchange, where, particularly in the early days of internet-based communication, it was assumed that access alone to NSs 'anytime, anywhere' would suffice to provide students with abundant opportunities for language learning and use (Blasing 2010). Of course, with no common goal, and no framing, it can be difficult for participants to collaborate (Pasfield-Neofitou 2014). As Leeman (1999) states, while there has been much said about the benefits of computer-mediated communication to increase L2 interaction and production (cf. Gonzalez-Bueno 1998, cited in Leeman 1999) learners (and instructors) do not necessarily know what to communicate about in such settings.

Hanna and de Nooy (2003) traced the journeys of four learners of French on newspaper discussion forums. They discovered that those who viewed the discussion as a form of language practice found it difficult to find willing interlocutors, but those who viewed the activity as participation in a discussion about the topics raised gained cultural knowledge and were able to engage more with NSs. Allen (2003), in a study of American students of French on study abroad in France, also found that while an overall increase in proficiency could be seen to result from time spent in-country, there were also clear examples where disincentives to communicate with locals impacted upon learner motivation.

We hypothesise that students on international exchange may experience a kind of vicious cycle. A lack of opportunities (either prior to departure, or in the country itself) to interact with NSs may exacerbate FLA, and FLA of course may in turn dissuade students from taking up opportunities to communicate with NSs (Wilkinson 1998) which they otherwise may have engaged in if they had more confidence in their language abilities.

Framework

Learning theories, and theories of online participation, along with other frameworks describing human participation in communities, often have in common notions of peripheral participation, cognitive apprenticeship or even 'lurking'. In Lave and Wenger's (1991) *Situated Learning*, they describe the ways in which newcomers become experienced members of a community group as 'legitimate peripheral participation'. According to the theory, learning not only involves the individual acquiring propositional knowledge; more significantly, it involves all participants in a discursive practice changing their patterns of social co-participation. Importantly, simulations are viewed as a good alternative where situated learning is not possible in the real world. This is consistent with another constructivist approach to language learning, i.e. cognitive apprenticeship which refers to the teaching of a skill of a master to an apprentice, supported by Bandura's (1997) theory of modelling in *Social Learning Theory*. In the context of NPCs, we view modelling as an important use for simulations while conversing with real NSs in this MUVE is hypothesised to equate to spoken conversation in real life. This hypothesis will be tested in the current research.

As our previous research has indicated (Grant et al. 2013, 2014), students perceive communication in the MUVE with NPCs differently to face-to-face interaction with their teacher and other students. In the present chapter, we propose that L2 communicative situations in the MUVE be thought of as situated along a continuum of less to more 'real', depending on the participants' perspectives. It is crucial to note that positions on the continuum are not fixed, and may vary somewhat both in terms of placement and distance from person to person, as individuals may place differing emphasis on physicality, immediacy, perceptions of 'Chinese-ness', voice or mode, and so on.

The Lesson

Participants in the study were undergraduate students enrolled in a beginner level Chinese language unit in an Australian university. The focus of the study was one of a series of three regular computer laboratory lessons conducted each semester. The lessons are conducted in Second Life, in a simulated 3D virtual Chinese township that has a range of venues used for task-based language learning such as a restaurant, a farmers market, a train station and a medical clinic, as described previously. In contrast to our earlier studies conducted in this environment, where students interacted conversationally with programmed NPCs using Chinese character text chat (Grant and Clerehan 2011; Grant and Huang 2010, 2012; Grant et al. 2013, 2014), the lesson that forms the basis of the current study involved an additional hour of voice-based communication with NS instructors based in

Taiwan. These task-based language learning scenarios were developed to complement material covered in the main textbook (Wu 2010).

A lesson plan was jointly developed by the Australian unit coordinator and the Taiwanese instructors that involved students working in teams to find their way through the maze-like streets to locate particular shops and then to identify the information contained within each shop. There were nine shops in total for students to find. Information in each of four key shops provided the answers to four questions about one of the Taiwanese instructors that could be then used to make a short story about the instructor in Chinese. The questions posed were as follows:

'Who is the instructor?' (老师是谁?)

'What is she going to do?' (她要做什么?)

'When is she going to do it?' (她什么时候要做?)

'Where is she going to do it?' (她要去哪里做?)

The class of twenty students was broken up into groups of four. Under the guidance of a Taiwanese instructor, each group broke into two subgroups. The first of these was given a map showing the roads and the shops in the small town (Fig. 7.4). Each shop on the map was labelled with a number out of sequence. The four key shops were also clearly labelled with one of the question words 'Who', 'What', 'When' and 'Where'. The other subgroup then moved to the entrance of the street maze. Using a private group voice call, the first group who remained outside the maze and out of visual contact with the second subgroup then gave the second group instructions in Chinese on how to proceed through the streets to find the key shops. As they moved through the streets, the second group could ask questions in Chinese of the first group for clarification and discuss how the information they found in the key shops related to the 'Wh-' questions they had to answer. This enabled students to practice giving, receiving and following directions in Chinese, a key element in the classroom-based lessons and lessons with the NPCs in the proceeding weeks. Throughout this process, the Taiwanese instructor supplemented instructions given by the group outside the maze and guided the students in the maze with discussion and questions in Chinese about the information they encountered in each of the shops (Fig. 7.5).

Once all the clues had been found, the subgroups then gathered together outside the maze of streets where a series of virtual blocks with each of the clues written on them in Chinese was placed in random order (Fig. 7.6). The members of both subgroups then had to work together to move each of the blocks into position to form a full and grammatically correct sentence.

Prior to the start of the main part of the lesson, each Taiwanese instructor guided students in their group through a practice run of explaining the task for the lesson. They then constructed a similar small story in Chinese using clues set out in two notecards that were distributed to each member of the group.

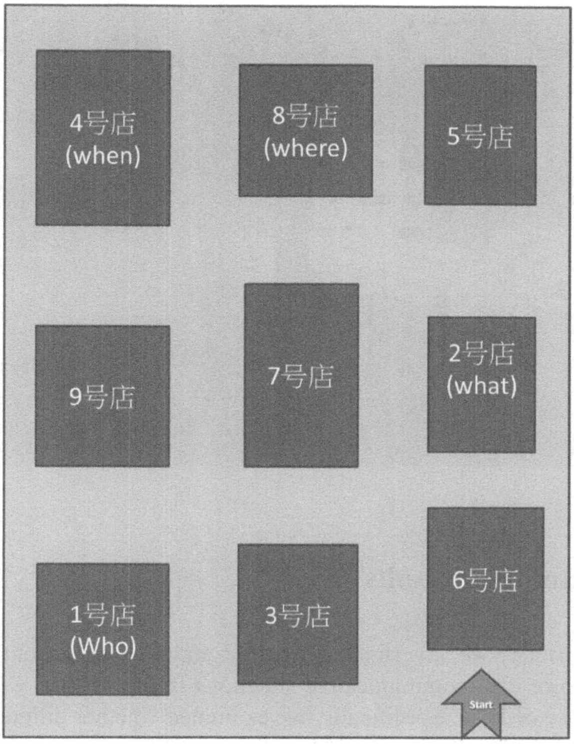

Fig. 7.4 Student map

Fig. 7.5 Shops with clues

Fig. 7.6 Making a sentence

The Study and the Results

In the present study, we investigated whether and to what extent the perceived 'realness' of voice chat communicative situations in the MUVE would affect students' experience of FLA. Specifically, we examined whether different groups with varied perceptions of 'realness' would experience different levels of FLA in two different environments (i.e. face-to-face classroom and MUVE). This focus extends our previous work (Grant et al. 2014) which examined perceptions of text-based communication with NPCs and found that a feeling of similarity between typed chat and verbal communication was correlated with student confidence.

Online questionnaires were conducted pre- and post-engagement in the online environment, and each consisted of the same 24 items in which students were asked to indicate their agreement or disagreement in relation to their language anxiety in different environments (i.e. in the face-to-face classroom and in the MUVE when using voice chat with NSs). The pre-questionnaire was completed before the lesson in Second Life (for lesson details see 'The Lesson' in the previous section) to seek students' response on their language anxiety in the face-to-face classroom while the post-questionnaire was conducted immediately after the students had the lesson in Second Life for their response in the MUVE. A total of 35 students and 37 students responded to the pre- and post-questionnaires, respectively. After matching the data, surveys from a total of 33 students who responded to both questionnaires were used for statistical analysis. Based on their responses in relation to how authentic they felt the conversations with NSs were in the MUVE as compared to 'real-life' conversation, respondents were divided into two groups:

- Group A: who do not believe in the authenticity of conversation in the MUVE, or believe less in it (n = 16)
- Group B: who believe in the authenticity of conversation in the MUVE (n = 17)

Detailed information on the participants can be found in Table 7.1. From Table 7.1, it can be seen that the students' profiles in the two groups are very similar except there are many more male students in Group B.

In order to examine what possible factors affect students' perception of the 'realness' of voice communication with NSs in the MUVE, a number of correlations were examined between student's feelings about the authenticity of voice conversation in the environment and their technical/computer skills, skill at navigating the MUVE, amount of computer and internet use, their self-perception of their own personality, as well as their age, gender and previous language learning background. The analysis using 2-tailed Pearson Correlations found no significant correlations between students' sense of the authenticity of voice chat in the MUVE and their computer and internet experience, perception of their own personality, or their age, gender, or previous language learning background (all $p > 0.05$). However, their sense of 'realness' of the voice chat in the MUVE is significantly but negatively correlated with technical anxiety and also their skill at using MUVEs (all $p < 0.05$). The more nervous or tense they feel when using a computer, the less authentic they feel the voice chat in the MUVE is ($r = -0.346, p < 0.05$). Likewise, their sense of the authenticity of voice chat with NSs in the MUVE is also negatively connected to technical anxiety in navigating the MUVE: the more anxious they feel about getting to Chinese Island or the more stress they feel reading Chinese characters in instant messages, the less authentic they feel the voice chat in the MUVE is ($r = -0.423$ and $r = -0.410$, respectively, $p < 0.05$). In contrast, if they found these things in the MUVE helpful, they felt the voice chat is more authentic, and comparable with 'real-life' conversations ($r = 0.371, p < 0.05$).

Prior to the examination of these differences, reliability tests were conducted, respectively, in each group for each test. The results found that all Cronbach's *alpha* coefficients were higher than 0.07 (0.80, 71 for Group A and Group B in classroom; 0.87 and 0.75 in MUVE), showing that the data were reliable in terms of being internally consistent.

In order to examine whether students with different perceptions of the 'realness' of the voice chat vary in their experiences of FLA in two different environments

Table 7.1 Demographic information of Group A and Group B

		Group A (those who did not believe in the authenticity of the MUVE)	Group B (those who did believe in the authenticity of the MUVE)	Total
Gender	Male	7	13	20
	Female	9	4	13
Age	18–23	14	15	29
	24 and above	2	2	4
Learned other language	Yes	10	9	19
	No	6	8	14

(i.e. the face-to-face classroom and MUVE using voice chat with NSs), paired T-tests were conducted to perform within-group analysis of the two different environments for each group. Given the small number of subjects in each group, we take effect size (eta^2) into consideration when looking at the significant difference in students' experiences of FLA. Specifically, those comparison results $eta^2 > 0.14$ (large effect size) are taken as statistically significant (Cohen 1988).

FLA Difference in Two Environments

According to Table 7.2, students in Group A, i.e. those who do not believe in or believe less in the authenticity of conversations in the MUVE, indicated that in the MUVE they were significantly less worried about their peers (Item 7), were less panicked when speaking without preparation in the MUVE (Item 8), less nervous about forgetting things they know (Item 9) and less afraid of their peers' laughter (Item 22) as compared to their perceptions of the face-to-face classroom experience. In addition, they appeared less afraid when the teacher was ready to correct their mistakes (Item 15), although interestingly, more nervous when they could not understand the teacher in the MUVE (Item 21). This last finding may be because of a lack of timely support from the teacher in the MUVE as the teacher may be unable to tell when a student is nervous in the environment unless the student explicitly communicates this.

Furthermore, Group A was found to have an overall higher level of technical anxiety, i.e. less confidence in dealing with the technical aspects of doing a lesson in the MUVE environment. This may partly explain their perception of the conversations in the environment as being less authentic and due to having to devote more mental resources to handling technical aspects of the lesson may have caused them to fear missing key information from the teacher about the lesson or the task. These reasons may explain why they reported that they would be marginally less inclined to attend more Chinese classes in the MUVE (Item 5). However, overall, this group indicated a lower level of FLA in the MUVE environment than in the face-to-face classroom.

The students in Group B, i.e. those who reported believing in the authenticity of conversations in the MUVE, showed not only less language learning anxiety but more confidence in the MUVE environment in most tested items as compared with that in face-to-face classroom (17 out of 24: i.e. Items 1, 2, 3, 4, 7, 8, 9, 10, 11, 14, 15, 16, 17, 19, 20, 21 and 24: except for Items 5, 6, 12, 13, 18, 22 and 23. For all the details, see Table 7.2). All of these results indicate that the students who believe more in the authenticity of the conversation in the MUVE feel much less anxious or more confident in completing language tasks in the environment. However, Group B students did not indicate much difference in their class engagement in the two different environments (Items 5, 6, 13), which means they have a very similar attitude to taking Chinese classes in either environment in spite of a very minor preference towards the traditional classroom. It is easy to understand why students

Table 7.2 Descriptives and within-group analysis

FLA Questions	Group A (who do not/less believe the authenticity of conversation in MUVE) ($N = 16$)							Group B (who believe the authenticity of conversation in MUVE) (N = 17)						
	in classroom		in 3D MUVE		t	*p*	*eta*^{2}	in classroom		in 3D MUVE		t	p	eta^2
	m	sd.	m	sd.				m	sd.	m	sd.			
1. I never feel quite sure of myself when I am speaking Chinese	3.75	0.77	3.56	1.03	−1.145	0.270	0.080	3.59	0.94	2.82	0.81	−2.889	*0.011*	*0.343*
2. I do not worry about making mistakes in Chinese	2.81	1.11	2.69	1.14	−0.565	0.580	0.021	2.53	1.07	3.65	0.79	3.951	*0.001*	*0.494*
3. I tremble when I know that I'm going to be called on	3.00	1.03	3.19	1.17	0.613	0.549	0.024	3.06	1.25	1.71	0.85	−3.625	*0.002*	*0.451*
4. It frightens me when I do not understand what the teacher is saying	3.56	0.81	3.31	0.87	−1.464	0.164	0.125	3.24	1.09	2.35	0.93	−3.273	*0.005*	*0.401*
5. It would not bother me at all to take more Chinese classes	3.44	0.96	2.88	0.81	−2.764	*0.014*	*0.338*	4.12	0.78	3.88	1.05	−0.655	0.522	0.026
6. I find myself thinking about things that have nothing to do with the course	2.94	1.06	2.38	1.09	−1.496	0.155	0.130	2.06	0.90	1.65	0.86	−1.444	0.168	0.115
7. I keep thinking that the other students are better at Chinese	3.69	1.14	3.31	1.01	−2.423	*0.029*	*0.281*	3.35	0.93	2.88	0.99	−2.704	*0.016*	*0.314*
8. I start to panic when I have to speak without preparation	3.75	0.86	3.44	1.09	−1.576	*0.136*	*0.142*	3.18	1.01	2.12	0.99	−3.246	*0.005*	*0.397*
9. I can get so nervous I forget things I know	3.38	1.09	3.00	1.15	−1.567	*0.138*	*0.141*	3.00	0.79	2.35	0.93	−2.678	*0.017*	*0.309*
10. I would not be nervous speaking Chinese with native speakers	2.63	1.20	2.25	0.86	−0.946	0.359	0.056	2.41	0.94	3.29	0.92	2.985	*0.009*	*0.358*
11. I get upset when I do not understand what the teacher is correcting	3.00	0.97	2.75	1.06	−0.889	0.388	0.050	3.06	0.97	1.76	0.66	−4.400	*0.000*	*0.548*
	3.13	1.09	3.19	1.05	0.324	0.751	0.007	2.53	0.94	2.35	1.00	−1.144	0.269	0.076

(continued)

Table 7.2 (continued)

FLA Questions	Group A (who do not/less believe the authenticity of conversation in MUVE) ($N = 16$)							Group B (who believe the authenticity of conversation in MUVE) (N = 17)						
	in classroom		in 3D MUVE		t	*p*	*eta*^{2}	in classroom		in 3D MUVE		t	p	eta^2
	m	sd.	m	sd.				m	sd.	m	sd.			
12. I feel anxious about Chinese class even if I am well prepared for it														
13. I often feel like not going to my Chinese class	2.50	1.03	3.06	1.18	2.183	*0.045*	*0.241*	1.71	0.59	2.00	1.00	1.159	0.264	0.077
14. I feel confident when I speak Chinese	2.81	0.91	2.88	1.09	0.222	0.827	0.003	2.76	0.75	3.53	0.72	4.190	*0.001*	*0.523*
15. I am afraid that my Chinese teacher is ready to correct my mistake	2.44	0.89	2.13	0.81	−1.576	*0.136*	*0.142*	2.47	1.12	1.94	0.66	−1.643	*0.120*	*0.144*
16. I can feel my heart pounding when I am going to be called on (or start a conversation with a teacher in MUVE)	2.88	0.89	2.94	1.29	0.251	0.806	0.004	2.94	1.03	1.47	0.80	−4.927	*0.000*	*0.603*
17. I feel very self-conscious about speaking Chinese in front of other students	3.38	1.20	3.13	1.09	−1.168	0.261	0.083	3.00	0.79	2.29	0.92	−2.509	*0.023*	*0.282*
18. Chinese class moves so quickly (or listening and understanding Chinese in MUVE takes so long) that I worry about getting left behind.	3.31	1.01	3.13	0.96	−0.716	0.485	0.033	2.94	1.09	2.65	1.00	−0.960	0.351	0.054
19. I feel more tense and nervous in my Chinese class) than in my other classes	3.19	0.98	2.81	0.83	−1.379	0.188	0.113	2.35	1.11	1.82	0.73	−1.643	*0.120*	*0.144*
20. I get nervous and confused when I am speaking in my Chinese class or doing so in 3D SE	3.13	1.02	3.06	1.06	−0.436	0.669	0.013	2.53	0.94	2.00	0.61	−1.941	*0.070*	*0.191*
	2.94	1.06	3.31	0.95	1.567	*0.138*	*0.141*	2.88	1.05	2.24	1.09	−2.678	0.017	0.309

(continued)

Table 7.2 (continued)

FLA Questions	Group A (who do not/less believe the authenticity of conversation in MUVE) (N = 16)							Group B (who believe the authenticity of conversation in MUVE) (N = 17)						
	in classroom		in 3D MUVE		t	*p*	*eta*^{2}	in classroom		in 3D MUVE		t	p	eta^2
	m	sd.	m	sd.				m	sd.	m	sd.			
21. I get nervous when I do not understand every word the Chinese teacher says														
22. I am afraid that the other students will laugh at me when I speak Chinese	2.56	1.15	2.25	1.00	−2.611	*0.020*	*0.313*	1.94	1.03	1.76	0.75	−0.765	0.455	0.035
23. I would probably feel comfortable around native speakers of Chinese (or around native speakers of Chinese in 3D SE)	2.50	0.89	2.63	0.89	0.522	0.609	0.018	2.82	1.13	3.24	1.03	1.329	0.203	0.099
24. I got nervous when the Chinese teacher asked questions which I had not prepared in advance	3.69	0.95	3.44	1.09	−0.939	0.362	0.056	3.71	0.99	2.53	1.12	−3.515	*0.003*	*0.436*

All highlighted boxes are specified as statistically significant with large effect size (eta^2 > 0.14) may still feel nervous as they cannot predict what the NS instructor will talk about even though they are well prepared (Item 12) and therefore still feel anxious when NSs are present in the MUVE (Item 23). This means they might be still anxious in being around or talking with NSs because of the unpredictability of the topics that may be raised by the NSs, something which might be less true of conversations with NPCs on pre-defined topics. Therefore, future investigation would be desirable to examine whether students' FLA differs when they converse with NPCs versus NSs in the MUVE. Even though Group B's anxiety in learning Chinese is significantly reduced in the MUVE, students still appear concerned about the pace of the class (Item 18), a concern which is not uncommon to face-to-face classes generally. Well-organised, well-paced classes appear important to reduce language learning anxiety in the environment. It is noted, however, that the fact that students in Group B did not report to any significant degree feeling less anxious about peer laughter might be attributable to a 'roof effect' (Item 22, see Table 7.2 for details). Anxiety about peer laughter appears very low in both environments for Group B students (1.94 and 1.76 out of 5, respectively, in classroom and in MUVE, the lowest score among all). This means the students who perceived the voice chat as being more 'real' in general did not consider laughter from peers a concern for them.

According to the analysis, the two groups' experiences of FLA were quite different in the two environments surveyed, i.e. the face-to-face classroom and the 3D MUVE with voice conversation with NSs. Only four items out of the 24 tested (Items, 7, 8, 9 and 15) yielded similar results from both groups in both environments, i.e. a small reduction in anxiety in the MUVE environment. This means that lessons in the MUVE are only helpful for both groups of students, regardless of their perception of authenticity of voice chat, in the reduction of anxiety about pressure from peers (Item 7) and teachers (Item 15) and also in the provision of a 'safe' environment for unprepared (Item 8) or forgetful students (Item 9). However, the students of Group B who believe in the authenticity of voice conversation in the MUVE reported much less FLA but more confidence in the environment than in the classroom,

It is interesting to note that both groups' attitudes in relation to Item 21 'I get nervous when I do not understand every word the Chinese teacher says' were statistically different across the two environments, but in opposite directions: Group A students, who did not believe strongly in the authenticity of the conversations in the MUVE, felt significantly more nervous in the MUVE as opposed to the face-to-face classroom in this situation, while Group B, who perceived the authenticity of the conversations in the MUVE more strongly, felt less anxious when they did not understand what the teacher said. We speculate that Group A's increased sense of anxiety in this case may be due to a fear of missing out on important information relating to the set task due to overall lower levels of confidence in the MUVE environment and higher levels of technical anxiety. It may be the case that the students in Group A, who were perhaps struggling more with the technology, had fewer opportunities to pay attention to what the teacher was saying in the MUVE, and felt less confident about their ability to ask for clarification.

Alternatively, it is also possible that these students felt that the absence of body language/gestures or other non-verbal clues negatively impacted their understanding. It is important to note that such clues do exist in the MUVE, such as the way the teacher's avatar is facing, what object they are clicking on, or via the use of basic, pre-set gestures, however, more research is needed to reveal to what extent students (from either group) are able to notice or interpret non-verbal cues, and any potential influence of prior experience, such as playing online games.

Conclusion

In summary, the study found that in terms of confidence about speaking Chinese, those who believe less or not at all in the 'authenticity' of interaction in the MUVE environment experienced no real difference between the classroom environment and the MUVE environment, aside from a minor reduction in FLA. Those who believed more in the 'authenticity' of spoken interaction in the MUVE environment on the contrary felt more confident in the MUVE environment. In terms of motivation to attend class and engagement in class, no significant difference was found between the two environments. Overall, both groups experienced less FLA in the MUVE environment, but the impact of the MUVE environment on reducing various factors causing FLA was much larger for those who believed more in the 'authenticity' of spoken interaction in the environment than those who believed less or not at all. This suggests that highlighting the benefits and potential transferability of language practice in the MUVE environment to other settings, and in particular to potential future in-country experiences, may be useful in modifying student perceptions of the 'authenticity' of this kind of practice and their motivation to participate. For students who may not have the opportunity to participate in study abroad at all, task-based learning in the MUVE environment could potentially provide an opportunity to experience target language use in contexts that are as close to authentic settings (the world outside the classroom) as possible but with reduced FLA and potentially fewer disincentives to engage. The key is their perception of 'authenticity' and confidence in use, so identifying and addressing the factors that may affect this perception provide opportunities for future research.

The study also found that the students' sense of the authenticity of spoken conversation is significantly related to their technical anxiety about using computers or using a 3D MUVE to communicate. In other words, developing students' confidence in generic computer skills, plus MUVE-specific technical skills, will help students to be more immersed in the environment and therefore more engaged in language activities, which in turn contributes to less worries and anxieties in learning a second language. These findings pose interesting implications for technical and pedagogical development of language lessons in the environment. When designing and implementing voice-based lessons in the 3D MUVE environment, careful consideration of the pace of interaction and activities and implementing protocols around ascertaining how students are coping with the pace could help to further reduce student anxiety. With experience, teachers will also be able to develop a range of strategies appropriate to the environment to check whether students have understood what they have said, potentially further reducing student anxiety.

In terms of future research, there remain a number of angles from which to explore the impact of FLA and MUVEs, including whether or to what extent prior experiences of communication in a MUVE environment affect student experience of FLA and engagement in later study abroad contexts, or even whether participation in a MUVE simulation influences students—positively or negatively—to participate in study abroad programs. In addition, we have identified a number of areas which are worthy of further investigation, including to what extent students are able to notice or interpret non-verbal cues in the MUVE environment, and whether activities such as playing online games influences this ability, to what extent an overall positive attitude to learning is related to positive evaluations of authenticity or utility of communication in both classroom and MUVE settings and a willingness to engage, and importantly, which factors most contribute to a sense of authenticity in MUVE-based L2 encounters. In this vein, further research will be conducted into differences in student perception of the authenticity of text-based communication with NPCs and voice-based communication with live NSs and the comparative impacts on the FLA they experience. Any reduplication is also sure to consolidate findings given the small number of participants of the study.

Acknowledgements Seed funding received from the Languages and Cultures Network for Australian Universities (LCNAU) provided the starting point for this research.

References

Allen, H. (2003). A mixed-methodology investigation of the linguistic and affective outcomes of summer study abroad. *Foreign Language Annals*.

Allen, H. W., & Herron, C. (2003). A mixed-methodology investigation of the linguistic and affective outcomes of summer study abroad. *Foreign Language Annals, 36*(3), 370–385. doi:10.1111/j.1944-9720.2003.tb02120.x.

Amit, V. (2010). Student mobility and internationalisation: Rationales, rhetoric and 'Institutional Isomorphism'. *Anthropology in Action, 17*(1), 618.

Bandura, A. (1997). *Social learning theory*. Englewood Cliffs, NJ: Prentice-Hall.

Blasing, M. T. (2010). Second language in second life: Exploring interaction, identity and pedagogical practice in a virtual world. *SEEJ, 54*(1), 96–117.

Bochner, S., Furnham, A., & Hutnik, N. (1985). The friendship patterns of overseas and host students in an Oxford student residence. *The Journal of Social Psychology, 125*(6), 689–694.

Carroll, J. (1967). Foreign language proficiency levels attained by language majors near graduation from college. *Foreign Language Annals, 1,* 131–151.

Cohen, J. (1988). *Statistical power analysis for the behavioral sciences* (2nd ed.). Hillsdale, NJ: Earlbaum.

Collentine, J. (2004). The effects of learning contexts on morphosyntactic and lexical development. *Studies in Second Language Acquisition, 26,* 227–248.

Dalgarno, B., & Lee, M. J. W. (2010). What are the learning affordances of 3-D virtual environments? *British Journal of Educational Technology, 40*(6), 10–32.

Dalgarno, B., Lee, M. J. W., Carlson, L., Gregory, S., & Tynan, B. (2011). An Australian and New Zealand scoping study on the use of 3D immersive virtual worlds in higher education. *Australasian Journal of Educational Technology, 27*(1). Retrieved from http://www.ascilite.org.auajet/ajet27/dalgarno.html.

DeKeyser, R. M. (1991). Foreign language development during a semester abroad. In B. Freed (Ed.), *Foreign language acquisition research and the classroom* (pp. 104–119). Lexington, MA: D.D. Heath and Company.

Dewaele, J., & Regan, V. (2002). Maitriser la norme socilinguistique en interlangue freancaise: Le cas du l'omission variable de "ne". *French Language Studies, 12,* 123–148.

DuFon, M. C. E. (2006). *Language learners in study abroad contexts*. Clevedon, England: Multilingual Matters.

Engle, L., & Engle, J. (2003). Study abroad levels: Toward a classification of program types. *Frontiers: The Interdisciplinary Journal of Study Abroad, IX*(Fall), 1–20.

Grant, S., & Clerehan, R. (2011). Finding the discipline: Assessing student activity in second life. *Australasian Journal of Educational Technology, 27*(Special issue, 5), 813–828.

Grant, S., & Huang, H. (2010). The integration of an online 3D virtual learning environment into formal classroom-based undergraduate Chinese language and culture curriculum *Journal of Technology and Chinese Language Teaching, 1*(1)

Grant, S., & Huang, H. (2012). 13. Learning a Second Language in Second Life. In T. Islam, O. Lee, J. Peterson & M. Piscioneri (Eds.), *Effectively implementing information communication technology in higher education in the Asia-Pacific Region*. Hauppauge, NY: Nova Science Publishers, Inc.

Grant, S., Huang, H., & Pasfield-Neofitou, S. (2013). language learning in virtual worlds: The role of foreign language and technical anxiety. *Journal of Virtual Worlds Research, 6*(1), 1–9.

Grant, S., Huang, H., & Pasfield-Neofitou, S. (2014). The authenticity-anxiety paradox: The quest for authentic second language communication and reduced foreign language anxiety in virtual environments. *Procedia Technology, 13,* 23–32. doi:10.1016/j.protcy.2014.02.005.

Gregory, S. (2011a). *Rethinking reaching and learning through machinima professional development on Sloodle*. Paper presented at the First Global Conference on Experiential Learning in Virtual Worlds, Prague, Czech Republic.

Gregory, S. (2011b). Teaching higher education students with diverse learning outcomes in the virtual world of Second Life. In R. Hinrichs & C. Wankel (Eds.), *Transforming virtual world learning: Cutting-edge technologies in higher education* (Vol. 4, pp. 333–362). Bingley, UK: Emerald.

Gregory, S., Lee, M. J. W., Ellis, A., Gregory, S., Wood, D., Hillier, M., & McKeown, L. (2010). *Australian higher education institutions transforming the future of teaching and learning through 3D virtual worlds*. Paper presented at the Curriculum, technology & transformation for an unknown future: Proceedings of the 27th ASCILITE Conference, Brisbane, Australia.

Hanna, B. E., & de Nooy, J. (2003). A funny thing happened on the way to the forum: Electronic discussion and foreign language learning. *Language Learning & Technology, 7*(1), 71–85.

Horwitz, E., Horwitz, M., & Cope, J. (1986). Foreign language classroom anxiety. *The Modern language journal, 70*(2), 125–132.

Isabelli-Garc´ıa, C. L. (2006). Study abroad social networks, motivation, and attitudes: Implications for SLA. In M. DuFon & E. Churchill (Eds.), *Language learners in study abroad contexts* (pp. 231–258). Clevedon, England: Multilingual Matters.

Kim, T. (2009). Transnational academic mobility, internationalization and interculturality in higher education. *Intercultural Education, 20*(5), 395–405.

Kinginger, C. (2008). *Language learning in study abroad: Case studies of Americans in France* (Vol. 1).

Kinginger, C. (2011). Enhancing language learning in study abroad. *Annual Review of Applied Linguistics, 31,* 58–73.

Lave, J., & Wenger, E. (1991). *Situated Learning: Legitimate peripheral participation*. Cambridge: Cambridge University Press.
Lee, M. J. W., & Dalgarno, B. (2011). Scaffolding discovery learning in 3D virtual environments: Issues and considerations for instructional design. In S. Hai-Jew (Ed.), *Virtual immersive and 3D learning spaces: Emerging technologies and trends* (pp. 138–169). Hershey, PA: Information Science Reference.
Leeman, J. (1999). Review of Un Misterio En Toluca. *Language, Learning & Technology, 3*(1), 31–41.
Masuda, K. (2011). Acquiring interactional competence in a study abroad context: Japanese language learners' use of the interactional particle ne. *Modern Language Journal, 95,* 519–540.
Meredith, R. A. (2010). Acquiring cultural perceptions during study abroad: The influence of youthful associates. *Hispania, 93,* 686–702.
Monk, N., McDonald, S., Pasfield-Neofitou, S., & Lindgren, M. (2015). Portal Pedagogy: From Interdisciplinarity and Internationalization to Transdiscipliarity and Transnationalization. *London Review of Education, 13*(3)
Pasfield-Neofitou, S. (2014). Language learning and socialization opportunities in game worlds: Trends in first and second language research. *Language & Linguistics Compass, 8*(7), 271–284.
Penn, T., Podvorska, A., & Segit, M. A. (2013). Shared Foreignness: Student experiences of social inclusion and exclusion during study abroad. *Reinvention, 6*(2). Retrieved from http://www.warwick.ac.uk/reinventionjournal/issues/volume6issue2/penn
Redden, E. (2013). International Study Up. *Inside Higher Ed.* Retrieved from http://www.insidehighered.com/news/2013/11/11/survey-finds-increases-international-enrollments-study-abroad#ixzz2vpuUaAkV
Regan, V. (2004). The relationship between the group and the individual and the acquisition of native speaker variation patterns: A preliminary study. *IRAL, 42,* 335–348.
Salisbury, N. (2013). The global MMO games market: Payments, intelligence and trends. *Global Collect Video Gaming Payments: Knowledge Series* (Vol. 2)
Tarrant, M., & Lyons, K. (2011). The effect of short-term educational travel programs on environmental citizenship. *Environmental Education Research, 18*(3), 403–416. doi:10.1080/13504622.2011.625113.
Wilkinson, S. (1998). Study abroad from the participants' perspective: A challenge to common beliefs. *Foreign Language Annals, 31*(1)
Wu, Z. (2010). *Contemporary Chinese for Beginners (textbook).* Beijing: Sinolingua.

Author Biographies

Scott Grant is an Assistant Lecturer in the Chinese Studies program at Monash University. He is the creator of the Monash Chinese Island language learning simulation in Second Life. He leads successful applications for three seed grants from the Languages and Culture Network for Australian Universities in 2012 and an Australian Federal Government OLT Seed Project grant in 2013–14. His publications on 3D virtual worlds include task-based language learning; foreign language and technical anxiety; assessment; self-efficacy; student cognition; integration of 3D virtual worlds into formal curricula; international collaboration; the role of non-character players; and pedagogical, task and environmental design.

Hui Huang is a Lecturer at School of Languages, Cultures and Linguistics at Monash University. She has been researching and publishing in the area of second language acquisition, language pedagogy, teaching Chinese as a second language and utilising ICT in teaching second language. Her recent publications cover the topics of educational uses of 3D MUVE environments, animation and learning of Chinese characters, the effect of intergenerational encounters on second language learning and identity reconstruction

Sarah E. Pasfield-Neofitou is an Adjunct Research Fellow at Monash, where until 2016, she held the position of Lecturer in Japanese, and was eEducation Coordinator for the Arts Faculty. She is the author of numerous papers on digital communication and language learning, as well as 'Online Communication in a Second Language' (Multilingual Matters, 2012). Sarah has worked with Scott and Hui on the LCNAU-funded Chinese Island project, and a paper from this project won the Silver Avatar at SLACTIONS, 2012. In 2013, Sarah and Scott worked with Patrizia Sambuco to develop a Virtual Prato in Second Life.

Chapter 8
Cognitive Engagement in Virtual Worlds Language Learning

Michael Henderson, Lyn Henderson, Scott Grant and Hui Huang

Introduction

Virtual worlds such as Second Life have a number of affordances for the teaching and learning of second languages and intercultural awareness. The virtual world can offer rich linguistically appropriate environments in which students can adopt roles and interact with others, including non-player characters (NPCs, also known as "bots"). Virtual worlds can support competency-based training such as vocabulary and grammar like other computer-assisted language-learning tools, but it can also support synchronous interaction with teachers, students and others, including native speakers in rich creative ways.

In a previous project, the authors had identified eight key affordances of virtual worlds for language learning (Henderson et al. 2012, pp. 402–403):

(1) Affective filter: In face-to-face classroom environments, student language learning outcomes can suffer from what has been termed foreign language classroom anxiety (Hauck and Hurd 2005; Zhao and Lai 2009). This affective filter arises because of learner perception of a threatening environment, in the form of negative feedback from classmates or the instructor, prompted by their attempt at producing output in the language being learned. The use of virtual

M. Henderson (✉) · S. Grant · H. Huang
Monash University, Melbourne, VIC, Australia
e-mail: michael.henderson@monash.edu

S. Grant
e-mail: scott.grant@arts.monash.edu.au

H. Huang
e-mail: hui.huang@monash.edu

L. Henderson
James Cook University, Townsville, QLD, Australia
e-mail: lyndhenderson@gmail.com

S. Gregory and D. Wood (eds.), *Authentic Virtual World Education*,
https://doi.org/10.1007/978-981-10-6382-4_8

worlds for language learning has been shown to reduce such anxiety (Grant et al. 2013; Peterson 2011).

(2) Persistent environments and persistent records: Virtual worlds are persistent, that is, the environment, Chinese Restaurant and the objects (Chinese menu), do not disappear at the end of the lesson, unless programmed to do so. Persistent records of interaction allow students to examine their own performance, as well as revisit and rehearse skills, and provide individual learners with feedback and critical self-appraisal on their language performance.

(3) Physical and linguistic copresence: Dalgarno and Lee (2010) pointed out that copresence allows learners to "engage simultaneously in shared tasks and/or produce joint artefacts by operating on the same objects in real time" which can "pave the way for rich and truly collaborative experiences that foster positive interdependence within a learning group" (p 0.22). The additional value of virtual worlds in relation to language learning is that it merges the physical copresence and linguistic copresence of the interlocutors (Schwienhorst 2002). For example, indexical language (*here*, *this*, etc.) is often problematic in teleconferencing or asynchronous forums.

(4) Avatar control and learner autonomy: In virtual worlds, students have a degree of autonomy over their avatar to explore and interact independent of the instructor. While limited by software and environmental design, it affords student-centred learning. In relation to language learning in virtual environments, Schwienhorst (2002) notes that learner autonomy can raise language and linguistic awareness as well as support complex thinking and critical reflection. Subsequently Collentine (2011) confirmed that there is a positive correlation between learner autonomy in 3D virtual environments and the learners' linguistic complexity and accuracy.

(5) The value of text interactions even in a virtual world experience: Simply because Second Life can support voice does not mean that it is always the most appropriate medium for the learning outcomes. Indeed, the research literature from language education in general, as well as computer mediated language education, reveals that writing not only improves written language skills, but also facilitates orality as well as linguistic and metalinguistic awareness (Chun and Plass 2000; Sykes 2005; Thorne 2008). For students learning character-based languages such as Chinese, text-based interactions also provide the opportunity to consolidate knowledge of Hanyu pinyin Romanisation and character recognition (Grant and Clerehan 2011; Grant and Huang 2012).

(6) Mediated environment: The virtual world acts as a mediator of the sometimes overwhelming rich linguistic and cultural information that can be found in real life experiences. Aspects of that rich information can be decreased, omitted, enhanced, synthesised, or otherwise changed to decrease learner cognitive load, heighten awareness and facilitate processing. The careful design of the immersive social environment can reduce the need for a layer of abstract thinking required in text-book and other formal learning situations (Carr 1995).

(7) Context sensitive interactions: Virtual worlds can interact in contextually appropriate ways with learners who can be greeted by a 'bot' whenever they enter a room (location context). That greeting can be sensitive to an endless number of variables, such as: the time of day, gender of the learner (or, more precisely, their avatar), formality of context and frequency of visits.

(8) Body language: Virtual worlds offer the opportunity for students to not only perform linguistically but to also "act" in culturally appropriate ways within the assumed roles within the virtual environment (Grant and Huang 2012). As virtual worlds increasingly become more graphically rich and the representation of avatars become more life-like, (including facial expressions and gestures), the affordance of body language becomes increasingly powerful. In language acquisition, body language enhances communication by adding layers of meaning to what is spoken which can aid comprehension as well as afford opportunities to explore mannerisms and gestures intimately linked with the target language and cultural practices (Allen 1999; Shi and Fan 2010).

Research literature indicates that virtual worlds can facilitate learning a second language (e.g. Chinese—Grant and Huang 2012; language in general—Levy 2009; English—Zheng et al. 2009) and for increasing intercultural awareness (Diehl and Prins 2008). Virtual worlds add much more than visual and auditory media; they provide instructors and students greater choices for collaboration, learner autonomy, creativity, experimentation, and identity formation. However, further research is required in all of these areas, but also in coming to understand the underlying cognition that is at the root of these outcomes, and that occur as a result of the virtual environment and related instructional designs. Although Schwienhorst (2002) concluded that text-based virtual worlds can support complex thinking, this line of inquiry has not been taken up in relation to 3D virtual worlds. As a consequence, this study investigates the impact of Second Life experiences on university-level student cognition. In particular, it utilises a well-established theoretical and methodological paradigm providing robust empirical data for the identification and evaluation of the cognitive processes utilised by students, in other words, learners' cognitive engagement.

Theoretical and Methodological Framework

This study draws on a cognitive perspective for its theoretical grounding. The cognitive theory asserts that learning is a conscious thinking process and that people are "active processors of information" (Woolfolk 1990, p. 229). The cognitive or thinking processes, by which we make sense of information, are essential in mediating learning (Jonassen 1992). By investigating the mediating processes arising from an instructional activity, some evaluation of its value as an instructional design can be made.

This qualitative empirical study utilised stimulated recall, an introspection-tracing methodology in order to identify participant in situ activity, for instance, what participants were thinking when completing a particular action or response in Second Life (Gass and Mackey 2000; Henderson and Tallman 2006). Stimulated recall is inherently grounded in information processing theory and the mediating process paradigm. Information processing theory describes how learning and remembering occur. In particular, it proposes that learning is a function of the interactions between sensory memory, short-term working memory, and long-term memory. Broadly, stimuli such as language prompts in Second Life are received by sensory memory, then either discarded or sent to the short-term working memory where it is processed and either discarded or sent to long-term memory for storage from which, when needed, it is recalled back to short-term working memory and then delivered as responses or learning outcomes. Such an outcome, in Scenario 1 of this study, was correctly ordering a meal suitable for four friends with differing dietary requirements.

The mediating processes paradigm is the conceptual framework. Each stage of the information processing model is mediated by cognitive processes. In particular, it provides us with a way of identifying the thinking processes of participants when carrying out a task in a virtual world. In effect, such processes mediate, or come between, the stimuli (e.g. lesson task) and outcomes (e.g. making soup dumplings) and are "the fine-grained elements of cognition through which, and by which, learning outcomes are realised" (Henderson et al. 1997, p. 163). This is different from the process–product paradigm in which thinking processes (e.g. recall) are assumed to have occurred because an outcome has been observed (e.g. using appropriate Chinese words to form a question). It cannot capture the choices, decisions, and judgements made by students during a learning activity nor what actually triggered these cognitive processes (Marland et al. 1992; Shulman 1986). In contrast, using stimulated recall within a mediating process paradigm we are able to identify the thinking processes employed by students while engaged in a Second Life lesson.

Although mediating processes are an essential part of an information processing model, this project does not attempt to study the entire system of information handling. The focus of this research is how learners make sense of the information given to them in a particular instructional setting; that is, what cognitive processes do learners employ to process and make meaning of the information. The information itself may be curriculum content (e.g. vocabulary, grammar, audiovisual designs in-world, etc.) but it may also be instructional interactions (e.g. instructions in-world and "real life"; exchanges between students, etc.) and in this case, technological interactions (e.g. dealing with computer-based prompts, managing the software, etc.). Despite the agreed importance of mediating processes, there is no definitive list. This is partly the result of an inherent inability of the cognitive perspective to clearly delineate how information is processed (Henderson 1996). However, a number of researchers have developed a list of commonly agreed upon thinking processes found in the research literature, validated in their own studies and cross-referenced to considerations of depth or quality of processing (e.g. Henderson 2005; Henderson et al. 2010; Henderson 1996; Marland et al. 1992).

The resulting list of twenty-two thinking processes was adopted by this study; however, as the aforementioned authors have noted, the list is not assumed to be definitive, nor is it expected that all processes will necessarily be evident.

In this study, each of the participants were video recorded during the Second Life computer lab lesson. Screen capture software (ScreenFlow) was used to record both the on-screen Second Life activity as well as the face of the participant (via the inbuilt web camera). This video was then replayed during the participant's interview. Both the participant and the interviewer had control over the video so that they could pause, fast forward, or rewind. The participant was encouraged to pause or stop the video and invited to recall what they had been thinking during that video segment. The researcher would also pause the video if an action or facial expression was observed that might indicate thinking that the student may not have reported. A major strength of using video in stimulated recall interviews is to explore the visual cues, such as frowning, posture changes or taking notes, that have been found as major indicators of mediating processes (e.g. Gass and Mackey 2000; Henderson and Tallman 2006). For a detailed description of stimulated recall (and other introspection tools) including issues of reliability, validity, and protocols for interviewing and analysis, see Henderson et al. (2010).

Coding the transcripts requires use of strict analysis protocols, including inter-coder reliability practices. In this particular study, each author coded the transcript of the same student's interview. This was swapped with another author and checked for accuracy. When there were differences, all authors discussed the differences until a consensus was reached. Each then completed two or three transcripts that were then double-checked. The most experienced coder then re-checked all for consistency of coding. Invalid data were discarded, namely, thoughts that occurred during the interview (and not during the actual lesson) or as a result of a leading question by the interviewer. Coded interviews were again checked and, if necessary, corrected by the most experienced coder when entering data tallies; only two instances required changing.

Participants and Lesson Designs

The first semester subject, *Chinese 1*, admits students who have not formally studied Mandarin Chinese. Each year it has an average of 150 students, with the majority (66% on average) having English as a first language. Apart from the use of Second Life in a series of 90 min lessons, the subject consisted of the traditional weekly lectures and tutorials, independent study based on textbooks and their associated language DVD. In terms of the Second Life lessons, the student's first lesson was largely devoted to learning how to use the technology, particularly their avatar. In the second lesson, the students engaged in Scenario 1: ordering food in a Chinese restaurant. In their third lesson, the students engaged in Scenario 2: getting directions and purchasing food ingredients. Both scenarios were specifically designed to reinforce language and culture content previously covered in the classroom and in the textbook. There was a month between the Second Life scenario lessons.

This research focusses on the experiences of 14 students who participated in Scenario 1 and eight students who participated in Scenario 2. The 22 students were interviewed using the stimulated recall method. There was only one student who was interviewed twice (i.e. for Scenario 1 and Scenario 2). All students in the Scenario 2 interviews had previously experienced Scenario 1.

In the Scenario 1 lesson, the activity was made authentic by asking students to work collaboratively to choose the most appropriate dishes for "people" sitting at their table. They were informed that their table included a Muslim, a vegetarian, a diabetic, someone who did not like spicy food, someone who was allergic to seafood, and a friend from Beijing. It required students to be able to: (a) understand the menu and other text, and then (b) make considered decisions among several possible alternatives, according to the description of each of the dishes and their negotiated understanding of the dietary context, including Chinese culture. In most cases, there was no clear single answer. In order to complete this task in time, the students were encouraged to form groups, organise themselves and collaborate through the group text chat facility. Students shared their ideas, compared their understanding of the appropriateness of the dishes and eventually ordered the chosen dish that was brought to their table by the waitress (a non-player character [NPC]). In this lesson, the students had a number of learning objectives aligned with those of the subject, for instance: the lesson aimed to strengthen student use of Chinese pinyin Romanisation to input Chinese characters on a computer as well as to be able to read Chinese characters (consequently, this lesson did not allow in-world voice communication).

Communication was centred around, but not limited to, practicing key vocabulary and phrases related to ordering food learned from the textbook and to extend on the textbook through new phrases introduced by the tutor or NPC. While most of the communication was through the text chat facility in Second Life, students could choose to communicate in the physical classroom to give each other help, especially in terms of using the software and in learning Chinese characters and phrases that they could use in-world. Successful completion of the activity (e.g. ordering appropriate dietary dishes) could only be achieved through reading, writing, and negotiating choices in Chinese text.

The Chinese restaurant in Second Life was not intended to replicate real life but rather to evoke a sense of immersion in a Chinese setting. For instance, Chinese-styled furniture and decorations were complemented by Chinese signs and a background recording of people talking in a real-life restaurant in China. Upon arrival, students were greeted in Chinese by an automated waitress (NPC) who also gave them a custom designed heads-up display (HUD) that is seen at the top of Fig. 8.1. This tool, designed specifically for this subject, enabled the avatars to access sound files, pinyin spelling, and Chinese character information for each of the dishes. Students clicked on a dish enabling them to hear the dish's Chinese name and see its spelling in pinyin and Chinese characters. The students could also

Fig. 8.1 Making dumpling soup in Second Life

obtain more information about each of the dishes displayed in the restaurant in the form of a notecard containing the main ingredients and a description of the dish.

In Scenario 2, the students played the role of foreign students studying on Chinese Island. In this scenario, the students had decided to invite their teacher to eat soup dumplings after class because that day the local Chinese were celebrating the Winter Solstice when dumplings are traditionally eaten. Their task was to work in pairs to buy two bowls of dumplings and take them back to their teacher. They were directed to go to the local restaurant (the same setting as Scenario 1) to find a friend of their teacher who worked as a waitress and buy the dumplings from her. This required the students to communicate with two waitresses by typing Chinese characters into to a private Instant Message (IM) window to establish which one was their teacher's friend and how to buy the dumplings. The waitresses were NPCs programmed to recognise and respond to Chinese character input from the students. The program was able to pattern match student input in the form of questions, statements, and answers and produce appropriate pre-programmed responses in Chinese text. An additional program also enabled the waitresses to display a limited range of body language during the conversation, such as lifting both arms in welcome.

The waitress, who was the friend of the students' teacher, was programmed to respond to student requests to buy dumplings by informing them that the restaurant had temporarily run out of Chinese cabbage which was needed for the dumplings. Students were asked to go and purchase a cabbage from a local farmer's market stall and bring it back to the restaurant's kitchen where they would make their dumplings.

Initially, students were not given specific directions on the route to the market by the waitress. They were required to ask for directions: the lesson instructions included sample phrases from their textbook to help them ask this and other questions. On receiving directions, students next had to utilise them to find the market and the market vendor who was selling Chinese cabbages. Like the waitress, the seller is also a programmed non-player character. Students then had to converse with the seller in Chinese character text chat and convey what they wanted to buy, find out how much, and then pay for the cabbage (from a virtual wallet they had been given containing mock PR China currency). Once they bought the virtual cabbage, the students had to return to the restaurant kitchen where they made the cabbages into virtual dumplings, cooked them in pots on stoves and served in bowls. These were then presented by each student to the lecturer's avatar as proof of task completion.

Students were given lesson plans, instructions, and additional resources on Moodle at the start of the lesson. The resources included a short illustrated passage in Chinese on the history of dumplings and the Winter Solstice. Their instructions were a mixture of English and Chinese that had previously been learned in the classroom. In addition, help signs were positioned at strategic points in various lesson-related locations. When clicked by students, the signs would give virtual notecards containing additional hints and reminders in Chinese text. Students were also given assessment criteria that included the teacher sighting the student's cooked dumplings, as well as demonstrating information that they had gathered from various other stages of the scenario tasks.

Results and Discussion

The twenty-two interview participants reported a total of 2,055 mediating processes stimulated by the one hour Second Life language lesson (either Scenario 1 or Scenario 2). The fourteen participants in Scenario 1 had an average of 76 while the eight participants of Scenario 2 had an average of 124 (see Table 8.1). However, Scenario 1 had participants with both the lowest (23) and highest (178) reported mediating processes (Scenario 2's range: 67–176). The degree of variance was greater in Scenario 1 with a standard deviation of 45.1 compared with Scenario 2's standard deviation of 38.9. While the small number of participants does not lend itself to statistical analysis, the reporting of variance does help to highlight that there was considerable variation while at the same time confirming that Scenario 2 appears more successful in stimulating a greater number of thinking processes. However, as Table 8.1 shows, despite these differences, both scenarios resulted in clearly similar patterns of frequency, namely the high frequency of the same five thinking processes.

Table 8.1 delineates the twenty cognitive processes identified from the coded transcripts; the bolded cognitions are rated higher level thinking processes and those italicised, the lowest level (as defined by Henderson et al. 2010; Henderson

Table 8.1 Reported cognition (thinking processes)

	Scenario 1 (ordering Chinese dishes) (14 students)			Scenario 2 (cabbage dumplings) (8 students)			Total	
Cognition[a]	Mean	Number	%	Mean	Number	%	Number	%
Affect	*15*	*208*	*19.6*	*27*	*216*	*21.7*	*424*	*20.6*
Strategy planning	*12*	*164*	*15.5*	*19*	*154*	*15.5*	*318*	*15.5*
Justifying	*8*	*105*	*9.9*	*19*	*151*	*15.2*	*256*	*12.5*
Evaluating	*11*	*149*	*14.1*	*12*	*96*	*9.6*	*245*	*11.9*
Metacognising	*8*	*105*	*9.9*	*14*	*112*	*11.3*	*217*	*10.6*
Comparing	3	46	4.3	5	41	4.1	87	4.2
Confirming	3	41	3.9	6	46	4.6	87	4.2
Generating	4	49	4.6	4	29	2.9	78	3.8
Anticipating	3	43	4.1	2	19	1.9	62	3.0
Diagnosing	2	29	2.7	3	27	2.7	56	2.7
Categorising	2	26	2.5	2	17	1.7	43	2.1
Recalling	2	21	2.0	3	22	2.2	43	2.1
Translating	1	13	1.2	2	17	1.7	30	1.5
Analysing	1	16	1.5	2	13	1.3	29	1.4
Linking	1	17	1.6	1	9	0.9	26	1.3
Deliberating[b]	1	13	1.2	1	10	1.0	23	1.1
Reflecting	0	4	0.4	1	11	1.1	15	0.7
Selecting	1	7	0.7	0	3	0.3	10	0.5
Imaging	0	3	0.3	0	2	0.2	5	0.2
Applying	0	1	0.1	0	0	0.0	1	0.0
TOTALS	76	1060	100	124	995	100	2055	100

[a]Higher order thinking processes are bolded; the lowest are italicised; the remainder are middle range (categorisation adopted from Henderson 1996)
[b]*Deliberating* occurred when the type of thinking was not disclosed (e.g. "I was just thinking about the dishes.")

1996; Marland et al. 1992). Overall, the two Second Life scenario lessons stimulated a pleasing number of higher level thinking skills; however, the most prevalent thinking was related to affect, or feeling, which is typically categorised as a low or surface-level thinking process. All participants demonstrated a range of different types of thinking processes (average 16; least reported 13, most reported 18). Despite the representation of different types of processes, it is striking that 71% of all instances were accounted for by only five types of thinking processes. These top five reported thinking processes and their implications are now discussed.

Table 8.2 displays a closer examination of the top five cognitive processes. When conducting research into the cognitive processes of students, it is natural to ask whether the reported thinking is in relation to the task or curriculum. Analysis of the reported cognitive processes reveals that 87.4% of the 1,460 processes reported for the top five were focused on the task (i.e. curriculum content, learning

Table 8.2 Context of cognitive process and source of stimuli

Cognition		Context		Source of Stimuli		Total
		On-task	Off-task	In-world	"Real world"	
Affect	Positive	188	13	175	26	201
		(12.9%)	(0.9%)	(12%)	(1.8%)	(13.8%)
	Negative	174	49	184	39	223
		(11.9%)	(3.4%)	(12.6%)	(2.7%)	(15.3%)
Strategy planning		289	29	238	80	318
		(19.8%)	(2%)	(16.3%)	(5.5%)	(21.8%)
Justifying		217	39	198	58	256
		(14.8%)	(2.7%)	(13.5%)	(4%)	(17.5%)
Evaluating		206	39	185	60	245
		(14.1%)	(2.7%)	(12.7%)	(4.1%)	(16.8%)
Metacognising		203	14	176	41	217
		(13.9%)	(0.9%)	(12%)	(2.8%)	(14.8%)
Total		1277	183	1156	304	1460
		(87.4%)	(12.6%)	(79.1%)	(20.9%)	(100%)

activity, procedural request from the instructor, etc.). The remaining 12.6% were classed as off-task (something other than curriculum or lesson, e.g. thinking about their avatar's clothing).

In this research, the lessons in Second Life were in the "real world" context of a formal class in a computer laboratory in the presence of the lecturer, and researchers. Consequently, we were interested to validate if the cognition was triggered by in-world (e.g. interactions with virtual environment) or "real world" (e.g. interactions with lecturer, textbook, other students) stimuli. Across both scenarios, the majority of the stimuli were in-world (79.1%) with the remaining (20.9%) arising from events, interactions, or resources, such as the lesson worksheet or reading the textbook from the "real world". The dominant "real world" stimuli were the lecturer who gave initial class instructions, announcements about time remaining, and roamed the classroom offering advice and answering questions. Consequently, the lecturer had a particularly influential role in mediating confusion arising from the intersection of the instructions, technology, virtual environment, and curriculum content.

Affect

Affect is defined at its simplest as feelings (Henderson et al. 2010). In this study, in both scenarios, affect was the highest reported cognitive process (20.6%, 424 instances, Table 8.1). It was the highest reported process for fourteen of the twenty-two participants and in the top three most frequently reported process for the remaining eight participants. Affect has been classified as low or surface-level thinking (Henderson 1996), although this does not mean to suggest that affect does not have a role to play in learning. In addition, affect can be viewed in terms of valence, that is, the subjective experience of a positive-to-negative state. In this study, each process was categorised according to whether it was broadly positive (e.g. feelings of excitement, satisfaction, pleasure), or negative (e.g. frustration, anger, embarrassment, and anxiety).

Approximately half (47%) of the reported affect were positive in nature, for example: "It's like going to a restaurant in China; it was really cool, that's what I felt!" It is interesting to note that a majority of the positive affect was on-task, that is, related to the task or curriculum, for example: "I was just laughing at the mistake I made; I said, 'I want to sell a cabbage instead of buy a cabbage!'" Such instances were often a result of a thinking process that led to perceived success, for instance, one student reported what they were feeling when they were observed to be smiling: "Yeah! It was my response for getting a successful response from the programmed robot. It was progress!" Positive affect was reported as motivating and, in the majority of instances, quickly led to other thinking processes, such as strategy planning, for example: "That was the dish I wanted! [student smiling in video recording] Okay, now I just have to fill in three others." It is noteworthy that not all positive affect are motivating, for example, amusement at a situation may not motivate further action (Harmon-Jones et al. 2013). However, in this study, the reported affect was largely in context of the students' own task behaviours (e.g. pursuing the curriculum) and, as a seeming consequence of this engaged state, the positive affect led to motivational outcomes.

The other half (53%) of the reported affect were negative in nature. The major cause for the negative affect was the limited range of vocabulary responses programmed into the NPC in both Second Life scenarios: "It's a robot. It's not a real person!"; "The most frustrating thing is to get: 'I'm sorry! Could you please repeat?'"; "I was starting to get really frustrated 'cause, like, there's no other variation of the same question that you can ask!" Such interactions caused panic for one student: "I won't get back in time to make the dumplings! I won't pass this assessment!" While most of the negative, affective cognitive processes were stimulated by interactions with NPCs, the remaining were largely related to clarity of instructions and relating those to the environment (for example, knowing where to click, to look, or where to walk). An interesting dynamic was that many of the reported instances of negative affect were also in the context of an awareness of limited time. Reference to time was often stimulated by lecturer comments about end of class (e.g. "ten minutes to the end of class") or self-reference to the worksheet which highlighted their (lack of) progress. This resulted in one student reporting thirty-eight instances related to time, such as: "I'm a bit scared of not finishing on time!" Being aware of limited time seems to intensify students' negative affect and often led to spontaneous courses of action or waiting for help from the lecturer.

Strategy Planning

Strategy planning is described as the process of generating ways to process or accomplish tasks, such as the learning objectives (Henderson et al. 2010). Strategy Planning was the second-most frequently reported cognitive process in both scenarios (318 reported instances, or 15.5%, Table 8.1). As with affective thinking, the majority of strategy planning were in relation to on-task activity (i.e. focussed on the learning activity) and stimulated by in-world media and interactions.

A typical example of strategy planning was: "I remember at this point thinking: 'I've put the characters together but the sentence still doesn't make sense!' [pause] So, then I thought: 'Figure out what the [Chinese] characters are. Figure out the different meanings, two or three different meanings for that sentence. Then choose!'" The high frequency of strategy planning is thought to be a result of the ongoing engagement of students who have to constantly make decisions about what to do next. In the virtual world lesson, students need to act. For example, a NPC will not guide students unless they have been asked the correct question. This is quite different from typical language tutorials in which students are generally guided or prompted by the tutor, who will continue with the lesson regardless of whether the answer is correct, incorrect, or even if no answer is provided. In such lessons, the students do not need to make frequent decisions and are presented with a limited number of opportunities to strategise about processing the content and accomplishing a task. However, while the instructional design of the two Second Life language lessons required students to frequently make decisions, requiring a high level of strategy planning (as well as justifying and evaluating), it is also apparent that a consequence is the significantly small frequency of other cognitive processes, such as reflecting (careful consideration of past action, response, and causality), and applying (considers something in terms of how it could be used elsewhere) (Table 8.1).

Again, awareness of time appears to have heightened the state of flow, making students particularly focussed on accomplishing the task, as opposed to, for example, reflecting, analysing, linking, or applying (see Table 8.1). An example of this is provided by a student who strategised different ways to accomplish a task, including following other students in-world (as opposed to reading the Chinese road signs themselves). Towards the end of the lesson he reported thinking:

I figured we were pretty much done in the Second Life workshop: 'I found the cabbage street stall vendor, bought a cabbage, returned to the restaurant and made it into dumplings; just need to present one to the lecturer.' So I thought, 'Okay! Well, I can do things a little bit more properly now. Like, look up the lesson plan to look up the word for 'dumplings'!'

However, awareness of restricted time also resulted in motivation and focus, for example: "Well, at this point I'm thinking like: 'Okay, these are the meals I need. I have, like, 35 min for seeing the food and 5 min to order!"

Justifying, Evaluating, and Metacognising

The three mediating processes of justifying, evaluating, and metacognising accounted for 35% of the total reported thinking. Each process is distinct. In this chapter, they are considered together as they reveal common implications for instructional design, particularly clarity of instructions, supporting resources, and linearity of activity sequences.

Justifying is defined as trying to prove that a proposed action/idea is reasonable or correct through self-argument (Henderson et al. 2010). For example, one student reported thinking to herself: "If I do it this way then I can finish earlier and it won't take so long, 'cause it takes quite a while to type Pinyin in". Scenario 2 had a noticeably higher frequency of "Justifying" over "Evaluation". This can be explained, in part, by the greater volume of decision making in Scenario 2 which not only required similar activities as did Scenario 1 (such as purchasing items) but also required students to navigate to locations and interact with multiple NPCs. However, the sequence of seemingly open-ended and necessary actions in order to complete Scenario 2 also resulted in students frequently reporting an internal dialogue that was justifying their actions or a course of action, such as: "randomly exploring" because "it's better than doing nothing". Indeed, while justifying is considered a deeper level thinking process, many of the instances in Scenario 2 were focussed on task completion (e.g. justifying a course of action in relation to finding the next milestone, such as the market vendor) rather than language content (such as justifying the use of a particular pinyin character).

Evaluation is defined as making judgements about the value or worthwhileness of something, including activities, content, and own point of view (Henderson et al. 2010). For example, one student reported thinking: "What's good about this Second Life thing that makes him think that it would be good for his students? [pause] But if he thinks it is good, then I will too!" Evaluating the worthwhileness of an activity or response for learning, or in terms of short-term goals, achieving the task objectives, was frequently reported by students in Scenario 2, for example: "It was a good challenge because looking at the characters and trying to understand what they were saying in an actual conversation made it easier to learn." While such instances were evident in Scenario 1, the higher frequency of evaluative thinking processes can be ascribed to the instructional design in which students were required to make evaluations about the worth or correctness of a menu item in terms of the needs of the customers (e.g. vegetarian).

Metacognising is defined as thinking about, evaluating, or directing one's own thinking (Henderson et al. 2010). There were two clear themes in the reported instances of metacognising: the self-realisation of students that (1) they did not know what they should be doing or where they should be, or (2) did not know how to do something. The first is related to the clarity of instructional design, particularly in terms of instructions and media-rich virtual world environments. For example, a number of students commented that they became confused about what they should be doing (instruction or task design) or where they were (interpreting the virtual world): "I was lost, I didn't know what to do!"; "I am finding it difficult … it isn't easy enough for me. It's not completely clear in my head what I am doing!" These instances of reported metacognition due to being "lost", both in relation to the task or in relation to the virtual world, led to acting or strategising about getting back on track. This is a useful skill for any student, but arguably would not be as frequent if the tasks and virtual world could be designed to reduce instances of being "lost."

The second theme in reported metacognition was that students went through a process of self-realisation that they did not know how to do something, such as answer a question, type a Chinese character, use a grammatical form in Chinese, etc. While some reported instances were related to off-task concerns, such as realising that they did not know how to make their avatar fly, the majority of metacognition was directly related to the learning tasks in-world. The following example reveals part of an inner monologue of a student exploring their own knowledge, the cause of their own lack of knowledge and the way in which they need to direct their own thinking in future:

> I know what I want to say… how do I say it? At this point I'm going: 'I should know these things; I (pause) and half of me is thinking I should know these things because of all the work that we've done in the course but, then, the other half of me is saying '… they haven't given us enough exercises in Chinese for us to run through this really easily, or… or if they have, I haven't been paying attention to that side of it!

This self-realisation, exploring one's own thinking to realise that current knowledge or process is not sufficient, is arguably an important component of self-directed learning. In the above instance, the student recalls knowledge and revisits the textbook and evaluates its success which, in turn, helps them to develop a further strategy: "This is easy! I know this! All I have to do is …". However, it is also clear from the transcripts that while students can generate strategies or engage in other thinking processes to lead to future actions, there is a clear need for supporting resources (textbook, in-world prompts, access to the lecturer, etc.) to facilitate students achieving the learning objectives. A significant factor in the frequency of both metacognitive themes was the linear design of the instructional design, requiring students to correctly perform a number of milestone hurdles (find the stall, purchase a cabbage, etc.).

Conclusion

Learners can be engaged with virtual worlds in a variety of ways, including cognitively. This chapter has focussed on the ways in which a designed series of lessons can influence learners' cognitive process which are, fundamentally, at the root of learning. As we have demonstrated, virtual worlds can support learning, including second language acquisition. This study has revealed a high frequency of cognitive processes stimulated by programmed lessons involving the use of curriculum knowledge and skills to successfully complete in-world tasks. However, some of the thinking processes, despite being related to the task or curriculum, were focussed on simply meeting the task requirement (e.g. getting to a location which could be accomplished by following other avatars), rather than engaging with the learning goal (e.g. using their knowledge to read the Chinese road signs).

In terms of affective thinking processes, it can be concluded that virtual world lessons comprising a series of in-world tasks, that immediately give feedback to students regarding their success (e.g. successful use of Chinese language to ask a question), can engender positive affect that motivates additional on-task cognitions and behaviour. In contrast, negative affect (leading to increased tension and dissatisfaction) can result from when instructions are not clear to the student or when the programmed environment does not react or interact in expected ways (e.g. the NPCs programmed to recognise only a limited range of queries frustrates students who cannot problem solve the situation). The incidence of negative affect also appears to be intensified in the context of time restrictions. Negative affect can be avoided or, as demonstrated in this study, ameliorated through increased clarity in instructions and supports (e.g. the lecturer roaming the classroom to answer questions).

Deep-level thinking processes, such as strategy planning, justifying, evaluating, and metacognition are typically desirable in any learning activity. However, as in the case of negative affect, the awareness of limited time can result in the thinking processes focussing on task accomplishment rather than learning goals. Nevertheless, this study revealed a large number of cognitive processes engaged with learning. It is clear that the design of in-world lessons requiring students to make frequent decisions in order to accomplish tasks (such as, choosing options, pathways, answers, etc.) can result in frequent strategising, justifying, evaluating, and metacognising, but at the same time may not facilitate other cognitive processes such as reflecting and applying.

The programmable nature of Second Life can enable instructional designs where students are required to frequently draw on their knowledge and skills to achieve learning goals and, in which, they are provided with immediate feedback. However, the reported instances of negative affect also show that limitations in instructional design can result in tension, frustration, and dissatisfaction. Nevertheless, despite such frustration, a number of students commented after the stimulated recall interview processes that the virtual world lesson was better than the regular language tutorials and workshops due to the ability to practice with a degree of independence. One student summarised this:

> During the seminars and tutorials, a lot of people speak over the teacher … I don't feel like I'm learning much. If I want to learn Chinese, I've got to put in the extra effort and do it myself at home. But, with this [Second Life], I can use my Chinese and actually learn things. Like, interact with other people and this way use it and then practice it and then I'll learn it, hopefully! Like, I'm more likely to remember how to write the characters after learning it here than just seeing them on the whiteboard to read … I find this [Second Life] is a better way to learn because you actually have to figure out how the Pinyin is, and how to type it, and recognise the characters and, then, if you get it wrong, it's not going to come up with the right answer. You have to do the work!

Such uses of virtual worlds, to shift the onus of thinking onto students, are clearly a positive affordance of the technology for student learning. Having to make frequent decisions resulted in greater frequency of deep-level thinking processes, such as: strategising, justifying, evaluating, and metacognising. However, it was also noted that the focus of the thinking was sometimes orientated to successful task completion (e.g. find the restaurant), rather than learning (e.g. what would the Chinese word for restaurant look like on the road signs?). As a consequence, it can be concluded that the alignment of the sequence of hurdle tasks needs to be carefully considered to ensure that the activity requires knowledge or skills valued in the curriculum. In-world exercises, including the transitions from one task or locality to another, should be treated as a series of learning opportunities. In addition, the study of the students' metacognitive processes also revealed a need to ensure clarity of instructional design, particularly in terms of instructions and the information provided in-world. This would reduce instances of being "lost", thereby reducing unnecessary metacognition dealing with thinking about instructions rather than thinking about content.

References

Allen, L. A. (1999). Functions of nonverbal communication in teaching and learning a foreign language. *The French Review, 72*(3), 469–480.

Carr, K. (1995). Introduction. In K. Carr & R. England (Eds.), *Simulated and virtual realities*. London: Taylor and Francis.

Chun, D., & Plass, J. L. (2000). Networked Multimedia Environments for Second Language Acquisition. In M. Warschauer & R. Kern (Eds.), *Network-based language teaching: Concepts and practice* (pp. 151–170). Cambridge, MA: Cambridge University Press.

Collentine, K. (2011). Learner Autonomy in a task-based 3D world and production. *Language Learning & Technology, 15*(3), 50–67.

Dalgarno, B., & Lee, M. J. W. (2010). What are the learning affordances of 3-D virtual environments? *British Journal of Educational Technology, 41*(1), 22. doi:10.1111/j.1467-8535.2009.01038.x.

Diehl, W. C., & Prins, E. (2008). Unintended outcomes in second life: Intercultural literacy and cultural identity in a virtual world. *Language and Intercultural Communication, 8*(2), 101–118.

Gass, S. M., & Mackey, A. (2000). *Stimulated recall methodology in second language research*. Mahwah, NJ: Lawrence Erlbaum.

Grant, S., & Clerehan, R. (2011). Finding the discipline: assessing student activity in Second Life. *Australasian Journal of Educational Technology, 27*(5), 813–828.

Grant, S., & Huang, H. (2012). Learning a second language in second life. In O. L. T. Islam, J. Peterson, & M. Piscioneri (Eds.), *Effectively implementing information communication technology in higher education in the Asia-Pacific Region*. Hauppauge, NY: NOVA Science.

Grant, S., Huang, H., & Pasfield-Neofitou, S. (2013). Language learning in virtual worlds: The role of foreign language and technical anxiety. *Journal of Virtual Worlds Research, 6*(1), 1–9.

Harmon-Jones, E., Gable, P., & Price, T. F. (2013). Does negative affect always narrow and positive affect always broaden the mind? Considering the influence of motivational intensity on cognitive scope. *Current Directions in Psychological Science, 22*(4), 301–307.

Hauck, M., & Hurd, S. (2005). Exploring the link between language anxiety and learner selfmanagement in open language learning contexts. *European Journal of Open, Distance and E-Learning, 2005*(2).

Henderson, L. (2005). *Video games: A significant cognitive artifact of contemporary youth culture.* Paper presented at the DiGRA 2005 Conference, Vancouver, Canada.

Henderson, L., Henderson, M., Grant, S., & Huang, H. (2010). What are users thinking in a virtual world lesson? Using stimulated recall interviews to report student cognition, and its triggers. *Journal of Virtual Worlds Research, 3*(1), 1–20.

Henderson, L., Putt, I., Ainge, D., & Coombs, G. (1997). Comparison of students' thinking processes when studying with WWW, IMM and text-based materials. In F. Verdejo & G. Davies (Eds.), *Virtual campus: Trends for higher education and training* (pp. 124–162). London: Chapman and Hall.

Henderson, L., & Tallman, J. (2006). *Stimulated recall and mental models: Tools for teaching and learning computer information literacy.* Lanham, MD: The Scarecrow Press.

Henderson, M. (1996). *Multimedia interactivity: An investigation into learners' mediating processes during click-drag activities.* Townsville, Qld: James Cook University.

Henderson, M., Huang, H., Grant, S., & Henderson, L. (2012). The impact of Chinese language lessons in a virtual world on university students' self-efficacy beliefs. *Australasian Journal of Educational Technology, 28*(3), 400–419.

Jonassen, D. H. (1992). What are cognitive tools? In P. Kommers, D. Jonassen, & J. Mayes (Eds.), *Cognitive tools for learning.* Berlin: Springer-Verlag.

Levy, M. (2009). Technologies in use for second language learning. *The Modern language journal, 93*(1), 769–782.

Marland, P. W., Patching, W. G., & Putt, I. (1992). *Learning from text: Glimpses inside the minds of distance learners.* Townsville: James Cook University.

Peterson, M. (2011). Digital gaming and second language development: Japanese learners interactions in a MMORPG. *Digital Culture & Education, 3*(1), 56–73.

Schwienhorst, K. (2002). Why virtual, why environments? Implementing virtual reality concepts in computer-assisted language learning. *Simulation & Gaming, 33*(2), 196–209.

Shi, Y., & Fan, S. (2010). An analysis of non-verbal behaviour in intercultural communication. *The International Journal - Language Society and Culture* (31), 113–120.

Shulman, L. (1986). Paradigms and research programs in the study of teaching: A contemporary perspective. In M. Wittrock (Ed.), *Handbook of research on teaching* (3rd ed., pp. 3–36). New York: MacMillan.

Sykes, J. M. (2005). Synchronous CMC and pragmatic development: Effects of oral and written chat. *CALICO Journal, 22*(3), 399–431.

Thorne, S. (2008). Mediating technologies and second language learning. In J. Coiro, M. Knobel, C. Lankshear, & D. J. Leu (Eds.), *Handbook of research on new literacies.* Mahwah, NJ: Lawrence Erlbaum.

Woolfolk, A. E. (1990). *Educational psychology.* Englewood Cliffs: Prentice Hall.

Zhao, Y., & Lai, C. (2009). Massively multi-player online role playing games (MMORPGS) and foreign language education. In R. Ferdig (Ed.), *Handbook of research on effective electronic gaming in education* (pp. 402–421). New York: IDEA Group.

Zheng, D., Young, M. F., Wagner, M., & Brewer, R. A. (2009). Negotiation for action: English language learning in game-based virtual worlds. *The Modern language journal, 93*(4), 489–511.

Author Biographies

Michael Henderson is an Associate Professor of Educational Technologies in the Faculty of Education, Monash University, Australia. Michael's research lies in the use of educational technologies, particularly Internet-based technologies in teaching and learning in schools and higher education contexts. Recent work has focused on the areas of instructional design and pedagogy in online learning including social networks and virtual worlds. In the last four years, he has spent time considering the role of social media in teaching contexts and has published academic and professional articles on risks, ethics and opportunities relating to social networks in education.

Lyn Henderson is an independent researcher having retired as Associate Professor in Educational Technologies in the Faculty of Education, James Cook University, Australia. Lyn's international research in Australia, the United States of America and Israel examined students' and teachers' cognitive and affective engagement with educational and recreational interactive technologies in early primary through to university levels. Recent work continues her focus in the areas of instructional design and pedagogy in online learning, and teaching and learning with social networks and virtual worlds.

Scott Grant is an Assistant Lecturer in the Chinese Studies program in the Faculty of Arts, Monash University. He is the creator of the Monash Chinese Island language-learning simulation in Second Life, part of the formal beginner-level curriculum at Monash since 2008. His publications on 3D virtual worlds include: task-based language learning; foreign language and technical anxiety; assessment; self-efficacy; student cognition; integration of 3D virtual worlds into formal curricula; international collaboration; the role of non-player characters; and pedagogical, task and environmental design.

Hui Huang is a lecturer at School of Languages, Cultures and Linguistics at Monash University. She has been researching and publishing in the area of second language acquisition, language pedagogy, teaching Chinese as a second language and utilising ICT in teaching second language. Her recent publications cover the topics of educational uses of 3D MUVE environments, animation and learning of Chinese characters, the effect of intergenerational encounters on second language learning and identity reconstruction.

Chapter 9
Anticipating Engagement: Pre-service Teachers' Perceptions of Virtual Worlds

Lisa Jacka and Matthew Hill

Introduction

Engagement has become a significant driver in the choice of resources that teachers utilise at both university and K-12 level. Educators and governments recognise that increasingly, students are being pushed away from school due to a lack of engagement at a time when the need to have a skilled and educated society is ever more pressing. Information communication technologies (ICTs) are often used as a means to provide engagement. With the now ubiquitous presence of ICTs in classrooms, homes and workplaces, the need to develop high quality learning experiences with ICTs is increasingly apparent.

Virtual worlds are an ICT that, when first encountered, offer what appears to be a highly engaging environment especially for young adults and children. Many virtual worlds have some level of game features such as multiple paths, user-level control, interaction, visuals, risk-taking, rules and goals (Baranauskas et al. 2001; Crookall et al. 1987; Gredler 1996). Malone (1980) suggests that there are four factors of games that contribute to the level of engagement; challenge, fantasy, complexity and control. However, for students at university, these features can possibly act as a motivator or as a deterrent. Most adult students have expectations about what they believe a learning experience should be. Due to the connection they make with games and having fun, games are not traditionally linked to serious learning.

L. Jacka (✉) · M. Hill
Southern Cross University, Lismore, NSW, Australia
e-mail: lisa.jacka@scu.edu.au

M. Hill
e-mail: matt.hill@scu.edu.au

S. Gregory and D. Wood (eds.), *Authentic Virtual World Education*,
https://doi.org/10.1007/978-981-10-6382-4_9

Background

In 2010 the virtual world of Second Life was introduced to students enrolled in the Bachelor of Education (Secondary) at a regional university in Australia. The students in the Secondary program are required to have content knowledge in at least one discipline that can be taught in secondary schools in Australia. Most of the students will have already completed an undergraduate degree in a specific discipline (Visual Arts, Music, History, Physical Education, Science, or Mathematics). They therefore have perceptions about what university education should be, yet are novices in terms of understanding pedagogy as it pertains to teaching with children.

Since the first introduction of Second Life, a variety of virtual worlds have been utilised in the university. These include OpenSim (JokaydiaGRID), Sim-on-a-Stick (SOAS) and Minecraft. The main discipline in which virtual worlds have been used is in Education.

Literature Review

The literature on engagement is extensive and is framed in various ways such as 'student engagement' (Reeve and Tseng 2011), 'school engagement' (Fredricks et al. 2004), 'learner engagement' (Romero 2012) and 'user engagement' (O'Brien and Toms 2008). The latter term is utilised in the context of human-computer interface or design literature whereas the first three terms are used specifically in relation to teaching and learning. Fredricks et al. (2004) presents the concept of engagement as one that is multifaceted and includes behavioural, emotional and cognitive aspects. For each of these aspects there are degrees of engagement that can vary in both intensity and duration. For example:

> (B)ehavioral engagement can range from simply doing the work and following the rules to participating in the student council. Emotional engagement can range from simple liking to deep valuing of, or identification with, the institution. Cognitive engagement can range from simple memorization to the use of self-regulated learning strategies that promote deep understanding and expertise (Fredricks et al. 2004, p. 61).

Reeve and Tseng (2011) add the notion of agentic engagement as a fourth aspect to the concept of engagement. Agentic engagement is defined as "students' constructive contribution into the flow of the instruction they receive" (Reeve and Tseng 2011, p. 258). Whilst the behavioural, emotional and cognitive dimensions can effectively capture how a student responds to a given learning task, the agentic dimension assists in developing an understanding of the extent to which a student is pivotal in the process of adapting or even formulating learning tasks.

Central to the focus of research on engagement is that it is linked to an improvement in learning outcomes and achievement levels of students and that it is critical in developing qualities such as commitment and active involvement thus preventing students dropping out or becoming alienated. As Fredricks et al. (2004)

point out, there is a presumption that engagement is malleable and as a result many interventions in education settings focus on improving engagement. In the context of this chapter, the focus is on the relationship between ICTs, specifically virtual worlds and the perception of engagement by university students.

Student engagement with ICTs, particularly in relation to game based environments (such as virtual worlds) and intelligent tutoring systems, is often taken as given. However as Rowe, Shores, Mott, and Lester (2011) suggest, there is a concern that such engagement does not necessarily translate to learning. Time on-task is not necessarily an indicator of engagement as learners' attention may be focussed on off-task thoughts that inhibit cognitive engagement (Romero 2012). In this view, the distracting entertainment features (Mayer and Johnson 2010) or the seductive details (Harp and Mayer 1998) promote engagement but not deep learning. Rowe et al. (2011) present research to refute this concern, finding in an empirical study of 153 high school age students that engagement with a particular narrative based learning environment was associated with improved learning outcomes. Rowe et al. (2011) suggest that the story and gameplay design elements are critical to ensure engagement leads to learning. Clearly there is a need to consider the design of both the particular ICT and the learning activity in order to maximise opportunities for engagement.

Arnone, Small, Chauncey, and McKenna (2011) emphasise the importance of curiosity in relation to interest and engagement when considering new media technology-pervasive environments. New media environments afford opportunities for new information and new experiences, however these environments can support or detract from curiosity. Arnone et al. (2011) suggest that "the curiosity episode, if resolved satisfactorily, initiates new learning [as in sense-making] but it is curiosity's power to both trigger and be triggered through the development and deepening of interest and consequently, the forms of engagement that result in deep learning and effective participation, collaboration, and affinity" (Arnone et al. 2011, p. 185). Further to this, personal, contextual and situational factors intersect with a students' experience with a new media environment and these need to be considered when seeking to leverage the potential of new media tools to create opportunities for students to experience deep learning (Arnone et al. 2011).

Whilst not directly linking engagement and learning, O'Brien and Toms (2008) deconstruction and definition of the term 'user engagement' does provide a useful framework for understanding how successful ICTs move from being merely usable, to engaging. They defined engagement as "a quality of user experience characterised by attributes of challenge, positive affect, endurability, aesthetic and sensory appeal, attention, feedback, variety/novelty, interactivity, and perceived user control" (O'Brien and Toms 2008, p. 938). Through exploring the experiences of users in relation to online shopping, web searching, education webcasting and video games, O'Brien and Toms (2008) revealed that engagement was a process that comprised of four distinct stages. They called these stages the point of engagement, sustaining engagement, disengagement and possible reengagement.

While O'Brien and Toms (2008) describe engagement as a process in which the participant moves through stages, Conrad and Donaldson (2011) developed a model of phases of engagement. Their model is designed to assist the instructor to facilitate the student through each of the four phases when engaging in the use of online learning resources. They make the assumption that the learner begins as the 'newcomer' and moves through the phases as 'co-operator', 'collaborator' and finally as the 'initiator or partner'. They define engaged learning as "a collaborative learning process in which the instructor and learner are partners in building the knowledge base" (Conrad and Donaldson 2011, p. vii). Their framework links with the work of Salmon (2002, 2004) in her five-stage model for effective online teaching and learning. Salmon et al. (2010) extended her research involving the stages model to the use of the virtual world Second Life. She describes the importance of students mastering skills and each level in order remain motivated and as a result engage with other students and in the virtual world activities.

Methodology

A mixed method approach using both quantitative and qualitative data collection and analysis was used to assist with the triangulation of emergent themes. The methodological framework was action research, as described by Kemmis and McTaggart (1988). Action research has previously proved productive in the gathering and evaluating of data in a virtual world environment (Carr et al. 2010; Gregory and Masters 2012; Kohler et al. 2011; McKeown and Sanders 2007; McKeown Orwin 2009). Cycles underpin the action research model in order that data may be collected and evaluated to facilitate changes in the subsequent cycles. The testing of different methods for engagement and participation in virtual worlds was made possible by the use of cycles over the three-year period with three cycles being undertaken, one for each iteration of the subject.

Data was gathered from an online survey, observations and blog posts. The survey was designed to capture the knowledge that students had about virtual worlds prior to their introduction to any content about virtual worlds in education. Observation was undertaken both in the virtual world and in face-to-face tutorials. The blog posts were an assessment requirement in which the students reflected on their perception and/or experiences of virtual worlds.

The participants were students enrolled in the Bachelor of Education (Secondary) course at a regional university in NSW, Australia. The use of virtual worlds was embedded in a subject focussing on new media and emerging pedagogies. Part of the requirements for this subject was to read literature about the use of virtual worlds and to attend a tutorial conducted in a virtual world. Over the three cycles a number of different virtual worlds were offered to the students including Second Life, OpenSim, Sim-on-a-Stick and Minecraft. The students made their own choices about their level of engagement and were free to reflect upon their experiences through their blog posts. Three hundred and eleven posts were logged over the three cycles and they contribute to the data analysed in this chapter.

The aim of this research was to ascertain the capacity for virtual worlds to engage pre-service teachers in thinking about the possibilities for virtual worlds in their future classrooms. A secondary consequence of the implementation of virtual worlds in pre-service teacher education was to facilitate a shift in pedagogy by the students to fully utilise the affordances of virtual worlds. From these aims the theme of engagement in virtual worlds emerged as a significant motivator for students making decisions to embrace or reject virtual worlds in education.

Analysis

Approximately 18% (n = 56) of all the students enrolled in the subject that included virtual worlds responded to the survey. They survey asked them:

(1) Whether they used social networking applications or played computer games;
(2) If they were familiar with the term virtual world and understood what a virtual world was;
(3) If they had visited a virtual world before; and
(4) If they could see the possibilities for virtual worlds in the classroom

Of those who responded 85% (n = 48) used social networking applications and 23% played computer games (n = 13). Familiarity with the term virtual worlds and what a virtual world is was relatively high at 78% (n = 44) of the respondents. Sixteen per cent (n = 9) were familiar with the term but not what a virtual world is, and 2% (n = 1) indicated that they were familiar with neither the term nor what a virtual world is. These response rates indicate that the students overall had a high level of awareness about virtual worlds. In response to whether they could see the possibilities for virtual worlds in the classroom 60% (n = 34) indicated that they could see the possibilities, 32% (n = 18) were unsure and 3.5% (n = 2) indicated that they couldn't see the possibilities. These figures indicate that while the majority of students (78%) were familiar with virtual worlds a smaller number (60%) could see the possibilities.

The blog post responses displayed patterns that became evident as phases of engagement with virtual worlds for education. These phases are different in nature to those identified by O'Brien and Toms (2008), Conrad and Donaldson (2011) and Salmon (2002) in their studies into engagement and online learning. The phases that are proposed indicate the extent to which the students felt compelled to realise the potential for virtual worlds in their studies and/or teaching through to the students embracing the virtual world as having the capacity to affect their pedagogy and to utilise the technology fully in the classroom. As such their level of willingness to engage with virtual worlds is being assessed and has been categorised in relation to their capacity to articulate how they would utilise virtual world in a K-12 classroom.

The term phase has been used as individuals demonstrated that they moved between each of these phases yet did not necessarily start at the first phase. The

Table 9.1 Characteristics from the blog posts used to categorise the comments into phases of engagement

Phase	Characteristics espoused in student feedback
Pre-realisation	Could not see the benefit of using virtual worlds in education Would not use virtual worlds in education
Realisation	Could see the benefit of using virtual worlds in education Stated a number of barriers that would restrict their actual use of virtual worlds in education Unlikely to use virtual worlds in education Demonstrated a conflict in perceived benefit versus barriers May not like virtual worlds themselves but can see that students will
Replication	Could see the benefit of using virtual worlds in education Likely to use virtual worlds in education Some barriers may still exist Demonstrated the ability to link the way they would use virtual worlds in education to their current pedagogy
Re-imagining	Excited about the use of virtual worlds in education Most likely to initiate the use of virtual worlds in education Could describe how they would use virtual worlds demonstrating innovative teaching practice Minimal or no barriers if barriers were discussed they were done so with solutions offered

students may have engaged with the readings and activities and then made a choice not to engage with the concept of actually using the virtual world in a classroom setting. The characteristics of the responses that were used to place the comments within each phase are indicated in Table 9.1.

Pre-realisation Phase

The pre-realisation phase is identified by responses that indicate that they would never use virtual worlds and they could not see any benefit of using them in an education setting. The percentage of students who were categorised as making responses in the pre-realisation phase was 12% of the total students (n = 37).

The students in this category may have fully engaged in the tasks required of them to complete their study of virtual worlds and then become disengaged in the concept of actually using virtual worlds in the classroom. O'Brien and Toms (2008) suggestion that engagement moves through phases that includes the point at which someone becomes disengaged is evident with the responses in the realisation phase. As one student stated:

> I can't say I really understand the point. Going even further, even despite our discussion in class, I can't really understand how Second Life could be functional or relevant to a high school setting. I do understand how the program can be used for students develop their technology skills, however I don't believe it holds a place in the classroom (Cycle 1).

This comment highlights the contextual issues that Arnone et al. (2011) state as impacting in students' engagement. The student took the first steps of engaging in the activities of reading the online resources and joining in the class discussion but when asked to engage with actually using virtual worlds in the K-12 classroom there were too many contextual barriers.

What was evident in the comments made by students who were categorised as pre-realisation was that they were not approaching the virtual world with negative perceptions but were trying to reconcile their own capacity to utilise virtual worlds in the classroom. The virtual world experience was often referred to as being fun, which they equated with students not studying in a serious manner or being off-task. The following comment illustrates the juxtaposition that the student made between learning and fun and what they felt was appropriate pedagogy:

> I understand that people learn best when they are having fun…. I don't think that this means everything in a classroom should be a game. Why isn't it fun for students to talk and interact face to face? I am tech savvy, I was and am a part of the technological revolution, and I still think virtual worlds should be played with in their own time (Cycle 1).

The media image of Second Life was a particular concern to those in the pre-realisation phase. The following response shows the way that the students found it difficult to reconcile the media image of Second Life and the potential use of virtual worlds other in an educational setting.

> While we were in Second Life we saw many weird and unsavoury characters that I would not like my students to meet or even see. I believe there could be a danger with using Second Life in schools, and I doubt many parents would like their children to be in that sort of environment (Cycle 1).

As a result of the responses from the group in Cycle 1 who expressed concern over the use of Second Life the type of virtual world used for tutorials was changed to a number of other virtual worlds that the students might perceive as less threatening. In Cycle 2 the students were given the option of exploring Second Life, JokaydiaGRID or the open-sim grid created as part of the Pathways for Learning, Anywhere, Anytime, a Network for Educators (PLANE) developed by the NSW Department of Education. In Cycle 3 they were given an introduction to JokaydiaGRID where there are two islands with work created by primary school children. From an analysis of the responses over the three cycles the percentage of students who were categorised as pre-realisation dropped. This indicated that the situational factors of the type of virtual world and the perceived appropriateness of that virtual world to an educational context played a significant role in the level of engagement that the student undertook.

Realisation Phase

The realisation phase is the phase after pre-realisation but it may be the point at which the student starts, rather than a movement occurring sequentially from one to the other. The indicators in the blog post responses that put the students in the realisation phase were that they could see the benefit of virtual worlds but also stated a number of barriers or concerns that would impact on their capacity to actually utilise virtual world in education. In their reflections, they either indicated that they were unlikely to use virtual worlds in education or they presented a number of issues that expressed that it would be extremely difficult for them to implement the use without a high level of support. Other factors that came through in the realisation phase was the ability to distinguish between their own feelings of discomfort or difficulty with virtual worlds but recognising that their future students will need to be aware of the ICTs and may well be already using them. The percentage of students who were categorised as making responses in the realisation phase was 42% of the total students (n = 129).

The realisation phase responses were most likely to have not reconciled their personal position and the perceived benefit of the virtual world. Comments such as the following make this point as they can 'identify the usefulness' and see that students would be engaged however they are concerned about 'online bullying and other associated issues.' The concern about online bullying represents a perception not founded in their actual experience but relevant in that it impacted on their capacity to engage in the concept. The following comment shows the conflict that the student had between using a resource that they believe would be engaging to their students and having emotional factors influencing them. Those factors of fearing what might occur in the virtual world based on their perceptions based on media reports and hearsay:

> After undertaking the module on virtual worlds I'm still undecided on my feelings towards the incorporation into the classroom. I can identify the usefulness of the virtual learning. It lends itself towards student's directed learning and allows the students to engage in a game-based type learning. I think this would engage students more. It would also allow a greater collaboration for students who cannot be in the actual classroom. However, this type of learning and world opens itself up to online bullying and other associated issues. If I were to employ this type of learning in my classroom I would need to ensure the students (online) safety with rules and expectations (Cycle 2).

The main difference that put the student in the realisation phase instead of the replication phase was that they were engaged in the concept of virtual worlds in education but were not engaged enough to actually take it to the step of implementing it in the classroom. They expressed that they would most likely use virtual worlds if others around them were doing so or if the barriers to use with removed.

> There really are endless possibilities with the use of virtual worlds, but I still don't think I am ready to embark upon that journey. Even though I would still be hesitant to use them with my students, mainly through my own lack of capabilities, I can certainly now understand and value their use (Cycle 3).

The realisation phase is an important phase as it is the place where most novice users of virtual worlds might start when trying to apply virtual worlds to education. From my analysis of the data it appeared that students who indicated this phase had engaged with the content provided as part of the topic in the unit of study. They had not always experienced the virtual world. If they did experience the virtual world, it tended to be only on the one occasion in the tutorial with the whole group.

Replication Phase

The replication phase was signified when the students' reflections demonstrated that they were engaged in the concept of virtual worlds in education to the extent that they were likely to use it in their future classroom. This phase was also signified when the students could make links to their current pedagogical practice, thus replicating current ways of teaching yet adding the virtual world as a resource or tool. They would be placed in the replication phase and not the re-imagining phase if they were still acknowledging barriers or if their description of use was still similar to current pedagogical practices. They were placed in the replication phase and not the realisation phase if they expressed a desire to implement the use of virtual worlds regardless of whether they felt they had the capacity yet to do so. The percentage of students who were categorised as making responses in the replication phase was 23% of the total students (n = 70).

The description in the following quote shows the student has been able to articulate how they could use the virtual world in the subject area of Physical Education. They state that:

> The PDHPE 7-10 syllabus has a strong focus on developing protective factors and behaviours around risk taking. Students are taught about road safety, drug and alcohol education and increasing resiliency, as well as many other important skills such as communication, decision-making and interacting. Designing activities that incorporate these aspects into virtual learning would be of great benefit to students and provide them with something new and interactive. I believe this would encourage student interaction, critical thinking and involvement in the tasks (Cycle 3).

However, the same student reflected on the issues that they perceived such that they felt that the virtual world "should be used sparingly, as an over reliance on ICTs can cause problems when issues arise with the ICTs" (Cycle 3). This type of concern in relation to ICTs in general indicates that the student was not engaged sufficiently that they would make extra effort to implement virtual worlds in their future classroom even though they can describe why and how they might use virtual worlds.

A consistent factor that motivated the students to show engagement in virtual worlds was their perceptions about their future teaching environment and their future students. Comments such as the following demonstrate this characteristic: "although I do feel that virtual worlds will not be used in many schools at present, I do think it is a thing of the future. A future that I will be teaching" (Cycle 3).

The following comment articulates both the personal engagement with the virtual world and the perceived engagement of their future students. The concept that their students would be engaged was highly motivating for the students and motivated many of them to engage with the virtual world to the point of being outside their own comfort zone:

> I must admit I was pretty fascinated interacting in the JokaydiaGRID world. The many benefits became evident. It can be used for all ages and enhances motivation and learning. Students are likely to become more interested and engaged in the work they are doing. Furthermore, as teachers we are able to guide and/or scaffold to a desired level throughout the assessment process. We can provide rewards for progress and completion of work. We and the students can access this, and interact with one another from any location (Cycle 3).

Re-imagining Phase

Reflections in which the students described experiences and environments that are difficult or impossible to create in real life signify the re-imaging phase. When students have either reached this phase or started in this phase they are most likely to fully utilise the affordances of virtual worlds. They will be describing the use of virtual worlds beyond the 'distracting entertainment features' (Mayer and Johnson 2010) or the 'seductive details' (Harp and Mayer 1998). They are describing ways to utilise the affordances of virtual worlds to create engagement in knowledge creation. The percentage of students who were categorised as making responses in the pre-reimagining phase was 24% of the total students (n = 70).

Students in this phase are generally excited about the use of virtual worlds in education and use words such as fascinating, exciting, astounding, wow, fun and inspired. Comments included "it was a fascinating experience and I enjoyed the experience more than I thought I would" or "I was inspired" or "I feel I need to reiterate how amazed I am by the educational possibilities of virtual worlds" or "the clip on virtual learning blew my mind! How fantastic would it be to have a school website that was a virtual world - gathering information could be fun and students hard work could be exhibited on a global scale" were synonymous with the engagement that the students experienced. The following comment succinctly expresses both the excitement of the student and their imagined possibility for their music class beyond what they had experienced or what was a reality in the classroom without virtual worlds:

> Wow! Again, I can't believe how much education has changed. I'm really looking forward to using these virtual worlds in my classroom. I can just imagine having a Jimi Hendrix-like avatar shredding it up on the virtual stage (Cycle 3).

From the evidence of these comments it does not require a lot of time experiencing virtual worlds to be at the reimagining phase. The students were able to describe different models of teaching and learning after only one experience or interacting with one resource. An important aspect of the reimagining phase was the ability of the student to articulate what they might do with virtual worlds in their future classroom. The types of examples that they provided included activities that are dangerous such as in science experiments where "it would allow them the freedom and confidence to conduct experiments and perform reactions in a virtual laboratory that may otherwise be considered too expensive, toxic or dangerous in the 'real' world" (Cycle 3). Activities that were otherwise impossible to undertake such as visiting the Sistine Chapel for "art students to experience one of the true master pieces without having to paying thousands of dollars to travel to Italy and see it in real life" (Cycle 1). Other activities included things such as stimulating students' imagination by using the virtual world "to give my students inspiration for writing, to perform plays, to script their own plays, to do all sorts of stuff" (Cycle 3). One student described a number of different ways that authentic experiences could be designed for students such as "virtual stores that could teach students about commerce in an environment where they can trade goods and services for real rewards" or "virtual governments could teach students about civics and responsibility. Historical characters can be brought to life and scenes re-enacted" or how "theoretical mathematics could be given real (virtual) world applications" (Cycle 3).

The students who were most able to reimagine the types of activities and the teaching-leaning process were those who experienced the virtual world, particularly if they had a positive experience that included interactions in spaces that revealed new ways of thinking about their discipline. Having had those experiences, they made comments such as: "the idea of having interaction and the almost game-like feel would be enticing to many students who many not normally feel as engaged in the typical pen to paper or whiteboard classroom scenario" (Cycle 1).

Differences Between Cycles

There are some distinct differences in the results when comparing the three cycles (see Fig. 9.1) that demonstrate the impact of changes made in the delivery of the unit over the three iterations. The percentage of students in the pre-realisation phase decreased from 19% in Cycle 1 (n = 19) to 11% in Cycle 2 (n = 9) and a smaller

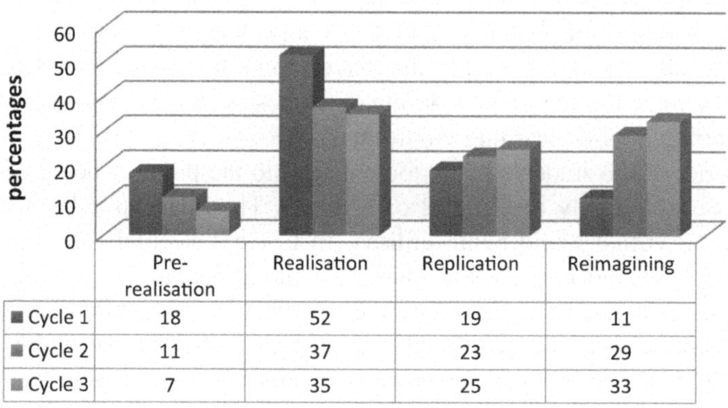

	Pre-realisation	Realisation	Replication	Reimagining
Cycle 1	18	52	19	11
Cycle 2	11	37	23	29
Cycle 3	7	35	25	33

Fig. 9.1 The variation in students categorised in each phase over the three cycles

decrease to 9% in Cycle 3 (n = 9). At the same time the number of students who demonstrated characteristics of the re-imagining phase increased from 11% in Cycle 1 (n = 12) to 40% Cycle 3 (n = 32). One of the possible explanations for this change in characteristics between cycles was the result of the change of delivery in the face-to-face lecture and tutorials. The emphasis on Second Life as the virtual world of choice was shifted to virtual worlds that the students perceived to be more appropriate for education (such as SoaS, JokadiaGRID, PLANE and Minecraft). The delivery of content in Cycle 2 and Cycle 3 was able to include an increase in examples of how virtual worlds were being used in primary schools due to the work that had begun by some of the students from Cycle 1. In Cycle 3 one of the students who had been using virtual worlds in local primary schools became one of the expert tutors and spoke with the students. The work undertaken by this student is discussed in Jacka and Booth (2012, 2013).

Barriers to Engagement

Patterns emerged from the data about the perceived barriers to the use of virtual worlds in education and as such the phase of engagement in which the students were currently situated in. The perceptions about their future students, virtual worlds in general and in the classroom as well as their personal experiences and apprehensions all impacted on their responses. These contextual and situational factors impacted on the level of engagement (Arnone et al. 2011). Some factors that were considered as barriers by some students were perceived as beneficial by the students who were most engaged.

In Cycle 1 the main barrier that was raised was that their future students would be too engaged by the virtual world to the point of being distracted and in turn would find it difficult to remain on task. This view is reflective of Rowe et al. (2011) suggesting that engagement does not necessarily translate to learning and that time on-task is not necessarily an indicator of learner engagement (Romero 2012). The aspects that the students found distracting were what Mayer and Johnson (2010) call the ‘entertainment features’ and Harp and Mayer (1998) refer to as the seductive details. There are studies that have shown that these ‘entertainment features’ can be linked to improved learning outcomes as students engage with what is often a ‘narrative based learning environment’ (Rowe et al. 2011).

The barrier of the students being too engaged to the point of being off-task was not expressed so highly in Cycle 2 or Cycle 3. This may have been due to the change in the virtual world being utilised. In Cycle 1 Second Life was the main virtual world. Second Life does not have the classic features of a narrative based environment as it can be designed by the teacher to be structured and to include game elements as well as traditional pedagogical tools. However, the ways that Second Life was used in Cycle 1 were very unstructured and exploratory in nature. The students were given free reign on the University’s education island, as a way to discover the tools, navigation and orient themselves. Many of them found that the space was highly engaging and entertaining and they expressed in their reflections that they found it difficult themselves to remain on task. Comments the students made about the level of engagement and being on-task included:

> The use of Second Life in the classroom has the potential to enhance student engagement and enrich teaching and learning activities, however, it is essential to include clearly defined learning outcomes to avoid off task behaviour (Cycle 1).

> Virtual Learning in this new digital age can offer students so much opportunity to experience different ways of learning and engagement. I believe teachers hardest task is keeping students focused on learning and not being side tracked (Cycle 1).

In response to the feedback about being on task, the structure of the tutorial in the subsequent Cycles was altered. In Cycle 2 the pre-service teachers were offered a number of virtual world options to explore including; Second Life, JokaydiaGRID and the Department of Education OpenSim - PLANE. As such the feedback about not being on task in tutorials and being concerned that their students would not be on task were not present in the Cycle 2 reflections. In Cycle 3 the students were instructed in the process of navigating and utilising virtual worlds in the OpenSim of JokaydiaGRID. The University space in JokaydiaGRID included work wholly created by primary school children.

Students in Cycle 3 started to consider that the level of engagement with the virtual world would in fact keep the students on-task as is evident in the comment that "I can see how powerful a tool it would be to motivate the students to stay on task" (Cycle 3).

Another student in Cycle 3 articulated that the virtual world was a space that the teacher could control and scaffold, unlike previous comments that stated the contrary as a concern. They said:

> The use of virtual and game based learning allows teachers to introduce a controlled learning environment, where the parameters of the task are clear and specific, therefore allowing students to focus more directly on individual learning and development of critical thinking skills (Cycle 3).

Other concerns that the students had were that either they or their student might become addicted to the virtual world due to the highly engaging nature of the environment. They typically related addiction to their own experience as these comments reveal:

> A lot of people can get so immersed in video games, such as WoW [World of Warcraft], that they lose touch with reality for days on end. I know some people that will spend an entire weekend playing, and not even shower or leave the house (Cycle 1).

> Given that I once caught my daughter feeding money into a game that would let her create flowers, I can just see an irate parent asking me what I was doing encouraging something that could be so addictive (Cycle 3).

Engagement was generally considered a positive affordance of virtual worlds but the loss of time due to engagement was generally viewed as a negative. They felt that they could have been doing more productive activities with their time. As in the comment that "I sat in our tutorial thinking that all I was doing was wasting time, when I could have been researching for our next assignment?!" (Cycle 1). The following comment illustrates the concern that engagement per se may not be enough: "My main concern would be to ensure that the purpose of the task is closely evaluated and that students are meeting the required outcomes, not just being actively engaged" (Cycle 1).

The Meta-Language of Engagement

As the participants were all students training to be teachers, the educational meta-language that they were being instructed in throughout their studies was prominent in the blog posts. An analysis of the frequency of particular words in the data gave the following results: metacognition (n = 21), imagination (n = 47), higher-order-thinking (n = 39), problem solving (n = 62), creativity (n = 77), communicating (n = 99), collaborating (n = 81), interacting (n = 217), engaging (n = 291) and creating (n = 345). Creating was the most frequently used term with engaging the second most used. The students' response to virtual worlds highlighted the connection that the students perceived between creating, engagement and virtual worlds. The following comments provide a sample of the way in which the students use the term 'engaging'.

> This is so much more engaging than reading a text, watching a movie, or listening to a boring teacher out the front of the classroom, and provides the venue for students to create their own lived experiences in the past (Cycle 3).

> As teachers we worry that our pedagogical practices aren't engaging, and are we really placing knowledge within our students' heads. Through implementing a VLE environment, we are creating a variety of engaging pedagogical practices, that further develop their learning (Cycle 3).

> Overall, I think game-based learning and learning through virtual worlds is one of the most promising ways to learn in the future. It accommodates to students in a sense that it increases engagement because the way of learning is extremely attractive to young minds and is not as traditional. This factor alone will make learning more enjoyable for students. Keeping this in mind, if students are engaged in the way they are learning, then it is likely that they will be more engaged in the content at hand (Cycle 2).

> I think there is a lot of potential for this technology to be used widely in schools to facilitate student learning and engagement in a way that has not been previously possible (Cycle 3).

Conclusion

The comments made by students studying to become secondary school teachers revealed that virtual worlds have the potential to engage students to think about the possibilities for virtual worlds in their future classrooms. The students' perception of the level of engagement that their future students would have was a highly motivating and influential factor in their own determination to pursue the use of virtual worlds. The students also made strong connections between perceived levels of engagement and the creative aspects of virtual worlds. Engagement from the university students further increased as students started to use virtual worlds in the authentic context of the primary school classroom. The action research cycles undertaken in this study assisted in the design and implementation of the virtual world activities and content. Being able to change the emphasise on particular virtual worlds helped to focus the students on what the virtual worlds could do rather than what barriers they might present.

From this longitudinal study we believe that virtual worlds, while still in their infancy in education, do have the capacity to engage both university and K-12 students. Furthermore, the types of engagement are varied and do not fit easily within existing categories or descriptors of engagement. This research has found that the initial and at times superficial perception by students that the 'entertainment features' or 'seductive details' will engage their future students has the capacity to motivate the university student to investigate the potential for higher level cognitive engagement. The barriers that may be preventing the student from engaging with virtual worlds can be overcome by continual redesigns that respond to the students' concerns. By increasing the students' knowledge about virtual worlds in both their capacity to use the ICT and to design meaningful learning experiences for their future students a higher level of engagement will emerge.

Whilst the findings from this research are derived from data collected from pre-service teachers, they tentatively could be applied to educators in general. The phases of realisation outlined in this chapter (pre-realisation, realisation, replication and reimagining) could usefully be transferred to understanding the level of readiness and/or preparedness for educators more broadly to incorporate the use of virtual worlds in their teaching practice. This research has shown that by providing best practice exemplars and alternative virtual worlds (which may not be stigmatised in the same way as Second Life, for example), the barriers to implementation are reduced. Such actions could easily be transferred to other education settings to promote the use of virtual worlds in education contexts more broadly.

References

Arnone, M. P., Small, R. V., Chauncey, S. A., & McKenna, H. P. (2011). Curiosity, interest and engagement in technology-pervasive learning environments: a new research agenda. *Educational Technology Research and Development, 59*(2), 181–198.

Baranauskas, C. C., Neto, N. G. G., & Borges, M. A. (2001). Learning at work through a multi-user synchronous simulation game. *International Journal of Continuing Engineering Education and Life Long Learning, 11*(3), 251–260.

Carr, D., Oliver, M., & Burn, A. (2010). Learning, teaching and ambiguity in virtual worlds. In A. Peachey (Ed.), *Researching learning in virtual worlds* (pp. 17–30). London: Springer.

Conrad, R., & Donaldson, J. A. (2011). *Engaging the online learner: Activities and resources for creative instruction* (Vol. 38). San Francisco: Jossey-Bass.

Crookall, D., Oxford, R., & Saunders, D. (1987). Towards a reconceptualization of simulation: From representation to reality. *Simulation/Games for learning, 17,* 147–171.

Fredricks, J. A., Blumenfeld, P. C., & Paris, A. H. (2004). School engagement: Potential of the concept, state of the evidence. *Review of educational research, 74*(1), 59–109.

Gredler, M. E. (1996). Educational games and simulations: A technology in search of a (research) paradigm. In D. H. Jonassen (Ed.), *Handbook of research on educational communications and technology* (Vol. 39, pp. 521–540). New York: Macmillan.

Gregory, S., & Masters, Y. (2012). Real thinking with virtual hats: A role-playing activity for pre-service teachers in Second Life. *Australasian Journal of Educational Technology, 28*(3), 420–440.

Harp, S. F., & Mayer, R. E. (1998). How seductive details do their damage: A theory of cognitive interest in science learning. *Journal of Educational Psychology, 90*(3), 414.

Jacka, L., & Booth, K. (2012). Pre-service teachers designing virtual world learning environments. *International Journal of Virtual and Personal Learning Environments, 3*(4), 16–26.

Jacka, L., & Booth, K. (2013). What about the firewall? Creating virtual worlds in a public primary school using Sim-on-a-Stick. *Australian Educational Computing, 27*(2), 13–17.

Kemmis, S., & McTaggart, R. (1988). *The action research planner.* Victoria: Deakin University.

Kohler, T., Fueller, J., Matzler, K., & Stieger, D. (2011). Co-creation in virtual worlds: The design of the user experience. *MIS Quarterly, 35*(3).

Malone, T. W. (1980). *What makes things fun to learn? A study of intrinsically motivating computer games.* Palo Alto: Xerox.

Mayer, R. E., & Johnson, C. I. (2010). Adding instructional features that promote learning in a game-like environment. *Journal of Educational Computing Research, 42*(3), 241–265.

McKeown, L., & Sanders, R. L. (2007). Promoting reflection through action learning in a 3D virtual world. *International Journal of Social Sciences, 2*(1), 50–55.

McKeown Orwin, L. (2009). Action learning in a virtual world. In J. Molka-Danielsen & M. Deutschmann (Eds.), *Learning and teaching in the virtual world of second life* (pp. 91–102). Trondheim: Tapir Academic Press.

O'Brien, H. L., & Toms, E. G. (2008). What is user engagement? A conceptual framework for defining user engagement with technology. *Journal of the American Society for Information Science and Technology, 59*(6), 938–955.

Reeve, J., & Tseng, C.-M. (2011). Agency as a fourth aspect of students' engagement during learning activities. *Contemporary Educational Psychology, 36*(4), 257–267.

Romero, M. (2012). Learner Engagement in the use of individual and collaborative serious games. In C. Wankel & P. Blessinger (Eds.), *Increasing student engagement and retention using immersive interfaces: Virtual worlds, gaming and simulation* (Vol. 6, pp. 15–34). UK: Emerald.

Rowe, J. P., Shores, L. R., Mott, B. W., & Lester, J. C. (2011). Integrating learning, problem solving, and engagement in narrative-centered learning environments. *International Journal of Artificial Intelligence in Education, 21*(1), 115–133.

Salmon, G. (2002). *E-tivities: The key to active online learning.* London: Routledge Falmer.

Salmon, G. (2004). *E-moderating: The key to teaching and learning online.* London: Routledge Falmer.

Salmon, G., Nie, M., & Edirisingha, P. (2010). Developing a five-stage model of learning in Second Life. *Educational Research, 52*(2), 169–182.

Author Biographies

Dr Lisa Jacka is a lecturer in the School of Education at Southern Cross University, NSW. She has been an adult educator for many years who works with pre-service and post-graduate education students to expand their knowledge and confidence to integrate innovative ICTs into their teaching practice. Lisa has expertise in virtual worlds in education having completed PhD research in this field as she introduced educators to the possibilities of virtual worlds. She has over 27 publications including book chapters, journal articles and conference papers and in 2015 was awarded a Vice Chancellor's citation for innovative design and delivery online learning experiences that facilitate education students' readiness to teach in learning environments of the future.

Dr Matthew Hill is the Course Coordinator of the Contemporary Music Program at Southern Cross University, NSW, Australia. He completed a PhD at James Cook University in the area of music technology and composition in a range of musical styles and completed his undergraduate music degree in guitar performance at Southern Cross University. His research interests include learner engagement in higher music education, collaborative music making practices, music analysis and screen sound.

Chapter 10
Utilising Second Life Machinima-Facilitated Narratives to Support Cognitive and Imaginative Engagement Across an Undergraduate Curriculum

Des Butler

The Traditional Approach to Legal Education and Impetus for Change

Like many disciplines, legal education in Australia has undergone substantial change in the past 20 or so years, with change accelerated with the advent of the digital age. Nevertheless, it is still the case that in many ways it has struggled to completely shed the shackles of a traditional model of learning and teaching. Keyes and Johnstone (2004) identified the dominant characteristics of this model as including a teacher-focus, in which academics transmit material from within their own expertise in specific areas of law to their students. In this model, "most teachers uncritically replicate the learning experiences that they had when students, which usually means that the dominant mode of instruction is reading lecture notes to large classes in which students are largely passive" (Keyes and Johnstone 2004, p. 239). The model is almost entirely focused upon transmission of content knowledge, an approach that can trace its pedigree to the late nineteenth-century attitudes exemplified by the declaration by English jurist Dicey in 1883 that nothing "can be taught to students of greater value, either intellectually or for the purposes of legal practice, than the habit of looking upon the law as a series of rules" (Allison 2013, p. 499). A hallmark of the traditional approach is the teaching of doctrine and legal rules from case law (Pearce et al. 1987).

A negative consequence of the teacher-focus of the traditional approach is that it is apt to lead to surface, rather than deep-level learning, a process that has often been described as involving that which is written on the lecturer's page being transferred to the student's page without passing through the mind of either

D. Butler (✉)
Queensland University of Technology, Brisbane, QLD, Australia
e-mail: d.butler@qut.edu.au

S. Gregory and D. Wood (eds.), *Authentic Virtual World Education*,
https://doi.org/10.1007/978-981-10-6382-4_10

(Eison 2010). By contrast, it has been extensively argued and indeed demonstrated that instruction that is more student-centred in design can lead to deeper understanding, an increased motivation to learn, greater knowledge-retention and an overall more positive attitude to the material being studied (Bonwell and Eison 1991; Johnson et al. 1991; McKeachie 1986; Meyers and Jones 1993). There may also be an implication inherent in a teacher-focus approach that success is to be measured by how well students regurgitate in assessment what they have been told in lectures (James 2000).

Another negative consequence is that governments and universities may be led to believe that the legal education may be provided for relatively little cost (Thornton 1991). Under the Australian system, the Commonwealth Government provides funding for public universities on the basis of a differential system, with different groupings or "bands" of disciplines receiving different levels of funding. At the same time, student contribution to the cost of higher education is also based on a differential system. Currently, legal education is in the lowest band for funding but assigned to the highest band for student fees. The result is that Australian law schools are starved of funding while their students pay full price for their degrees (Keyes and Johnstone 2004). This has had serious implications that have impeded the development of curricula for decades (LCA 2008). In particular, it has generally impeded law schools from deviating from the traditional approach (Johnstone and Vignaendra 2003). However, despite calls for reform (e.g. Pearce et al. 1987), this funding model persists today.

Nevertheless, the traditional approach faces challenges on a number of fronts. From as early as the 1990s, there was a series of reports in the USA (ABA 1992), England (ACLEC 1996) and Australia (ALRC 1999) that were critical of the content focus of the traditional approach—what lawyers need to know—and urged a shift to include an inclusion of skills and values acquisition and training in law curricula—what lawyers need to do. Nonetheless, with a few exceptions, these pleas failed to produce real change (Kift 2008).

There has been a rapid increase in the number of law schools in Australia since 1989. In the period from 1855 to 1989, there were twelve law schools. By 2014, there were 36, for a country which has a population approaching 23.5 million people. This growth has had a number of implications. It has meant that more students of varying backgrounds are undertaking law degrees. This, together with the high price of a law degree, has led to a commodification of legal education, with some law schools seeking to emphasise their distinctiveness and to distinguish themselves from other law schools, especially their local competition (Johnstone and Vignaendra 2003). At the same time, the legal profession has itself undergone dynamic change, driven by factors such as globalisation, competitiveness and competition reform, information and communications technology and a shift away from adversarial court proceedings as the main form of dispute resolution (Kift 2008). This climate and the close association that remains between the legal profession and law schools (Keyes and Johnstone 2004) have provided powerful stimuli for change.

A further powerful stimulus has been a climate change of another nature. The demands of modern students, particularly those born into the digital age, in terms of their preference to study when, where and how they want, have been well canvassed (e.g. Frand 2000; Kift 2009; Oberlinger 2003). Modern students also exhibit changed patterns of engagement and disengagement (Kift 2008), often leading to low attendance in traditional transmissive lectures. Low attendance may additionally be attributable to students now juggling the competing time commitments of their work (in many cases necessitated by the high student contributions that they must pay), study and leisure (Moreau and Leathwood 2006; Tarrant 2006).

Machinima-Facilitated Narratives

The use of narrative is part of the human condition. Bruner described it as a "natural expressive form for any age and culture" (1990, p. 43). Narrative has been recognised as being able to assist in the development of cognitive abilities and the organisation of knowledge (Schank 2000). According to Wertsch (1998, p. 81): "The cognitive function of narrative form is not just to relate a succession of events but to body forth an ensemble of relationships of many different kinds as a single whole". Similarly, Ricoeur (2005, p. 278) saw the activity of narrating as involving the construction of "meaningful totalities out of scattered events". Dettori and Paiva (2009) considered the configuration created by relationships among narrative elements to be a crucial aspect for promoting active thinking and providing support for the construction of meaning.

A narrative may not only convey important information. It may also provide "contextual cues" that enable information to be recalled in comparable situations (Ferguson et al. 1992). Rowe et al. (2007, p. 1) described the unique ability of stories to "draw audiences into plots and settings, thereby opening perceptual, emotional and motivational opportunities for learning". Narratives are capable of facilitating students' semantically encoding new information, as well as committing material to long-term memory (Ormrod 2004). In addition to aiding cognition, narratives can promote intrinsic motivation by encouraging active involvement and stimulating curiosity and imagination (Malone and Lepper 1987; Rowe et al. 2007).

Narratives are not limited in their nature or the language that they use. Accordingly, they may be true or invented, and depicted by words, text, static or moving pictures or a combination of these (Dettori and Paiva 2009). Technology, including 3D graphics and animation, is able to take advantage of, and enhance the learning potential of narrative in a variety of ways and for a variety of purposes (Dettori and Paiva 2009). It has been recognised that technology is capable of being an effective alternative to real-life learning experience such as clinical exercises, without the need to sacrifice the essential authentic context (Herrington and Oliver 2000). The use of 3D graphics and animations enables virtual characters and virtual settings to present essential information and set tasks in a simulated environment and may therefore be an effective means of creating such an authentic learning environment (Agostinho 2006).

While professional 3D graphics and animation productions may be a stretch for many or most tertiary education budgets, especially the budgets of Australian law schools under current funding arrangements, machinima is relatively cost-effective means of creating effective learning environments (Middleton and Mather 2008). Machinima—a portmanteau of machine and cinema—has variously been described as "animated film-making within a real-time virtual 3D environment" delivered as digital video (Daly-Swanson 2007, p. 1), "real-world filmmaking techniques applied within an interactive virtual space where characters and events can be either controlled by humans, scripts or artificial intelligence" (Dellario and Marino 2005) and "making animated movies in real-time with the software that is used to develop and play computer games" (Lowood 2006, p. 26). Middleton and Mather (2008) suggest that machinima emerged in 2001 as a means of gamers sharing and celebrating their first-person shooter exploits with fellow gamers. However, its true origins as a narrative platform may be traced to a group called "The Rangers", who in 1996 made a video called "Diary of a Camper" using the *Quake* game to incorporate a storyline and characters (Kastelein 2013; Lowood 2006).

While a number of virtual worlds may be capable of supplying the necessary 3D graphics, such as *The Sims* and *The Movies*, the range of functionality provided by the Second Life virtual world, including the freedom to customise not only characters but also the props and indoor or outdoor environments in which they interact, and the way they are animated together with the camera angles with which to view the action, makes it highly adaptable to producing machinima for the purposes of incorporating narrative in learning (Bardzell et al. 2006).

Machinima in the QUT Undergraduate Law Curriculum

Development of machinima-based programs in the QUT undergraduate law curriculum has not been the result of an integrated master plan but rather has proceeded as a progressive evolution, the success of earlier programs paving the way for the development of further programs. The first program, *Air Gondwana*, was introduced into the then first-year undergraduate law subjects, Contracts A and Contracts B, in 2007 as a means of teaching the skill of negotiation. Since then, seven more machinima-based programs have been implemented across seven different subjects. All utilise machinima created using the Second Life virtual world, with screen activity recorded using the FRAPS video capture program. Voices for characters have been provided by the author and other members of the law school staff, students and friends (a total of 48 characters being voiced by 35 different people) and recorded separately using the Audacity program, with video and audio then edited by the author using Sony Home Studio software. Still images were created using the in-built snapshot feature in Second Life. Apart from the voice work by colleagues and others and, where necessary, advice or input from colleagues concerning substantive content in areas of law outside of his expertise, all of the programs have been solely created by the author, without the need for formal training or background in multimedia or film production, and without the need for technical support in software or multimedia development. Online components of programs are accessed by students via modules created using Articulate Storyline 360 authoring software which are uploaded to the university's Blackboard Learning Management System.

The programs not only embrace a variety of areas of law across different stages of the degree but also range in focus from substantive content (e.g. criminal law and contract law) to practical skills (e.g. negotiation and interpretation of statutes), and ethical awareness and professional responsibility. They also vary in the degree of integration in subject curricula, some only addressing discrete portions of subjects while others range across multiple weeks or entire semesters. Some are used for formative purposes only while others facilitate summative assessment.

The programs are stand alone in the sense that each may be undertaken independently without requiring the prior completion of any of the other programs. Nonetheless, in the light of the promotion of engagement achieved through the use of narrative in *Air Gondwana*, and notwithstanding the absence of an overarching plan, programs developed subsequently are linked by storylines forming part of a common narrative featuring recurring characters, forming a universe of virtual people, settings and relationships that are collectively dubbed "The Complex Narratives Project" (see Fig. 10.1).

Where necessary "flashback" sequences are used to pick up elements of narrative from previous programs so that students do not need to remember those previous elements or be at a disadvantage if they did not do the previous programs (e.g. if they transferred from another university). A brief survey of the programs and the storylines running through them is warranted to explicate the wide potential offered by machinima and the narratives that it may portray.

In their Introduction to Law subject in the first semester of their first year, students undertake *Indigo's Folly* which facilitates their study of the skill of statutory interpretation. This is a skill that is crucial for legal practice, with the ever-increasing proliferation of statute laws, but one with which is notoriously difficult to engage students using traditional approaches. The program uses machinima videos to depict a narrative involving Ian Indigo, the owner of a warehouse property, who seeks advice from Jess Astrild, a lawyer with the fictional Odin's Lawyers law firm, concerning the interpretation and application of the variety of statute laws governing the conversion of the property into a night club, "The Sapphire Club". These machinima videos are complemented by a range of documents such as simulated Acts of Parliament and Hansard (the reports of proceedings in parliament), with their interpretation and application being discussed in small group tutorial classes. The program also includes several modules of multiple-choice questions, created using the Articulate Storyline 360 program, which comprise fact scenarios also based on the Indigo narrative, illustrated by Second Life images as a means of assisting cognition of the facts, and which provide feedback on both correct and incorrect responses.

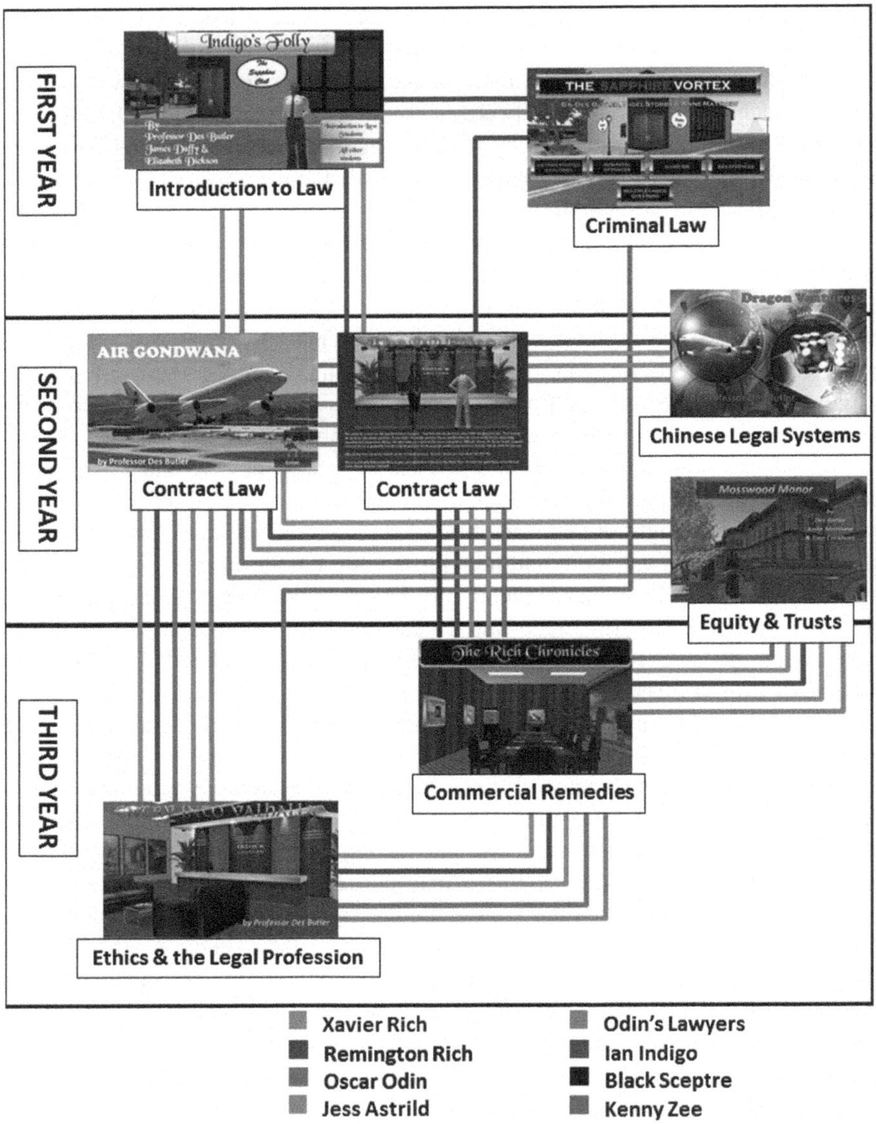

Fig. 10.1 "The Complex Narratives Project": Second Life machinima programs in the QUT undergraduate law curriculum showing the storylines (by character) that link the programs

The Sapphire Vortex in the second semester of first year Criminal Law subject uses a 15-min machinima video to depict a series of connected events occurring at the Sapphire Club, including a rape, a glassing (of the owner, Indigo), a one-punch homicide, a stabbing, and drug and property offences. This video is supplemented by machinima videos of the various subsequent court proceedings, which depict prosecutors and defence barristers making submissions to judges and magistrates.

These videos facilitate discussion in small group tutorial classes, in which students effectively role play the various judges and magistrates in making rulings on the various submissions. The program also includes modules of multiple-choice questions similar to those in *Indigo's Folly.* In the second year, Contract Law subject students undertake *Air Gondwana.* The first four modules of this program utilise a cognitive apprenticeship-style approach, with elements such as modelling, coaching, scaffolding, reflection and exploration (Brown et al. 1989; Collins 1991) for the teaching of negotiation skills to Contract Law students. This part of the program is used as a means of enabling students to obtain experiential learning of the practice of contract formation in parallel with their learning of the legal principles related to contract formation. The program is based on the contractual dealings of a fictional airline, Air Gondwana. It is set against a narrative involving a wealthy businessman (Xavier Rich) who, as a test of business acumen, installs his youngest son (Remington) as the head of one of his companies (the airline). The first three modules are completed online while the fourth involves an in-class activity. Instruction on negotiation theory in Module 1 is done by means of a 20-min video featuring a real-life narrator and includes vignettes which illustrate the various points made in the instruction and in which real-life actors portray a storyline involving the hiring of a pilot. The vignettes also model both poor and sound negotiation practice. The balance of the program utilises Second Life machinima. Modules 2 and 3 are completed online and use Articulate Storyline 360 as a platform. In Module 2, students practise the application of negotiation principles across a series of short scenarios (such as the commissioning of a new wardrobe for airline staff, the purchase of flight booking software and charter contracts), all of which are illustrated by Second Life images. Feedback is provided for each questions against which students may compare their answers. In Module 3, students practise the application of negotiation principles in the context of a single, more complex fact situation (the purchase of a supersonic aircraft). This immersive simulation involves interactivity akin to gameplay. It utilises machinima video, which includes some of the characters that appeared in the Module 1 storyline with the actors reprising their roles by lending their voices to avatars created in their likeness in the new adventure. The video stops at various points where students are asked questions concerning the application of negotiation principles in the context of the story. Feedback is again provided on the questions against which students may compare their answers. Module 4 is the culmination of the negotiation aspect of the program and requires students to engage in an in-class face-to-face role play involving negotiations over the use of a Pacific island on which the airline proposes to build a holiday resort. This exercise is facilitated in part by a "corporate video" showing the attractions of the island depicted by way of machinima. Personalised feedback on negotiated agreements is complemented by general feedback delivered by a machinima video shown in class, which features Remington Rich explaining the kinds of solutions students may have included in their agreements. The final module, Module 5 consists of *The Hercules Trilogy,* a trilogy of mini-modules featuring a storyline involving the airline's charter of a helicopter to service a fly in-fly out contract and combining machinima videos and simulated documentation (including contracts, letters, emails and diary notes) to facilitate the in-class discussion of interpretation of contract terms. Together the two phases of *Air Gondwana*—the negotiation phase (Modules 1–4) in which students are actively involved in the authentic task of negotiation and risk allocation in contract formation and the Hercules phase (Module 5) in which they are involved in the real-world activity of contract interpretation—engage students in authentic tasks that closely resemble those typically encountered in legal practice.

In Contract Law, students also undertake *The OO Files*, a suite of five modules of multiple-choice questions packaged together using Articulate Storyline 2. This online program comprises of over 150 short fact scenario questions, each of which is illustrated by a Second Life image as a means of assisting cognition of the facts, and which provide formative feedback on both correct and incorrect answers. It is based on the fictional Odin's Lawyers law firm, with each module involving the student as a clerk assisting either the senior partner Oscar Odin or senior associate Jess Astrild to provide advice on contract law issues to a different client (including a construction company, Ian Indigo as the owner of The Sapphire Club nightclub, the Air Gondwana airline and a rock band called Black Sceptre). Due to its success, this program sets the pattern for the inclusion of similarly styled multiple-choice learning tools in programs subsequently developed (like *Indigo's Folly* and *The Sapphire Vortex*).

In *Air Gondwana* and *The OO Files*, a romantic relationship develops between Remington Rich and the lawyer Jess Astrild. This relationship is further featured as an important plot device in *Mosswood Manor* in the second semester second-year Equity and Trusts subject. This program was originally designed to facilitate the next stage development (after *Air Gondwana*) of students' negotiation training, which required exposure to a multi-party negotiation in the context of conflict. It did this by a negotiation exercise concerning conflict surrounding a family trust. This exercise was facilitated by machinima videos depicting the volatile relationships between three generations of the Mosswood-Rich family, leveraging students' familiarity with the relationship between Xavier and Remington Rich gained through the *Air Gondwana* program to build a bridge not only between the narrative but also the material being studied. A curriculum review in 2014 led to the negotiation training role being removed from the subject. However, trust law is a notoriously abstract area of law to which students traditionally find difficult to relate. While the program was primarily directed to negotiation training, it was found to have had an additional incidental positive impact on student's understanding of, and engagement with, the substantive trust law content of the subject. Consequently, the program was reconfigured in a fashion similar to *The Hercules Trilogy*, with its machinima video being redesigned and re-edited as a means of contextualising the abstract law relating to trusts complemented by simulated documents including trust deeds, wills, letters, emails and newspapers, to facilitate small group class discussions of that law. This reconfiguration highlights the adaptability of machinima-based programs, with the raison d'être of the program changing but the design strengths of the original iteration of *Mosswood Manor*, including the continuation of the narrative from *Air Gondwana*, the authentic simulation in a real-world context and involving students in problem-solving activities, being maintained.

The same formula of machinima videos depicting narrative supported by simulated documents is also used in *Dragon Ventures* in the second-year Chinese Legal Systems elective subject. The Chinese Legal System is a complex interaction of communist ideology and a codified civil law influenced by the laws of the former Soviet Union and as such would, if taught by traditional means, be conceptually daunting for students whose training is otherwise focused on the Australian judge-based common law system. Instead *Dragon Ventures* utilises the narrative of Air Gondwana and the Xavier Rich companies as a device to explore the challenges of companies trading in China and thereby provides an authentic setting for an exploration of the practical impact of laws in that country. Machinima videos depicting a narrative supported by simulated documents and multiple-choice questions in the style of *The OO Files* are also used in *The Rich Chronicles* in the third-year Commercial Remedies subject, which in part depicts a continuation of the storyline in *Air Gondwana* Module 3 in which the supersonic aircraft purchased by the airline is involved in a number of legal disputes to the embarrassment of Remington Rich and otherwise involves members of the Mosswood-Rich family featured in *Mosswood Manor* in a variety of scenarios.

In their third year, students also undertake *Entry to Valhalla*, a suite of modules in the Ethics and the Legal Profession subject. Apart from self-test multiple-choice questions illustrated by Second Life images, it includes machinima videos to depict multi-layered real-world ethical dilemmas and wellness issues confronting legal practitioners in the fictional law firm, Odin's Lawyers. These include dilemmas concerning the romantic relationship between the lawyer Jess Astrild and her client Remington Rich, the conflict of interests arising from a dispute between Remington Rich and his father Xavier over the running of Air Gondwana due to the failed supersonic aircraft venture depicted in *The Rich Chronicles*, and ethical issues arising from a scenario involving one of the original *Sapphire Vortex* defendants allegedly subsequently framed by a police officer. *Entry to Valhalla* accordingly draws together various storylines running through the other programs. Each video features a lawyer in the law firm approaching the two senior partners of the firm seeking advice concerning the ethical dilemma they are confronting. In class discussions, students role-play the senior partners in relation to the appropriate advice they should give.

In addition to these programs in the undergraduate law degree, also worthy of mention for its different use of machinima is the *Black Sceptre* program in Entertainment Law, a subject taught as part of a Bachelor of Entertainment degree at QUT. This program replicates the learning activities in the negotiation phase of *Air Gondwana*, albeit in a scaled-down format, in order to teach negotiation skills to Entertainment students. *Black Sceptre* is based on the contract negotiations of a fictional rock music band, Black Sceptre. Unlike *Air Gondwana*, which was made with the benefit of a small learning and teaching grant that enabled the production of the Module 1 instructional video, *Black Sceptre* was unfunded. In place of the real-life instructional video and real-life actors of the former program, the 20-min instructional video in Module 1 of *Black Sceptre* utilises Second Life machinima, and features instruction on negotiation theory by an avatar-narrator and vignettes starring avatars to depict that theory in practice by way of a scenario involving the band negotiating the use of a venue for a concert. The avatars also model poor and sound negotiation practice, including the appropriate use of body language. In addition, the program includes Second Life images to assist cognition of the facts by illustrating scenarios in a practice module, and machinima video to help facilitate an in-class role play activity by providing background briefing information necessary for a negotiation between the band and a film production company. The success of *Black Sceptre* as a means of engaging non-law students in the study of law led to the development of *Limelight Crux*, a program that combines machinima that periodically stops for questions (in the same fashion as Module 3 of *Air Gondwana*), those questions being in the style of the multiple-choice questions in *The OO Files*.

This collection of programs demonstrates that machinima may be successfully employed in a wide variety of ways, including the depiction of a background narrative to "set the scene" for the purposes of student activity such as a research assignment, to facilitate in-class activities such as workshop discussions or role plays, providing instruction and/or feedback, modelling behaviour and enabling aspects of gameplay. It can be used in conjunction with other cost-effective multimedia, such as simulated documents, letters and newspapers to enhance authenticity. It can also be used to teach both substantive content and skills, and for both formative and summative purposes (see Table 10.1). In addition, the collection illustrates the use of connected narratives running through programs in multiple subjects.

Reflections and Directions

Student Reaction

The success of Second Life machinima, videos and still images, as a means of facilitating authentic learning and engaging students, can be seen in the quantitative and qualitative results of surveys of each of these programs. A snapshot of the quantitative results to surveys conducted using a Likert scale (with the responses Strongly Agree, Agree, Agree, Neither Agree or Disagree, Disagree and Strongly Disagree) is provided in Table 10.2.

Authentic learning and engagement are among the themes typically emerging from students' qualitative comments. Students have commented on the ability of Second Life machinima to "humanise" characters in problems and to bring those problems "alive", making them easier to comprehend and more engaging, and making their learning more effective. One student said of *Entry into Valhalla*: "It puts [ethics] into a real-world perspective, putting faces to names, seeing the people, makes it easier to relate to the situation." Another student observed in

Table 10.1 Uses of machinima in the QUT undergraduate program

Program	Content (C) or Skills (S)	Formative (F) or Summative (S)	Background storytelling	Combined with mock documents	Instruction	Modelling	Gameplay aspects	Provision of feedback	Facilitate class discussions	Facilitate class activities	Illustrate facts to aid cognition
Air Gondwana	S	F + S	✓	✓			✓	✓	✓	✓	✓
Black Sceptre	S	F + S	✓		✓	✓				✓	✓
Dragon Ventures	C	F	✓	✓					✓		
Entry into Valhalla	C	F		✓		✓			✓		✓
Indigo's Folly	S	F	✓	✓					✓		✓
Limelight Crux	C	F	✓				✓				
Mosswood Manor	C	F	✓	✓					✓		
The OO Files	C	F									✓
The Rich Chronicles	C	F	✓	✓					✓		✓
The Sapphire Vortex	C	F	✓						✓		✓

Table 10.2 Snapshot of survey results

	Strongly agree/agree	Strongly disagree/disagree
Air Gondwana (2007) (n = 367)		
Helped me to understand the application of negotiation principles in real-world practice	**91%**	1%
Realistic setting for me to understand the principles of negotiation	**85%**	2.1%
Enabled me to gain an understanding of basic negotiation theory and practice	**95%**	0.8%
Enjoyed using as part of studies	**78%**	3%
Entry into Valhalla (2010) (n = 106)		
Helped me to relate my understanding of legal ethics to real-world situations	**82%**	7%
The law firm storyline helped my learning of legal ethics	**81%**	8%
Enjoyed using as part of studies	**72%**	11%
The OO Files (2011) (n = 263)		
Assisted my understanding of contract law	**96%**	0%
The law firm storylines were a valuable aspect	**68%**	5%
Will be a useful review tool for the exam	**95%**	0%
Mosswood Manor (2012) (n = 363)		
Helped me to see the real-world relevance of the unit content	**88%**	5%
Helped me to understand the relevance of negotiation to real-world practice	**88%**	3%
Helped me to understand the relevance of trusts in real-world practice	**85%**	5%
Challenged me to exercise skills in identifying which issues required a legal solution and which required a non-legal solution	**88%**	3%
Challenged me to synthesise my legal knowledge with my knowledge of negotiation theory	**87%**	2%
Enjoyed using as part of studies	**77%**	6%
Indigo's Folly (2014) (n = 186)		
Helped me to engage with the skill of statutory interpretation more than I think I usually would.	**85%**	2%
Encouraged me to think about the skill of statutory interpretation more than I think I usually would.	**87%**	1%
Helped me to see the real-world relevance of the skill of statutory interpretation.	**86%**	2%
Helped me to understand the skill of statutory interpretation in real-world practice	**86%**	2%
Enjoyed using as part of my studies	**83%**	2%

relation to *The OO Files*, which uses Second Life images to illustrate scenarios involving clients confronting contract law issues: "Legal discourse can seem quite sterile … the imagery gives the exercise character, context and a reminder that people are involved." A student commented in relation to *Mosswood Manor*:

> The entire thing just seemed more "real". Rather than having a page of facts presented to us, the use of various types of media (the videos, newspapers, emails, etc.) made me think "well this is (to an extent) just what I see clients bringing in all the time at the legal centre. This is about as real as it gets."

A student said of *Indigo's Folly*, the program designed to teach the otherwise abstract, notoriously unengaging, but nonetheless essential skill of statutory interpretation:

> I realised the extent to which legislation impacts the lives and choices of ordinary people. That helped to give a broader context to my studies. I realised how important it is to master the skill of statutory interpretation.

Another emphasised the ability of the same program to engage students:

> It was engaging. It was motivating. It was unlike any other tool I have used to learn. The program allowed me to maintain interest in statutory interpretation. The program also allowed me to really question and understand statutory interpretation. The idea of an interactive program allowed me to WANT to learn.

Student responses commonly include a large number who report that they find the programs to be interesting, imaginative, engaging and/or fun. In relation to the overall learning experiences created by the programs, a student said of *Mosswood Manor* that:

> The videos … were a really engaging way to deliver the information needed to complete the assignment, I would even go far as to say it made it fun. Answering a problem about the family made it a much more "real life" scenario and I felt it was a much more engaging experience than my other subjects.

These qualities lead to improvements in student learning. A student thought that *Mosswood Manor*: "Gave me a good idea as to working in a real-life problem in trusts and showed me the relevance of it … I've taken more of an interest in the subject itself since the [program]" while another felt that "it kept me entertained and interested … I remembered more than I usually would." A student said of *Air Gondwana* that: "I felt as if I was "learning" but it wasn't obvious that I was learning … I felt completely involved in the process."

As noted, the continuation of the *Air Gondwana* narrative in *Mosswood Manor* was based on the hypothesis that building a bridge between the storyline might help build a bridge to the subject matter being studied. That approach resonated with over half of the respondents, with only 12% disagreeing. Among the comments of those who agreed were observations that familiar faces made it easier to connect with the program; that it made the program interesting, entertaining and amusing; that it made the program more comfortable to do and that it helped give a depth and context to the program that made it feel more real world. Others went further and indicated that the continuing story made them think how different areas of law linked together while others thought it made it easier to revise the previous negotiation skills that they had learnt. As one student stated: "I loved the continuity … it seemed as though the program was advancing with me and my skills … it also just made the whole thing more fun."

By contrast, a third of respondents felt that while the continuity in the story was interesting, it was not essential to the exercise and a new set of characters would have worked just as well. By contrast, a handful of this group of respondents reported that it had been so long since that they had studied contract law that they did not remember *Air Gondwana.* The significant portion of respondents who stated that they saw value in the continued narrative between *Air Gondwana* and *Mosswood Manor* may be seen as support for the hypothesis that engagement may be promoted by storylines featuring the same characters in multiple programs. Further research into the potential cognitive benefits that may be achieved by such an approach may therefore be indicated.

Machinima and a Willing Suspension of Disbelief

The effectiveness of Second Life machinima as a means of simulation depends in part upon the degree to which students are prepared to undergo what the poet Samuel Taylor Coleridge first described a "willing suspension of disbelief". As Herrington et al. (2003) stated:

> There is increasing evidence that in order to fully engage with an authentic task or problem based scenario, students need to engage with a process that is familiar to moviegoers throughout the world – the suspension of disbelief. For example, consider the suspension of disbelief that audiences must undergo to enable them to become engaged with movies such as Star Wars, Mad Max, The Matrix, The Truman Show, and Back to the Future. Audiences need to accept the worlds that have been created, no matter how unlikely. Once the initial suspension of disbelief has occurred, it is only inconsistencies within the parameters of the plot itself that cause dissonance in the viewer. In other words, once the viewer has accepted the fundamental basis for the simulated world in which he or she is immersed, engagement with the story and message of the film is entirely feasible.

The extent to which Second Life machinima can facilitate a suspension of disbelief, and as a consequence the effectiveness of the learning environment, may depend upon the degree to which the notion of machinima as involving "real-world filmmaking techniques" (Dellario and Marino 2005) is embraced. Middleton and Mather (2008) noted that machinima may be sophisticated, artistic productions or, at their simplest, rudimentary "fly on the wall" CCTV-type recordings. While artistic productions of a type commonly seen in machinima contests may demand skill sets beyond those commonly held by most academics, little specialist film-making expertise is necessary to create productions that are superior to mere "fly on the wall" recordings. Machinima featuring avatars exhibiting no more than the default Second Life standing or sitting animations, for example, will seem less natural and as a consequence likely be less engaging than that of avatars exhibiting customised animations of a kind that may be obtained freely or purchased for a moderate price either "in world" or from the Second Life marketplace website. Similarly, taking care when providing voices for avatars can assist in facilitating the suspension of disbelief. There is always a risk when voices are provided by non-actors that they will sound like they are merely reading from a script. For an audience that may largely comprise modern-day students who have grown up having watched countless television programs and films, this may sound unnatural and be a barrier to engagement. By contrast, all voices for the various programs at QUT discussed above, while provided by non-actors, were recorded separately from the corresponding video. Audio and video were later synchronised in the editing process. Not infrequently, such recordings may require more than one take, and editing may be more challenging if the voices are to be closely synchronised with lip movement, but it is a means by which avatar dialogue can be made to sound and appear natural and engaging. Indeed, in formal surveys, students often comment favourably regarding the voice work in these programs.

Machinima can be further enhanced and made more engaging by basic film-making techniques that, as in the case of programs at QUT, have not required specialist background or training but rather can be simply gleaned by the machinima maker paying careful attention to television or film productions and the techniques they use. These techniques include the use of "establishing shots" (wide shots that are often the first shot of a scene designed to show the audience where the action is taking place and perhaps all of the characters in the opening of the scene); a mixture of camera angles such as close-ups, midshots, reverse angles, over-the-shoulder shots and shots showing two or more characters; and not "crossing the line" (i.e. the imaginary line between subjects in a scene which if crossed can disorientate and confuse the viewer when reversing the camera angle in consecutive shots). Basic instruction and tutorials regarding such techniques are, in any event, also freely available on the Internet (see, e.g. http://www.mediacollege.com). Video may also be made seem more authentic if some effort is made to "dress" the scenes appropriately in the same way that settings are prepared for the purposes of real film-making. In other words, in the case of an office scene, for example, there is value in enhancing the scene by placing a variety of office supplies on the desk and populating the room with other office furniture to help create a realistic feel to the setting. For instance, in the case of Air Gondwana the detail added to a desk in an office scene extended to a coffee cup on a saucer with a spoon, holiday photographs featuring Remington Rich and Jess Astrild in desk picture frames and printed business cards bearing his name and details, which all incidentally appear at one time or other in various shots.

Finally, machinima may be further enhanced by the addition of sound effects, such as those freely available from specialist repositories of Creative Commons audio samples (see, e.g. http://www.freesound.org) and music, such as that available from other specialist websites offering Creative Commons resources (see, e.g. http://www.freemusicarchive.org).

Following these techniques can be more time consuming than rudimentary fly on the wall real-time recordings of academics providing voices for their own avatars.

However, it is an investment of time which can produce immersive and engaging learning environments for students, as attested to by students who have used the programs at QUT who frequently comment positively concerning the production values of the programs. For example, in contrast with the sentiments expressed by Walsh (2011) that Second Life machinima lacks fidelity because only human actors can convey non-verbal communication, a student observed in relation to *Entry into Valhalla* that the advantages of machinima over text-based questions included "nuances of tone, body language more accurately portrayed, so easier to understand" while another stated that "the video can depict more easily the non-verbal cues among parties". These techniques can promote a willing suspension of disbelief and produce a high level of imaginative engagement.

Moreover, multimedia productions featuring human actors are not without their shortcomings, most notably in terms of cost in the context of the limited funding available for universities. Limited budgets translate into limitations on the kinds of productions possible if human actors were to be used, including locations and cast size. By contrast, the machinima components of *Air Gondwana*, for example, include scenes in an office, an executive jet, an open road, an air field and aircraft hangar in the Ukraine which includes a supersonic jet fighter that is integral to the narrative, and a ballroom featuring a large number of "extras" dancing in the background. It also features a wide variety of scenes on a Pacific island, including beaches, caves, bushland and underwater (Fig. 10.2). Second Life offers a rich canvas for storytelling for little or no cost, whereas attempting to portray the same narrative using human actors would be beyond the reach of available university funding, even if it were practicable to find comparable locations in real life.

Nevertheless, even if these techniques are employed, machinima videos will never enjoy universal approval among students. Formal surveys of the programs at QUT have generally shown a very small number of critics of the programs, who tend to fall into one of two camps. The first group consists of students who would appear to be gamers themselves. It would seem that for them no production with graphics less than the latest quality first-person-shooter games will be considered to be satisfactory. However, in 2013, the executive producer of one instalment in the

Fig. 10.2 Selection of scenes from *Air Gondwana* illustrating the potential of Second Life machinima as a means of portraying narratives

Call of Duty computer game franchise commented on the ballooning budgets now needed for so-called "AAA" game development, observing that they were becoming harder and more expensive to make due to the demand for better graphics and "more realistic looking art assets" and that only bigger studios may soon be able to afford the "scary" cost of development (Makuch 2013). While it may be difficult to confirm exact figures, since published costs may also include marketing and distribution expenses, it would seem that development budgets for such games could be between $20 and $60 million (Superannuation 2014), with a game like *Star Wars: The Old Republic* in 2011 being described in a LA Times as perhaps "the largest entertainment production in history", having involved 800 people and costing an estimated $200 million to develop (Fritz and Pham 2012). Accordingly, expectations of AAA game standard graphics are unrealistic and cannot be accommodated by university productions developed on meagre budgets.

The second group consists of students who view machinima as "cartoonish" and therefore not appropriate for university study. Research has shown that a small number of both students and staff will spurn such innovations in technology, particularly game-based design, for a complicated mix of personal conceptions concerning play and learning (deWinter et al. 2010; Gee 2003). Such resistance is likely to manifest itself in an unwillingness to suspend disbelief, which is needed for cognitive realism. Without sufficient cognitive realism, these students may regard the learning environment as being artificially situated and as a consequence perceive the technology to be an impediment that is distracting them from their learning (Matthew 2012). An appropriate response to the concerns of such students may be the simple provision of at least print-friendly versions of transcripts of the videos as an alternative means of providing them with the content of the narratives that form the basis of the relevant study activity.

Sustainability and Maintaining Continuity

If properly designed, machinima can be a sustainable resource. This is because machinima can depict fact scenarios that continue to be realistic and relevant year after year, thereby forming the basis of class discussions and other activities for successive year groups. Thus, while, for example, laws may constantly change, the application of those laws may be left to be discussed in class rather than requiring repeated changes to the machinima.

However, a challenge that may need to addressed in the case of multiple programs linked by a common narrative is if there is change in one or more of the subjects in which those programs reside, which may have impact on the continuity of that narrative. Such a change may occur in different ways, including a change in teaching staff in a subject in which a machinima-based project resides accompanied by a change in learning and teaching philosophy that has a different attitude to such initiatives, and more structural changes such as a course curriculum review that has flow-on implications regarding when and/or how particular subjects are taught.

The latter challenge arose in relation to the programs at QUT. A review of the undergraduate law curriculum implemented from 2015 rearranged the order of several subjects and therefore the order in which students encounter the various storylines. To a large extent, the strategy of designing the programs as stand-alone exercises and using flashback sequences to convey any necessary foundation for the continuing storyline can provide a measure of protection for the overall narrative from the loss of a program through changes to individual subjects. Further, as already noted, the curriculum changes that removed the negotiation training aspect from the Equity and Trusts subject were addressed by removing the negotiation component from *Mosswood Manor* and reconfiguring the program so that it instead focuses on trust law issues and facilitates class discussions of this abstract and difficult-to-comprehend area of law.

Changes to the order that students encounter certain subjects may be a greater challenge to maintaining continuity. For example, a reordering might have a significant impact on the continuity of a connected narrative, such as a character now dying in one program and then reappearing in good health in a subsequent program. Reordering of subjects under the curriculum review at QUT did not have such a dramatic effect, but nonetheless required changes in script and voice work and re-editing of some machinima. Indeed, in some cases, the reordering strengthened the connections between some of the programs. This was, however, more a matter of good fortune rather than design: while the programs were acknowledged by the architects of the new curriculum as valuable components of the respective subjects, it could not be expected that maintenance of continuity in the narrative running through them would figure in the factors taken into account when settling the new curriculum. The risk of subsequent changes to curriculum is therefore one to be borne in mind when designing programs featuring connected narratives.

Conclusion

Virtual simulation allows students to benefit from experiential learning (Middleton and Mather 2008) and is inclusive of a range of learning styles (Burbules 1999). The use of narratives depicted by machinima can be a cost-effective means of promoting imaginative engagement, assist cognition, provoke active thinking and provide contextual cues that aid later recall.

The experience of multiple programs linked by storylines featuring recurring characters in the undergraduate law degree at QUT provides a valuable case study of the positive outcomes that such programs may produce for student engagement and authentic learning. It demonstrates that machinima may be used in a variety of modes for both summative and formative purposes and to teach both substantive content and skills, as a component of a blended learning environment that can provide a learning experience that is adapted and appropriate for modern-day students. Machinima, if properly designed and created using basic film-making techniques, is capable of promoting a willing suspension of disbelief and enables the creation of authentic learning experiences. It can enable an environment in which students take an active, practical role in their learning and can appreciate the relevance of the material they are studying to their future professional careers.

Acknowledgements The author wishes to acknowledge the Office of Learning and Teaching (formerly the Australian Learning and Teaching Council), an initiative of the Australian Government, for its support for his fellowship. The views expressed in this chapter do not necessarily reflect the views of the Office of Learning and Teaching.

References

Advisory Committee on Legal Education and Conduct (ACLEC). (1996). *First report on legal education and training*. London: HMSO.

Allison, J. W. F. (Ed.). (2013). *A.V. Dicey: The law of the constitution*. Oxford: Oxford University Press.

American Bar Association (ABA). (1992). *Legal education and professional development—An educational continuum*. Chicago Illinois USA: ABA (the 'MacCrate Report')

Agostinho, S. (2006). Using characters in online simulated environments to guide authentic tasks. In A. Herrington & J. Herrington (Eds), *Authentic learning environments in higher education* (pp. 88–95). Hersley: PA: Information Science Publishing.

Australian Law Reform Commission (ALRC). (1999). *Managing justice: A review of the federal civil justice system Report 89*. Sydney: ALRC.

Bardzell, J., Bardzell, S., Briggs, C., Makice, K., Ryan, W., & Weldon, M. (2006). Machinima prototyping: An approach to evaluation. In *Proceedings of the 4th Nordic Conference on Human-Computer Interaction: Changing Roles* (Vol. 189, pp. 433–36) Oslo, Norway.

Bonwell, C. C., & Eison, J. A. (1991). Active learning: Creating excitement in the classroom. ASHE-ERIC Higher Education Report No. 1. Washington, DC: George Washington University.

Brown, J., Collins, A., & Duguid, P. (1989). Situated cognition and the culture of learning. *Educational Researcher, 18*(1), 32–42.

Bruner, J. (1990). *Acts of meaning*. Cambridge, MA: Harvard University Press.

Burbules, N. (1999). Technology in education: Who, where, when, what & why? *International Journal of Educational Technology 1,* 1 Retrieved from http://www.ed.uiuc.edu/ijet/v1n1/v1n1feature.html.

Collins, A. (1991). Cognitive apprenticeship and instructional technology. In L. Idol & B. F. Jones (Eds.), *Educational values and cognitive instruction: Implications for reform* (pp. 453–494). Hillsdale, NJ: Lawrence Erlbaum.

Daly-Swanson, B. (2007). Second Life machinima for libraries: The intersection of instruction, outreach and marketing in a virtual world. Paper presented at the World Library and Information Congress, 73rd IFLA General Conference and Council, August 19–23, in Durban, South Africa. Retrieved from http://www.ifla.org/IV/ifla73/papers/133-DalySwanson-en.pdf.

deWinter, J., Griffin, D., McAllister, K. S., Moeller, R. M, & Ruggill, J. E. (2010). Computer games across the curriculum: a critical review of an emerging techno-pedagogy. *Currents in Electronic Literacy.* Retrieved from http://currents.cwrl.utexas.edu/2010/dewinter_et_al_computer-games-across-the-curriculum.html.

Dellario, F., & Marino, P. (2005). Academy of machinima arts and sciences: Machinima FAQ. Retrieved from http://www.machinima.org.

Dettori, G., & Paiva, A. (2009). Narrative learning in technology and enhanced environments: An introduction to narrative learning environments. In N. Balacheff, S. Ludvigsen, T. de Jong, A. Lazonder, & S. Barnes (Eds.), *Technology-enhanced learning: Principles and products*. Dordrecht: Springer.

Eison, J. (2010). *Using active learning instructional strategies to create excitement and enhance learning*. Retrieved from http://cte.cornell.edu/documents/presentations/Eisen-Handout.pdf

Ferguson, W., Bareiss, R., Bimbaum, L., & Osgood, R. (1992). ASK systems: An approach to the realization of story-based teachers. *Journal of the Learning Sciences, 2*(1), 95–134.

Fritz, B., & Pham, A. (2012). *Star Wars: The Old Republic—the story behind a galactic gamble*. Retrieved from http://herocomplex.latimes.com/games/star-wars-the-old-republic-the-story-behind-a-galactic-gamble/#/0.

Frand, J. (2000). The information age mindset: Changes in students and implications for higher education. *Educause Review, 35*(5), 15.

Gee, J. (2003). *What Video games have to teach us about learning and literacy*. New York: Palgrave/Macmillan.

Herrington, J., Oliver, R., & Reeves, T. C. (2003). Patterns of engagement in authentic online learning environments. *Australian Journal of Educational Technology, 19*(1), 59–71.

Herrington, J., & Oliver, R. (2000). An instructional design framework for authentic learning environments. *Educational Technology Research and Development, 48*(3), 23–48.

James, N. (2000). A brief history of legal critique in Australian legal education. *Melbourne University Law Review, 24*(3), 967.

Johnson, D. W., Johnson, R. T., & Smith, K. A. (1991). *Active learning: Cooperation in the college classroom*. Edina, MN: Interaction Book Company.

Johnstone, R., & Vignaendra, S. (2003). *Learning outcomes and curriculum development in law* Canberra: AGPS.

Kastelein, R. (2013). *The rise of machinima, the artform*. Retrieved from http://insights.wired.com/profiles/blogs/the-rise-of-machinima-the-artform#ixzz2TyrAOCUC.

Keyes, M., & Johnstone, R. (2004). Changing legal education: Rhetoric, reality, and prospects for the future. *Sydney Law Review, 26*, 537–564.

Kift, S. (2008). 21st century climate for change: Curriculum design for quality learning enhancement in law. *Legal Education Review, 18*(1), 1–30.

Kift, S. (2009). *Articulating a transition pedagogy to scaffold and enhance the first-year learning experience in Australian higher education*. Canberra: Australian Learning and Teaching Council.

Law Council of Australia (LCA). (2008). *Review of Australian Higher Education Discussion Paper*. Canberra: LCA.

Lowood, H. (2006). High-performance play: The making of machinima. *Journal of Media Practice, 7*(1), 25–42.

Makuch, E. (2013). *Call of Duty: Ghosts producer on "scary" cost of AAA development*. Retrieved from http://www.gamespot.com/articles/call-of-duty-ghosts-producer-on-scary-cost-of-aaa-development/1100-6414781/

Malone, T., & Lepper, M. (1987). Making learning fun: A taxonomy of intrinsic motivations for learning. In R. Snow & M. Farr (Eds.), *Aptitude, learning, and instruction: III* (pp. 223–253). Erlbaum, Hillsdale, NJ: Cognitive and affective process analyses.

Matthew, A. (2012). Managing distraction and attention in diverse cohorts: 21st century challenges to law student engagement. *QUT Law and Justice Journal, 12*(1), 45–65.

McKeachie, W. (1986). *Teaching tips* (8th ed.). Lexington, MA: Heath & Co.

Meyers, C., & Jones, T. B. (1993). *Promoting active learning: Strategies for the college classroom*. San Francisco: Jossey Bass.

Middleton, A., & Mather, R. (2008). Machinima interventions: Innovative approaches to immersive virtual world curriculum integration. *ALT-J, Research in Learning Technology, 16*(3), 207–220.

Moreau, M., & Leathwood, C. (2006). Balancing paid work and studies: working (-class) students and higher education. *Studies in Higher Education, 31*(1), 23–42.

Oberlinger, D. (2003). Boomers, gen-xers millenials, understanding the new students. *Educause Review, 38*(4,) 37.

Ormrod, J. (2004). *Human learning* (4th ed.). Upper Saddle River, NJ: Pearson Education.

Pearce, D, Campbell, E., & Harding, D. (1987). *Australian law schools: A discipline assessment for the Commonwealth Tertiary Education Commission* (the 'Pearce Report') Canberra: AGPS.
Ricoeur, P. (2005). *Hermeneutics and the human sciences* (17th ed.). In J.B. Thompson (Ed.). Cambridge, MA: Cambridge University Press.
Rowe, J., McQuiggan, S., & Lester, J. (2007). Narrative presence in intelligent learning environments. In *Working Notes of the 2007 AAAI Fall Symposium on Intelligent Narrative Technologies*, Washington DC.
Schank, R. C. (2000). *Tell me a story: Narrative and intelligence*. Evanston, IL: Northwestern University Press.
Superannuation (2014). *How much does it cost to make a big video game?* Retrieved from http//: www. http://kotaku.com/how-much-does-it-cost-to-make-a-big-video-game-1501413649.
Tarrant, J. (2006). Teaching time-savvy law students. *James Cook University Law Review, 13,* 64–80.
Thornton, M. (1991). Portia lost in the groves of academe wondering what to do about legal education. *Australian Universities' Review, 34,* 26–32.
Walsh, M. (2011). Narrative pedagogy and simulation: Future directions for nursing education. *Nurse Education Practice, 11,* 216–219.
Wertsch, J. V. (1998). *Mind as action*. New York: Oxford University Press.

Author Biography

Des Butler is a Professor of Law in the Faculty of Law, Queensland University of Technology (QUT), Brisbane, Australia, where he served as Assistant Dean, Research (1997–2002). He is an Australian Learning and Teaching Fellow and a Senior Fellow of the United Kingdom Higher Education Academy. He has developed technology-based programs for enhancing the learning of law since 1990 and has received numerous awards for his work, including an Australian Award for Teaching Excellence and the Australasian Law Teachers Association Award for Excellence and Innovation in the Teaching of Law in 2008 (inaugural award) and 2014. He is, in addition, the author or co-author of 21 books and numerous articles on topics including technology-based innovations in legal education, contract law and media law.

Chapter 11
Decision-Making Supported by Virtual-World Systems Vis-à-Vis Enterprise Systems' Uncertainty and Equivocality

Amit Rudra, Bjørn Jæger and Kristine Ludvigsen

Introduction

For business decision-making at the tactical and strategic level in a distributed environment, it is crucial that the information system used facilitates mediation of tacit knowledge. From a social constructivist perspective, the environment fosters an associated community, where the goal of expanded knowledge is reached though cooperation (Anderson 2004; Vygotsky 1978). The quality of the cooperation, therefore, depends on the user-to-user interactions. The last decade has seen an increased focus on mediated collaboration in a distributed environment, with recent research studies by Datar et al. (2010), Pappano (2012) and Ratcliffe (2012) pointing to the skill needs of business students. However, traditional-mediated environments, like video conferencing and document sharing tools, are hampered by reduced quality of interaction when compared with face-to-face interaction. This entails a need for creating environments suited to collaboration and decision-making in a geographically distributed environment. The basic conditions for a good distributed computer-based system supporting tacit knowledge exchange are the same in both real-world and virtual-world situations. Kreijns (2004), for example, emphasised how feelings of social presence and group membership played a significant role in mediated environments; while Zhao et al. (2005) found

A. Rudra (✉)
Curtin University, Perth, Australia
e-mail: Amit.Rudra@cbs.curtin.edu.au

B. Jæger
Molde University College, Molde, Norway
e-mail: Bjorn.Jager@himolde.no

K. Ludvigsen
University of Bergen, Bergen, Norway
e-mail: Kristine.Ludvigsen@psych.uib.no

S. Gregory and D. Wood (eds.), *Authentic Virtual World Education*,
https://doi.org/10.1007/978-981-10-6382-4_11

that interactions among students, as well as between students and teachers, contribute to their goal of learning.

The growth of global business activities increases the need for tools supporting distributed business decision-making in international markets (WTO 2013; Galbraith 2012; Jæger et al. 2015). To succeed in such a competitive market place, an organisation needs to have a robust information processing infrastructure. Further, the operational and management levels have different information processing requirements in conducting international trade operations. At the operational level, transactions require detailed information of the goods traded, in addition to information of the logistical and legal parties involved. Enterprise systems help in making the information complete by export/import wizards (e.g. SAP Export/Import Cockpit), as well as tools to analyse and act on the information. Thus, enterprise systems help in eliminating the uncertainty involved by ensuring the information is complete. At the management level, trade operations have additional information processing requirements. At this level, management decisions are established on both explicit and tacit knowledge. No matter how much information are collected, a decision will still be based on negotiations between the companies (e.g. closing a deal between a buyer and a supplier company). This is attributed to the psychological interplay among the business actors. The term equivocality is used to describe this inherent ambiguity. While at the operational level, an organisation supports its trades through automated global business transactions using an enterprise resource planning (ERP) system; its management level meets an increase in the use of collaborative systems to support virtual teams (Roberts et al. 2006). A virtual-world environment is seen as a tool with unique properties for supporting management level decisions where the parties are geographically dispersed (Rudra et al. 2011; Jaeger et al. 2011; Jaeger et al. 2015).

In the first part of this chapter, we justify the unique properties of virtual-worlds as a tool in making management trade decisions by referring to two cases. First, at the management level, the case involves presentations and negotiations with geographically distributed team members communicating using Second Life. Business school students from two countries collaborate in this case. The second case, at the operational level, involves execution of business trade transactions (export and import) communication using the leading business enterprise system (SAP ERP system). Classes at two universities in two countries collaborate to run these two cases. For the management case, we discuss role-playing using virtual-worlds involving communication of both explicit and tacit knowledge. This is contrasted with role-playing using ERP systems handling explicit knowledge only.

In the second part of this chapter, we present a model of the role concept in user-to-user communication. We follow this up by a case study describing how the selection of an avatar reflects the user's role, and how an avatar situates the user in a business environment. Before the entrance of virtual-worlds, traditional distributed applications like distance education proved to lack interaction qualities compared with real face-to-face interactions. One example is Hirschheim (2005) who pointed out that instant and spontaneous interaction where students meet face-to-face disappears in distance-learning environment. Angelino, Williams and Natvig (2007) found that being separated from a physical classroom makes some students feel isolated and disconnected. With the advent of the Internet and online gaming, avatars emerged as the primary object for interaction. Avatars create new opportunities for effective, synchronous computer-mediated communication. In this regard, Bolter and Grusin (1999) observe that there are two main mediation categories. The first one seeks to make the technological medium transparent to users such that the experience resembles face-to-face communication. In this category, users are said to be "looking through" the technology. Video conferencing is a typical example. The other category considers the medium itself as the central communication component, with users "looking at" the technology. In this case, three-dimensional (3D) virtual-worlds are the most common technology, which is our focus in this study. In a 3D virtual-world, many geographically distributed users are connected via the Internet. A 3D virtual-world is accessible via a computer interface, where the term 3D refers to both sounds and images projected in a spatial context providing the user a feeling of being in a 3D environment. Roads, houses, trees, benches, animals and interiors are examples of visual artefacts constituting virtual-world places and spaces (Prasolova-Førland 2008). Compared to other communication technologies, 3D virtual-worlds offer a unique sense of simultaneity and presence (Edirisingha et al. 2009). 3D virtual-worlds also enable simulations and activities that would otherwise be too expensive, too dangerous or too difficult to access in other ways (Dickey 2005; Ludvigsen 2011). In this chapter, we explore avatars and how they affect roles and role expectations in a business decision-making situation. Following an ethnographic approach, we use an exploratory case study of learning activities at the virtual campus Kamimo Island in Second Life—including qualitative research interviews, lecturing observations and educational activity participation.

Broadly, the remainder of this chapter has two parts, laid out as follows. The first part covers the suitability of virtual-worlds as a tool in making management trade decisions. While in the second, using a case, we present a model of the role concept in user-to-user communication.

Role-Playing

Role-playing in the context of educational settings has been distinctive of student-centred learning (Vasileiou and Paraskeva 2010; Aldrich 2005; Bloom 1956; de Freitas 2006). For us, when creating environments for learning, a leading principle has been that it must inspire student involvement. Regarding student involvement, Astin (1985, p. 36) observes, "The effectiveness of any educational policy or practice is directly related to the capacity of that policy or practice to increase student involvement". While role-playing, our students contribute actively in learning activities. Throughout a role-play, participants involve themselves in stories. Depending on the learning situations, these stories could be defined either by a manuscript, or be open-ended, or a combination of both. In our case study, we used a combination of both with students demonstrating their understanding by improvising the open parts. Role-play can also be viewed as a social activity. Here, players act on specific roles assigned to them. Thus, in order to convince the other party, players express their feelings, ideas and arguments. This provides the players with opportunity for both sharing their knowledge and further, extending their knowledge by learning from others. For educational domains which may require skills such as group communication, critical thinking, decision-making and negotiating, role-play may be valuable providing higher learning. Two domains that stand to gain from such role-plays are information systems management and business education. In classes where the emphasis is upon choices, role-play exercises focusing on decision-making are ideal for supporting an educator's training needs (de Freitas 2006). With developments of immersive applications like Second Life, it is now possible to design more sophisticated online role-play environments which both simulate real-world environments more faithfully than before, and go beyond what is conceivable in real-world realms (Jones 2007; Aldrich 2005).

The Role Case at the Management Level

In this case, we targeted three learning dimensions. The first dimension—acquiring knowledge pertaining various ERP systems; the second—a comprehension of selection criteria for buying information systems and lastly, training in decision-making in a virtual or simulated business environment—whether as sales representatives or as a purchasing team. The particular role-play selected for the management level is response to Request-For-Proposal (RFP) for an enterprise system. The description of this role-play is in a textbook by Sumner (2005) on ERP systems and is commonly used in classes all over the world. It addresses the complicated issues of procurement, implementation and use of an ERP system. The background of the role-play relates to a fictional small and medium enterprise (SME), Wingate—a manufacturing company. This company manufactures small electric motors and uses a set of conventional computer applications that control information management needs of the company. However, over time these applications have become fragmented, unwieldy and costly to run. Consequently, to resolve this issue, Wingate is deliberating on procuring a new ERP system. The new ERP must have functions that allow financial and accounting procedures including accounts payable/receivable and posting on the general ledger. Further, for manufacturing and production planning, it should support the option for supplementing such modules. The company releases a RFP, which defines its needs of an ERP system. In response to the RFP, competing ERP vendors announce their interest in offering a proposal. These could be any three of Oracle, Microsoft and SAP; and an ASP solution or application service provider. After a presentation by each vendor, Wingate analyses, through a decision process, to resolve upon a winner. In a particular class, we organise the role-play into sets of four teams; with each sales team having three students for each of the three vendors and one purchasing team having either three or four members representing a panel of executives from Wingate Electric. We can organise 12 to 16 students in this way to participate in each set allowing the decision-making scenario to be conducted for a class in a limited time.

Throughout the preparation phase, each team, generally, has to conduct a thorough literature search and subsequent actions such as contacting the vendors in order to gather information and to develop particular deliverables to be used during the role-play. This grounding phase is essential for the learning outcome associated with specific topics studied (i.e. features of ERP systems). For the team playing the role of a purchaser, a deliverable is a scorecard based on several established selection criteria along with a weighted scoring method for evaluating available alternative ERP systems. A sales team, on the other hand, develops and prepares a sales presentation based on the ERP system it is going to sell. To help them with their preparation, teams are provided with Wingate's company background together with team directions. Further, a list of roles, their backgrounds, each role's job title and pointers to related literature are also given to prepare them for the role-play. While enacting its role, a sales team makes a sales presentation marketing the ERP system they sell by displaying slides on a virtual video projector in Second life. The purchasing team, representing the buyer company Wingate Electric Inc., asks questions to the sales team and records scores against selection criteria on their scorecard. Upon completion of all the sales teams' presentations, Wingate, the purchasing team, summarise scores to support their decision on a winning ERP vendor. While announcing the winner, the purchasing team provides feedback to each of the sales team as to how effective the sales team's presentation had addressed the stipulated selection criteria.

The Role Case at the Operational Level

During role-play at the operational level, each student acts as a supply chain manager in a company that is part of a global supply chain with four companies. The manager being responsible for both export and import operations, executes all transactions in this role-play. Each student uses the SAP ERP system of their company to execute their internal order cycles, while exchanging the external export and import messages with their trading partners using e-mail. The messages exchanged with the customer and the vendor are shown in Fig. 11.1 for one of the companies, the Dallas Bike Company, Dallas BC assumed to be in USA.

Each student operates one instance of a company in the global supply chain. The other companies have the same structure and the same type of messages exchanged. Some of the details needed to conduct the role include pricing information, product information in terms of product identifier and demand information in terms of quantity as shown in Fig. 11.1. Students must handle the export/import information required by fetching master data from the ERP system and entering transaction data

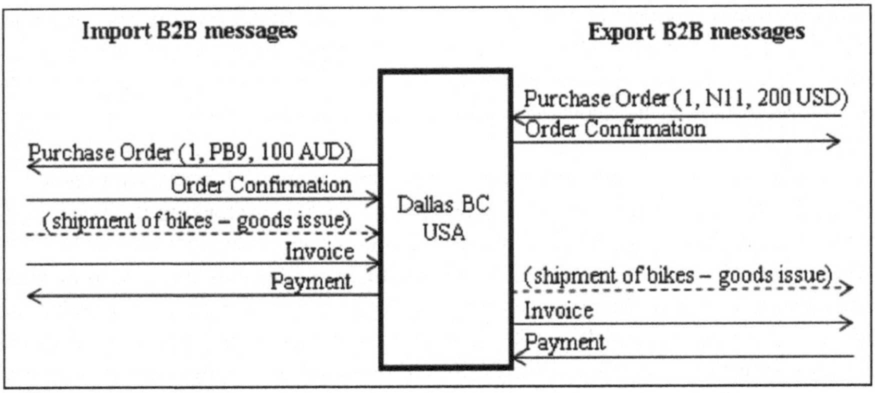

Fig. 11.1 Export and import messages exchanged in Business-to-Business (B2B). Purchase order parameters are quantity, product identifier and price

into the ERP system. This includes using the export cockpit wizard to help the student in ensuring that the information is complete. Thus, uncertainty is removed by using the system to verify that the information required is complete.

Explicit and Tacit Knowledge

Generally, a purchasing manager makes his decisions based on past data and experience, i.e. using both explicit and implicit/tacit knowledge. Giunipero, Dawley and Anthony (1999) found that executives, while making purchase decisions, used roughly equal extents of historical data and tacit knowledge. Knowledge that relates to individual experiences is termed tacit. Further, it represents knowledge that is used in decisions, evaluation and commitments, while expressing one's opinions or points of view. Codifying implicit knowledge is challenging as it is difficult to articulate. According to Von et al. (2000), a face-to-face communication and interaction is possibly the only powerful and effective means for transferring tacit knowledge. Typically, in a face-to-face situation, body language and gestures are used to exhibit emotional reactions.

Over the last decade or so, well after the monumental works of Von et al. (2000), we have witnessed the emergence of Second Life and other virtual-world environments. Second Life supports a combination of a real and a virtual presence of users. While voice communication allows us real presence, rudimentary gestures of an avatar can simulate some body language including lip synchronisation. At the moment, these gestures are fairly limited. However, the presence of avatars permits virtual face-to-face interaction combined with voice—thus, allowing us sharing of ideas and knowledge. Introducing a team-oriented role-play in Second Life allows the students to meet in a common virtual place for sharing and expressing opinions and ideas. Undertaken on a regular basis, interacting, meeting and participating can enable the participant to gain tacit knowledge. Providing regular feedback also leads to effective transfer of tacit knowledge in a virtual-world environment. Moreover, for training students, using a simulated or virtual business environment in Second Life can help preparing them for real business situations. For reviewing students' performances during the sessions in Second Life, one can easily record all the activities by using a screen and sound capturing software and analyse the activities afterwards one by one or in a group setting.

Compared to tacit knowledge, explicit knowledge is knowledge that has been codified (Kumari 2001). A purchase manager, in order to make a good decision, needs a lot of explicit knowledge. Vendor websites, online library resources, marketing and trade publications are the sources of such knowledge. Besides such explicit knowledge sources, a purchaser, in order to close a business deal, may also need tacit knowledge. Inexperienced purchase managers and students characteristically break societal norms and are likely to miss subtle cues, which experienced buyers take for granted. In order to make them aware of such subtleties, as teachers, we would like to introduce our students to the importance of tacit knowledge in both selling and making buying decisions. Role-playing has been found to be a useful method in imparting people-facing skills including training purchasing and sales people.

Role-Playing in Second Life

Second Life is claimed to be suited for role-playing in a virtual environment (Linden Labs 2014). The primary object for communication and interaction among users of Second Life is via avatars.[1] An avatar represents a user. Second Life users are dispersed all over its virtual-world, and real-time interaction among its avatars is facilitated through voice chatting, text and even using embedded video tools. Avatars are mobile, and Second Life allows them to walk or fly to explore different virtual-worlds enabling them to communicate, participate and collaborate in various activities. Human characteristics, including facial expressions and very importantly speech, allow an avatar to transfer expressions in the affective domain. Additionally, in a virtual-world environment, users are also able to trade and exchange services. Thus, we found Second Life to be a suitable medium appropriate for conducting virtual role-plays. Other communication technologies, such as video conferencing, do not support meeting at a common venue and interact as participants are situated in different geographic locations. Moreover, such environments inhibit performing negotiations, making team presentations and coordination of

[1]1. Hinduism—a manifestation of a deity on earth; Sanskrit—*ava* = down, below and *tara* = tread (Apte 1969);
2. An icon or figure representing a particular person in a computer game (Oxford Dictionary, 2014).

various group activities. In contrast, virtual-worlds allow creation of common virtual meeting places. One is able to create lifelike environments that are familiar to participating team members, enabling them to group together just as they would in the real world. A range of communication facilities, such as group and private conversations, are at their disposal to if needed. The key features of merging 3D world, Community, Creation and Commerce (3D3C) in a virtual-world environment, which resemble the real-life environment, allow education providers to use the virtual-world environment as a role-play (Sivan 2008).

Cost-Efficient Implementation

Compared with real-life environments, Second Life has the capability of building a varied range of learning environments that is extremely cost effective. A real-life role-play would be significantly more expensive due to the overheads of allocating or renting professional meeting rooms, co-locating participants, changing the appearance of the participants into a business style and arranging recording capabilities. Further, for virtual-world settings, another promising opportunity is the prospect of inviting leaders and guest experts from businesses and other organisations at no cost. Professionals, being experts in their field, can participate in role-plays that make it possible for students to interact directly with these business experts. Some of the studies that have reported participation of virtual guest professionals in mediated teaching settings found that students were motivated by the prospect of holding discussions with the guest experts, and vice versa—the guest's professionals were keen to spend time sharing their knowledge and expertise with young minds (Wearmouth et al. 2004; Kumari 2001).

During the preparation stage of the role-play, professionals in four Norwegian companies were asked to participate and all four agreed to join as guest experts at no cost. These business professionals were from four companies—DnB NOR, Ernst and Young, Wise Consulting and The Norwegian Labour and Welfare Administration (NAV). They were all experts in using ERP systems with vast experience in procuring and marketing complex software systems. The professionals were enthusiastic in using, for the first time, a virtual-world software to have direct interactions with the students. Apart from their corporate social duty, they also sensed a prospect of recruiting future incumbents. It also allowed them to test new innovative business opportunities and experiment with the use of Second Life as a tool for collaborative team work.

Framework Used

We follow an iterative problem-solving framework for our learning environment. This framework seeks to create innovations using information systems where design is seen as both a process and a product. Adapted from Kolb's Experiential Learning Cycle (Kolb 1984), the learning environment is our design product and

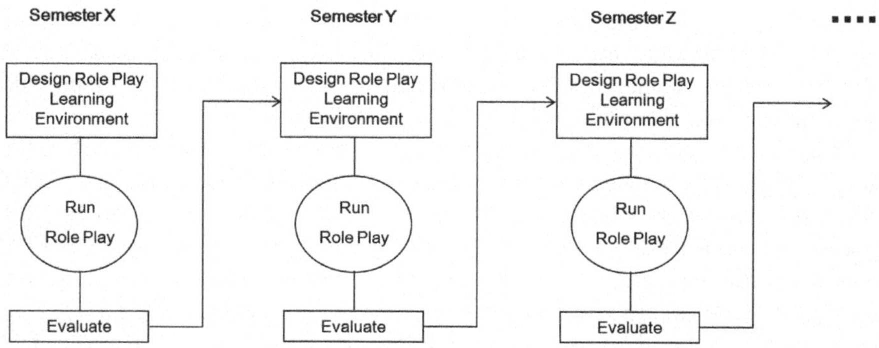

Fig. 11.2 Framework for development of the learning environment over several semesters

our design process and consists of the activities—design, run and evaluate as illustrated in Fig. 11.2.

The last step of evaluation provides feedback and an improved understanding of the learning environment in order to refine both the role-play assignment and the environment. We used a qualitative approach combining three methods. Our first method was a questionnaire with both numbered answer alternatives and open-ended questions. We used the questionnaire to get an impression of student perceptions and their reflections on using Second Life for the role-play. The second method was informal discussions with students and teachers at both campuses to get their perceptions and experiences. The third method was the use of playback of recorded sessions in Second Life to support feedback. Second Life, being a mediated technology via a computer, inherits the intrinsic property of mediated technologies that they can be recorded, stored and played back with little effort and cost. Second Life does not provide effective recording options; however, one can use screen-recording programs that record all activities including sound into a movie file. Popular recording tools are Camtasia (2010) and Fraps (2010). These tools enable a post-exercise reflection of the virtual-experience and a debriefing of the experiences, which is important for the learning outcome (de Freitas 2006). Further, the recording tools provide a valuable feedback not only to the teachers but also to the learning environment designers.

The design-run-evaluate sequence in Fig. 11.2 is repeated over several semesters. It goes on as long as the role-playing takes place to incorporate technological innovations and lessons learned from each previous semester. In this chapter, we report on our experiences from the semester February–April 2010, where we included international collaboration.

The Management Role-Play Experiment

Role-plays are an effective pedagogic strategy frequently used in information systems and business classes for addressing complex problem-solving issues. Since the publication of the role-play exercises (Sumner 2005, pp. 52–53), the author of the text, Mary Sumner had conducted a similar role-play on three occasions at Molde University College in 2005, 2006 and 2007. In this section, we provide details of how our role-play exercise was carried out.

Prior to a role-play session, the instructor must determine a play story. The play story is a meeting among business executives in the purchasing firm and senior sales executives from Microsoft, SAP and SAP ByDesign/Oracle. Normally, this type of meeting is held in a high-end executive meeting room since buying an ERP system is often the single largest investment a company undertakes with a time horizon of ten to twenty years. Figure 11.3 shows an executive meeting room that we created in Second Life to make the role-play look and feel more realistic. The Second Life environment is in many ways so different from real life that it is useful to spend some time in the field in order to ask the relevant questions. Based on traditional ethnological methods, Hine (2000) created selected research principles on data-mediated environments. She called these principles *virtual ethnography*, with one part referring to the data-mediated interaction with the informants and the other referring to the ethnographer's own interaction with the media she was researching. By being present with our own avatar in the observation, we gather first-hand knowledge about the field and a greater understanding of the experience of being there (Boellstroff et al. 2012). On the other hand, we sacrifice objectivity.

As we adhere to the realistic nature of the role-play exercise, the students were asked to familiarise themselves with the business etiquettes and code of conduct required in business dealings and negotiations. This included requiring avatars to have a formal dress code in a typical executive style aligned with the real-world environment. The students were provided with suitable business wardrobes to select from. Avatar appearance is one cue from the real world that can be mimicked in the virtual-world. We assume that the first impression largely defines "who" an avatar is—the three-second first-impression—just like in the real world (Lavington and Losee 1998). Figure 11.3 shows some examples of professionally dressed avatars.

Fig. 11.3 Avatars in business attire; negotiations in virtual mode

Fig. 11.4 A typical sales team (SAP) presentation in progress

The students were given a choice of enacting the role-play either in Second Life or participate in classroom-based face-to-face role-play. We had students from one class in Perth, Australia, and one class in Molde, Norway, participate in the same role-play forming true virtual teams. The virtual team role-play got more realistic as the students in Australia and Norway did not know each other beforehand. In total, 28 students participated—22 students in Molde and 6 students in Perth volunteered for the virtual team role-play. The students in Perth formed two sales teams, while the rest of the teams were from Molde. Figure 11.4 shows a presentation by a SAP Business ByDesign sales team in a Second Life presentation. Just as in real life, a virtual team is able to present slides in Second Life in a virtual-world environment. Further, when someone wants to communicate without disturbing an ongoing presentation, Second Life supports private voice and/or chat. This is a very useful feature, particularly for teachers from Australia and Norway, who observed the role-play sessions via their avatars. This enabled the coordination of activities without being intrusive—something that is not possible in real-life presentations and with other technologies such as video conferencing.

Evaluation of Feedback from the Management Role-Play Experiment

The method used for evaluating the participants' impressions was a combination of informal discussions with teachers and students and a questionnaire together with feedback from recordings of the sessions. A 7-point Likert scale was used for the numbered answer alternatives. The students were also given an opportunity to provide as many comments as they desired. All six in Perth and eighteen of the 22 students in Molde answered the questionnaire providing a total of 24 respondents. The questions with numbered alternatives for the answers, the scoring scales and the average scores from the results of responses from the students are shown in Table 11.1.

As Table 11.1 shows, the average scores from both Molde and Perth students are almost identical; hence, we deliberate on their combined scores (the last row in Table 11.1). Question A received a score of 5.1 indicating that the students considered the role-play as useful and that it could be used by real businesses. Question B received 4.4 indicating that the students perceived that they got a feeling of presence/got a good feeling of presence. For question C, the students considered the amount of work required for the role-play in Second Life as about the same or less than performing the role-play in real life. We conclude that the students show a positive attitude towards using Second Life for a virtual team

Table 11.1 Questions, with numbered alternatives 1–7 and the average scores of students' responses for each country and the average of both countries combined

Question	A. My general impression of using Second Life for doing a Virtual Team Role-play is that it's ___	B. When doing the role-play, I experienced a feeling of presence with the other participants __	C. As compared to traditional (face-to-face) projects on campus the workload in preparing for the role-play in Second Life required __
Scale	1.Totally useless	1. Not at all	1. Quite a lot more work
	2. Useless	2. Only to a very small extent	2. Much more work
	3. Mostly useless	3. Somewhat	3. More work
	4. Useful	4. Yes, I got a feeling of presence with the others	4. About the same amount of work
	5. Useful, this can be used by real businesses	5. I got a good feeling of presence.	
	6. Very useful	6. It was almost like in real life	6. Much less work
	7. An indispensable tool	7. Just like real life	7. Quite a lot less work
Molde	4.9	4.4	4.5
Perth	5.2	4.3	5.2
Combined	5.1	4.4	4.8

role-play. This is especially so when we consider the minimal exposure and training in Second Life (approximately, a total of one hour) before the role-play.

As we had encouraged students to provide comments about their learning experience, some students did so. These additional comments were on the open-ended questions, and the positive remarks were as follows:

- It was quite a new experience.
- It was efficient and real-time business decision-making.
- I learnt something useful this way. My attitude towards Second Life is quite positive.
- It [Second Life] has many advantages and provides a good feeling of presence, as it is 3D.
- Gives a feeling of presence and of real life. A very good experience.
- No stage fright to worry about. So easier to time presentation precisely.
- I did not have any faith in it when we made our avatar but was impressed when we did our presentation.
- Feeling of distance was less than expected.

It is apparent that students who were not confident speaking in public (due to lack of fluency being from a non-native English speaker) preferred the use of the virtual-world environment. However, few remarks were guarded, bordering on caution:

- Do the participants need a new round of clarification, explanations regarding the contents of the meeting?
- I would get best training for this type of assignment.
- I think a requirement for it [Second Life] to work in practice is that the participants have established a relation before its use.
- This means the participants have met each other and created a minimum level of confidence.
- It also depends on what will be at stake. That is, what significance such a "meeting" will have. What consequences will consensus have for the remaining part of the process?
- Will there be any form of doubt?

While most of the students were quite enthusiastic, there were a few who reported issues and concerns. Mainly, these were not being able to see the other participants' face and expressions. Technical issues were also a major concern and came in the way of the meetings.

- You don't have the feeling of seeing the person and his/her facial expressions.
- Need better Internet connection. Sometime it does not work because of the distance. (It was noticed that possibly due to Second Life server locations there were disruptions in communication between countries. For example, in one instance, the Perth students were able to communicate among themselves and could listen to their counterparts in Molde, the vice versa was not true; that is, the Molde students could not hear their Perth collaborators.)

- Bad sound and fast talking presenters—I had problems to get everything that was said.

Some casual observations from instructors were that, in general, in comparison with female students, younger male students preferred to use the technology. As a result, they were learners much keener to explore various facilities offered by the environment. Whereas, more matured ones tended to be less at ease with the technology.

Mediated Environments Supporting Decision-Making

Since written contracts and documents of a business organisation do not remove all uncertainties, one of the reasons for a business meeting is to help decision-making by eliciting more information from the other party. In this context, uncertainty, according to Galbraith (1973, p. 5), is "The difference between the amount of information required to perform the task and the amount of information already possessed by the organisation". Since Galbraith's model (1973) relating structural design to information processing requirements was proposed, it has been accepted that to reduce uncertainty organisations process information. Still another connected concept is equivocality, which is defined as the ambiguity inherent in the task caused by conflicting and inconsistent interpretations and expectations (Daft et al. 1987). However, having more information cannot always eliminate the inherent equivocality of a negotiation.

These are some of the reasons why knowledge management issues have been in the forefront lately. Knowledge is necessary for making right decisions at the company level and for aligning the decisions with higher system levels like supply chains in our case. We denote the factors contributing to human knowledge creation as soft inputs to the decision-making process, while data and information processed by computer-based information systems entail hard inputs. Humans can handle both soft and hard inputs, while machines can handle hard inputs only. The necessity of a soft and hard input combination is underlined by study (Giunipero et al. 1999), which reveals, that purchasing managers utilise approximately the same amount of hard inputs in the form of data and information processed by computer technologies, as the soft ones in the form of managers' tacit knowledge in decision-making. Galbraith (1973) and Galbraith (1974) provide an information processing model that relates the amount of information available to the uncertainty faced by decision-makers. Galbraith (1973, p. 2) states that "the greater the uncertainty of the task, the greater the amount of information that must be processed between decision-makers during the execution of the task to get a given level of performance". It has become accepted that organisations process information to reduce uncertainty. Organisations can reduce uncertainty through better planning and

Fig. 11.5 Model of information processing requirements (adapted from Galbraith 1973)

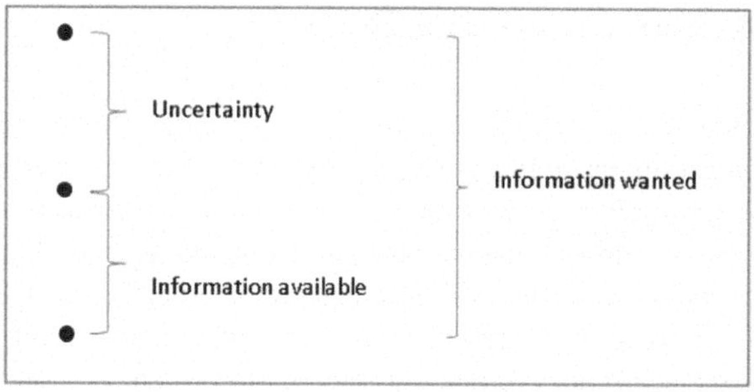

coordination supported by rules, clearer hierarchy, appropriate goals and right information systems. This is illustrated in Fig. 11.5.

However, for some decisions like the ones based on negotiations, increasing the amount of information will only help to some extent to support the decision. Providing more information cannot eliminate the inherent equivocality of a negotiation. The inherent equivocality of a negotiation cannot eliminate more information. Equivocality is defined as the ambiguity inherent in the task caused by conflicting and inconsistent interpretations and expectations and cannot be reduced by getting more information (Daft, Lengel and Trevino 1987). For example, in sourcing, when negotiating the contract with suppliers, the purchaser has to reach a decision. Uncertainties can be reduced by acquiring more information, but the inherent equivocality of negotiations result from a tussle of give and take that cannot be eliminated by getting more information. This is illustrated in Fig. 11.6. Popular tools to handle inherent equivocality are risk management and practices based on gaming theory.

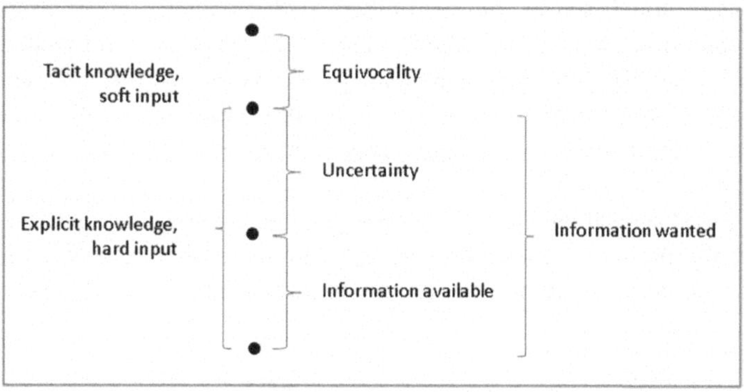

Fig. 11.6 Uncertainty, equivocality and information wanted to make a decision

Avatars, Users and Roles

One of the key elements for creating a sense of presence and simultaneity in a social environment is the use of avatars. We define *avatar* in this context as: *an artefact representing the user on the screen, making the user visible both to the user and to others.* Through the avatar, a user can move around in the virtual environment and, at the same time, communicate with others connected to the same environment. Users communicate via voice, text and avatar behaviour. This behaviour visualises aspects of non-verbal communication such as nodding, head shaking, showing someone something by pointing at it and demonstrating how something can be done. When logging into the virtual-world, the avatar situates the user in a shared 3D visual environment, such as a classroom or meeting situation. The visual environment forms a social context, which can be more or less pronounced by avatar appearance, for example, by age, gender or dress code as applicable to the role of a student, a teacher or other roles.

Mediating communication using avatars raises challenging research and design issues, such as how avatars affect student–teacher, student–student and teacher–teacher communication. Since our focus is on the communication aspects, we first develop a simple model introducing the role aspect in three steps. First, in face-to-face situations, mediation is through the air without using any electronic devices (Fig. 11.7).

Figure 11.7 illustrates user-to-user communication with no mediation technology. This can also be said to be the goal of the "looking though" the mediation category. However, introducing an avatar as a self-representation of each user creates an indirection level as illustrated in Fig. 8.

Figure 11.8 illustrates the user-to-user communication where the mediation technology is controlling the communication. Here, users are "looking at" the technology, which is typical of 3D virtual-worlds and allows an enhanced virtual reality. It utilises our senses as well as our ways of expression. Sight, hearing and, to some extent, touch senses, but also others such as smell, can be used. Typical ways of expression are oral, text, body language, appearance and technologies to emit gas (for smell). Introducing avatars in 3D virtual-worlds creates an extra indirection level since both users in Fig. 11.8 adopt different positions or *roles* as represented by their respective avatars. This extra level of indirection is illustrated in Fig. 11.9.

A user's avatar portrays the user in some way, either in a role that is as close as possible to the particular user's true identity, or in another selected role. A user selects expressions to communicate, providing information from which receiver can

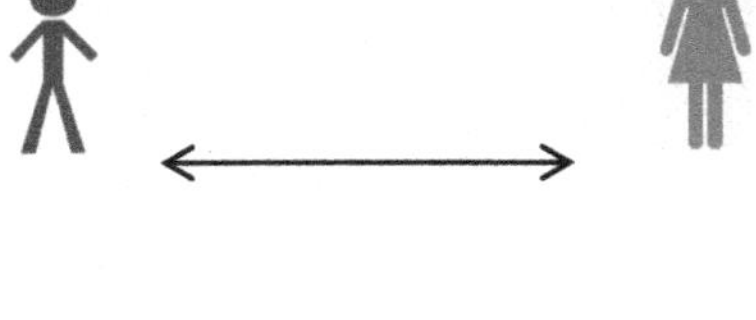

Fig. 11.7 User-to-user communication in a face-to-face situation

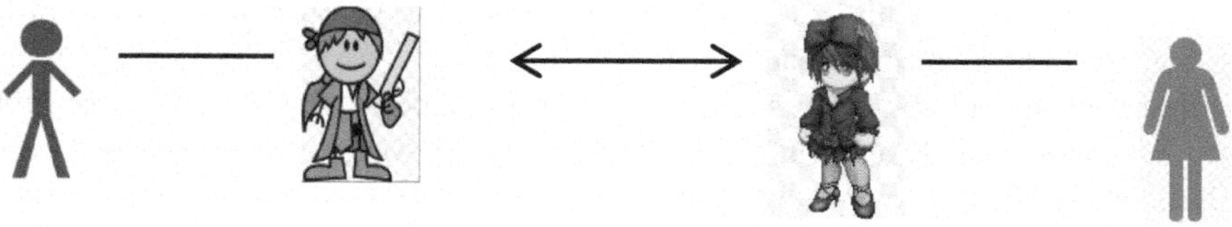

Fig. 11.8 User-to-user communication via avatars

User – Role – Avatar —— Avatar – Role – User

Fig. 11.9 User-to-user communication via avatars assuming different roles

infer the content of the communication. The interpretation by one or more receivers leads to role expectations. To see oneself represented as an avatar gives the person a third-person perspective on what one is doing, and a visualisation of one's own participation. Thus, acting through an avatar allows the user to take different roles when communicating with others. We look specifically at user roles in business decision-making.

How does using an avatar affect roles and role expectations in a distributed decision-making context?

Findings are presented and discussed under the following themes:

(a) Choosing an avatar reflecting the user's role
(b) Situating the user in an environment by applying an avatar

The four instructors interviewed will be referred to as Messing, Solo, Molo and Krokus, while the two students in the sample are referred to as Lemming and Cotton. The names differ from the actual avatar names to make the actors anonymous.

(a) Choosing an avatar reflecting the user's role

The avatar is in itself a primary artefact for communication, representing the self as it relates to the avatar's appearance, its place in the virtual environment and its behaviour. The informants agreed that 3D environment self-representation is of great importance for how you are perceived by others and contributes to setting others' expectations. Everyone has a relationship to their avatar; that is, how it should be and what they wish to communicate through it, as illustrated by one actor's expression: "I want the avatar to represent me in the best way possible". Common among all actors was that they modified their avatars as soon as they got them by, for example, buying new clothes, changing the hair or body shape. However, after the initial creation, they did not change them to any great extent: "I have deliberately not done anything to my avatar. I bought clothes once". The actors have different needs regarding their avatars, though one common feature is that they wish to be authentic in representing themselves, unless they participate in a role-play. This was expressed most strongly by Solo, "I don't want to represent myself through my avatar as something I am not (…). I don't want to be especially,

I don't know, fancy, with lots of muscles, I just want to be ordinary; I just want to be me. Nothing more than that".

Despite Linden Labs' slogan "Be who you want to be", it seems that it is not that easy for users to create an avatar that reflects how they see themselves (Linden Labs 2014). Many actors mention this, and tied it first and foremost to age, ethnicity and physical appearance. Cotton had problems creating an avatar the same age as her: "At first I felt like creating one that looked like it was around 40 years old, since I am (…), but that was impossible, at least for me".

Lemming was unsure whether her avatar should reflect her real age, as she did not want to stand out: "then I thought that maybe there weren't that many women my age (54 years) who look like that, so I thought that maybe it was better to choose one that looked younger".

Since Messing uses his avatar in many different situations, he would like it to reflect his role, with the result that he has spent a lot of time modifying it. He mentions having difficulties finding what he needs: "But it has been hard finding Afro-American skin and hair—even grey hair". Messing also says that there is little ethnic diversity in the Second Life environment: "unfortunately, in this virtual environment there is a kind of *vanilla look* to the way people look".

Solo also reflects over this: "Why does someone who's Afro-American create a white avatar?" The ideal for how one should look in the physical world is reflected in Second Life: "It looks like a … younger and … fitter version of me". They all relate the avatar to themselves and the way they look, as expressed by Solo: "Someone I know, when she saw me for the first time face-to-face, she said: 'You are the first person I have met who actually looks better in real life than your avatar'".

Technological limitations are also used as an explanation as to why it can be difficult to create an accurate avatar. To change, the avatar takes time and knowledge. To the actors in the sample, the purpose of the avatar is to communicate and not to experiment with appearance. All the same, it is clear that they all have a relationship with their avatar.

(b) Situating the user in an environment by applying an avatar

The avatar helps participants navigate and organise themselves in the virtual environment. Even when the avatar is passive, it represents a presence that communicates participation to others. For instructors, offering distance learning in social environments where they can meet students is their most important motivation. One of the project's aims was to create a place designed for the experience of being in a group in a commonplace, "The only person who is really here is Christian. The others are spread out over different cities in the world. And we have the ability to meet as if we were sitting looking out the window in Molde". Christian, the real name of another actor also in Second Life using a PC, located in a separate room on the same campus.

Here, teachers use Second Life to meet with students as if they were sitting around the same table. Both parties are assuming the behaviour, identity and mannerisms of their own identity as a teacher or student as illustrated in Fig. 11.10 by stating the roles. Examples of different aspects of this are provided next.

Student – StudentRole – StudentAvatar — TeacherAvatar – TeacherRole – Teacher

Fig. 11.10 Student-to-teacher communication via avatars

Cotton speaks of a *presence* depending on what she does in the virtual environment: "When I was to present something, it was almost as if I was there, I was all in a tangle!" In activities where she is the focus, the sense of being present in the virtual environment increases: "I was just as nervous as if I would have been standing there alone in front of a group of people". This might indicate that the environment in itself was not the only ground for experiencing social presence—the activity and the motivation for being there was also crucial. She is absorbed by what she is doing when the experience of personal relevance and possibility for interaction is heightened. It is hard to say what it is about the environment that creates the strongest experience of *co-presence*. The actors refer to it in both visual ("when I see you sitting here and I see myself around you...") and aural ("...and hear your questions...") terms ("...it's like we are sitting around the same table"). Being able to speak is central to the social presence experience (Warburton 2009). Solo expresses this as he talks about communicating in Second Life: "it is almost impossible not to react to each other as if we were sitting around the same table in the physical world". The sounds are spatial and can also make the experience more realistic. A statement such as this illustrates the feeling of co-presence: "it's a meeting place *where you can actually meet*". Molo says that using avatars makes the communication visible and the distributed meeting experience more personal. This allows for presence and involvement in the meeting.

Many actors consider the *interface functionality* when they describe their experience of presence. Lemming refers to the screen: "when I look at the screen, it becomes very alive, as if I was sitting with you here now"; or the image: "when I sit here looking at the image, it's as if I was in Molde, it feels like I'm sitting here". Molo refers to the camera: "when I look around with the camera from my position and see you sitting there, it's like we share this space". He also points to the interface information regarding who is logged in at any given time as a form of presence: "Every time I'm here, at least one or more of my students are logged in". Hence, he experiences a common presence with others who are logged in, even if they are in a totally different place in Second Life.

The informants do not express that technology has a prominent role in the social presence experience. Lombard and Ditton (1997, p. 1) call this "an illusion that a mediated experience is not mediated". Even if the informants express *co-presence,* they also sometimes refer to the real world. For example, Cotton relates the real-world situation to what she sees in Second Life: "What I see are not your real movements, it's not the way you sit, and I don't sit like that either, and I'm not wearing those clothes, so to me it's a bit artificial, really". Here, the lack of scenic realism reduces the presence experience.

Conclusion

We have presented a study of the suitability of virtual-worlds for business decision-making over distance involving the exchange of tacit knowledge to support decisions at the tactical and strategic management layers. A model of the role concept in user-to-user communication framed the importance of the avatar as the primary interaction object. Our case studies presented how the user's role affected the selection of an avatar, and how the avatar situates the user in a business environment. The avatar was found to fulfil the role of the communicator and to support the role expectations from real-life situations. We conclude that the unique properties of virtual-worlds support tacit information exchange for decision-making in a distributed business environment supporting organisations in adapting to an increasingly global and distributed business environment.

References

Aldrich, C. (2005). *Learning by doing*. San Francisco, CA, USA: Pfeiffer.

Anderson, T. (2004). Toward a theory of online learning. In T. Anderson & F. Elloumi (Eds.), *Theory and practice of online learning*. Athabasca, Canada: Athabasca University Press. Retrieved from http://cde.athabascau.ca/online_book/ch2.html.

Angelino, L. M., Williams, F. K., & Natvig, D. (2007). Strategies to engage online students and reduce attrition rates. *The Journal of Educators Online, 4*(2), 1–14. Retrieved from www.thejeo.com/Volume4Number2/Angelino%20Final.pdf.

Apte, V. S. (1969). *Sanskrit-Hindi Shabdakosh*. Delhi, India: Motilal Banarasi Das.

Astin, A. W. (1985). Involvement: The cornerstone of excellence. *Change, 17*(4), 35–39.

Bateson, G. (2005). *Mentale systemers økolologi: skridt i en udvikling / Gregory Bateson; in Danish language*. København: Akademisk Forlag.

Bayne, S. (2008). Uncanny spaces for higher education: Teaching and learning in virtual worlds. *Association for Learning Technology Journal, 36*(3) 197–205. Retrieved from www.informaworld.com/smpp/title ~ db=all ~ content=g906960349 ~ tab=toc.

Bloom, B. S. (1956). *The taxonomy of educational objectives: Classification of educational goals handbook 1: The cognitive domain*. New York: McKay Press.

Boellstroff, T., Nardi, B., Pearce, C., & Taylor, T. L. (2012). *Ethnography and virtual worlds—A handbook of method*. Princeton, NJ, USA: Princeton University Press.

Bolter, J. D., & Grusin, R. (1999). *Remediation: Understanding new media.* Cambridge, MA: The MIT Press, 295 pp.

Camtasia. (2010). Retrieved from www.softwarecasa.com/.

Carey, J. (2007). Expressive communication and social conventions in virtual worlds. *The DATA BASE for Advances in Information Systems, 38*(4), 81–85. Retrieved from portal.acm.org/citation.cfm?id = 1314249.

Clow, D. (2012). The learning analytics cycle: closing the loop effectively. In S. Buckingham Shum, D. Gasevic, & R. Ferguson (Eds.), *Proceedings of the 2nd International Conference on Learning Analytics and Knowledge* (LAK '12), ACM, New York, NY, USA, pp 134–138.

Daft, R. L., Lengel, R. H., & Trevino, L. K. (1987). Message equivocality, media selection, and manager performance: Implications for information systems. *MIS Quarterly*, 355-366.

Datar, S. M., Garvin, D. A., & Cullen, P. G. (2010). *Rethinking the MBA: Business education at a crossroads*. Boston, MA: Harvard Business Press.

de Freitas, S. (2006) Learning in Immersive worlds. *Joint Information Systems Committee (JISC) e-Learning Programme*, UK higher education, further education and skills sectors' not-for-profit organisation for digital services and solutions. Retrieved from http://www.jisc.ac.uk/media/documents/programmes/elearninginnovation/gamingreport_v3.pdf.

Dickey, M. (2005). 3D virtual worlds and distance learning: Two case studies of Active Worlds as a medium for distance education. *British Journal of Educational Technology, 36*(3), 439–451. Retrieved from www3.interscience.wiley.com/journal/118683361/abstract.

Dreyfus, H. (2009). *On the internet*. Abingdon, UK: Routledge.

Fraps. (2010). Retrieved from www.fraps.com.

Edirisingha, P. Nie, M., Pluciennik, M., & Young, R. (2009). Socialisation for learning at a distance in a 3-D multi-user virtual environment. *British Journal of Educational Technology. 40*(3), 458–479. Retrieved from www3.interscience.wiley.com/journal/122324744/abstract?CRETRY=1&SRETRY=0.

Galbraith, J. (1973). *Designing complex organizations*. USA: Addison-Wesley Publishing Company.

Galbraith, J. R. (1974). Organization design: An information processing view. *Interfaces, 4*(3), 28–36.

Galbraith, J. R. (2012). The future of organization design. *Journal of Design, 1*(1), 3–6.

Garcia, A. C., Alecea, I. S., Bechkoff, J., & Cui, Y. (2009). Ethnographic approaches to the Internet and computer-mediated communication. *Journal of Contemporary Ethnography, 38* (1), 52–84. Retrieved from jce.sagepub.com/cgi/content/abstract/38/1/52.

Giunipero, L., Dawley, D., & Anthony, W. P. (1999). The impact of tacit knowledge on purchasing decisions. *The Journal of Supply Chain Management, 35*(1), 42–49.

Good, J. Howland, K., & Thackray, L. (2008). Problem-based learning spanning real and virtual words: A case study in Second Life. *Association for Learning Technology Journal, 36*(3), 163–172. Retrieved from http://www.informaworld.com/smpp/title ~ db=all ~ content=g906960349 ~ tab=toc.

Herold, D. (2009). Teaching media studies in second life. *Journal of Virtual Worlds Research, 2* (2), 1–17.

Hine, C. M. (2000). *Virtual ethnography*. London, Great Britain: Sage.

Hirschheim, R. (2005). The Internet-based education bandwagon: Look before you leap. *Communications of the ACM, 48*(7), 97–101. Retrieved from http://portal.acm.org/citation.cfm?id=1070844.

Holmberg, K., & Huvila, I. (2008). Learning together apart: Distance education in a virtual world. *First Monday, 13*(10). Retrieved from www.uic.edu/htbin/cgiwrap/bin/ojs/index.php/fm/article/viewArticle/2178/2033.

Jæger, B., Rudra, A., Aitken, A. M., Chang, V. S., & Helgheim, B. (2011). Teaching business process management in cross-country collaborative teams using ERP. In *ECIS2011—ICT and Sustainable Services Development*, Helsinki: Finland.

Jæger, B., Rudra, A., Aitken, A. M., Chang, V. S., & Helgheim, B. (2015). Bridging the knowing-doing gap in global supply chain education. *Communications of the Association for Information Systems, 36*(1), 21.

Jones, S. (2007). Adding value to online role-plays: Virtual situated learning environments, In: R. Atkinson, C. McBeath, A. S. S. Kit & C. Cheers. (Eds), *The 24th Annual Conference of the Australasian Society for Computers in Learning in Tertiary Education "ICT: Providing Choices for Learners and Learning*". 2–5 December, Singapore 2007.

Kolb, D. A. (1984). *Experiential Learning: Experience as the source of learning and development*. Upper Saddle River, NJ, USA: Prentice Hall.

Kreijns, K. (2004). Sociable CSCL environments: Social affordances, sociability, and social presence. *PhD Thesis,* Open University of the Netherlands, Nederland. Retrieved from https://www.ou.nl/documents/Promoties-en-oraties/Promoties/Promoties2004/Dissertation_Karel_Kreijns_040510.pdf.

Kumari, D. S. (2001). Connecting graduate students to virtual guests through asynchronous discussions—Analysis of an experience. *Journal of Asynchronous Learning Networks, 5*(2), 53–63.

Lavington, C., & Losee, S. (1998). *You've only got three seconds: How to make the right impression in business and social life*. New York, USA: Broadway Books.

Linden Labs. (2014). Second Life—What is Second Life? Linden Lab, San Francisco, USA. Retrieved from http://secondlife.com/whatis.

Lombard, M. & Ditton, T. (1997). At the heart of it all: The concept of presence. *Journal of Computer Mediated Communication, 3*(2). Retrieved from jcmc.indiana.edu/vol3/issue2/lombard.html.

Ludvigsen, K. (2009). Nærvær på avstand. Et utforskende kvalitativt studie av tredimensjonale virtuelle læremiljøer som støtte for fjernundervisning. *Masteroppgave i pedagogikk høsten 2009, Det Psykologiske Fakultet, Universitetet i Bergen*. Retrieved from master.anorakk.net/.

Ludvigsen, K. (2011). L3D—Læring, kommunikasjon og brobygging i en tredimensjonal verden på Internett (in Norwegian). *L3D-SecondLife Project Report*, University of Oslo. Retrieved from http://www.uv.uio.no/intermedia/english/research/projects/l3d/documents/Review-SecondLife-v2.pdf.

McKee, H., & Porter, J. (2009). Playing a good game: Ethical issues in researching MMOGs and virtual worlds. *International Journal of Internet Research Ethics 2*(1) 1–37. Retrieved from ijire.net/issue_2.1/mckee.pdf.

Molka-Danielsen, J., Carter, B., Richardson, D., & Jæger, B. (2009). Teaching and learning effectively within a virtual campus. *International Journal of Networking and Virtual Organisations, special issue Toward Virtual Universities, 5*(6), 476–498.

Muilenburg, L. Y., & Berge, Z. L. (2005). Student barriers to online learning: A factor analytic study. *Distance Education, 26*(1), 29–48.

Oxford Dictionary. (2014). Retrieved from http://www.oxforddictionaries.com/definition/english/avatar.

Pappano, L. (2012) The Year of the MOOC, *New York Times*. Retrieved from www.nytimes.com/2012/11/04/education/edlife/massive-open-online-courses-are-multiplying-at-a-rapid-pace.html?ref=edlife

Prasolova-Førland, E. (2008). Analyzing place metaphors in 3D educational collaborative virtual environments. *Computers in Human Behavior, 24*(2), 185–204.

Ratcliffe, R. (2012). Top UK universities launch free online courses. *The Guardian*. Retrieved from www.guardian.co.uk/education/2012/dec/14/top-uk-universities-launch-free-online-courses?INTCMP=SRCH.

Roberts, D., Wolff, R. & Otto., O. (2006). The impact of display system and embodiment on closely coupled collaboration between remote users. In: R. Schroeder, & A-S. Axelsson. (Eds), *Avatars at work and play—Collaboration and interaction in shared virtual environments*. Springer, Dordrecht, The Netherlands, pp. 131–150.

Rudra, A., Jæger, B., Aitken, A., Chang, V. & Helgheim, B. (2011). Virtual team role-play using Second Life for teaching business process concepts. In *Proceedings of the 2011 44th Hawaii International Conference on System Sciences (HICSS '11). IEEE Computer Society*, Washington, DC, USA.

Sivan, Y. (2008). 3D3C real virtual worlds defined: The immense potential of merging 3D, community, creation, and commerce. *Journal of Virtual Worlds Research, 1*(1), 1–32.

Sumner, M. (2005). *Enterprise Resource Planning*. New Jersey, USA: Prentice Hall.

Vasileiou, V. N., & Paraskeva, F. (2010). Teaching role-playing instruction in Second Life: An explorative Study. *Journal of Information, Information Technology and Organizations, 5*(1), 25–50.

Von, K. G., Ichijo, K., & Nonaka, I. (2000). *Enabling knowledge creation: How to unlock the mystery of tacit knowledge and release the power of innovation*. Oxford, New York: Oxford University Press.

Vygotsky, L. S. (1978). *Mind in society, the development of higher psychological processes*. Cambridge, MA: Harvard University Press.

Warburton, S. (2009). Second Life in higher education: Assessing the potential for and the barriers to deploying virtual worlds in learning and teaching. *British Journal of Educational Technology, 40*(3), 414–426.

Wartofsky, M. W. (1979). *Models: Representation and the scientific understanding* (Vol. 129). Springer Science & Business Media.

Wearmouth, J., Smith, A. P., & Soler, J. (2004). Computer conferencing with access to a 'guest expert' in the professional development of special educational needs coordinators. *British Journal of Educational Technology, 35*(1), 81–93.

WTO (2013). World trade developments. World Trade Organization (WTO). Retrieved from http://www.wto.org/english/res_e/statis_e/its2013_e/its13_highlights1_e.pdf.

Yin, R. (2003). *Case study research: Design and methods*. Thousand Oaks, CA: Sage.

Zhao, Y., Lei, J., Yan, B., Lai, C., & Tan, H. S. (2005). What makes the difference? A practical analysis of research on the effectiveness of distance education. *Teachers College Record,* 107 (8), 1836–1884. http://www.tcrecord.org/library ID Number: 12098. Retrieved from www.tcrecord.org/library/abstract.asp?contentid=12098.

Author Biographies

Amit Rudra is a Lecturer with the School of Information Systems, Curtin Business School at Curtin University in Perth, Australia. He has a PhD in Computer Science from Curtin University. Amit's research interests and publications are in the areas of ERP in Education, Big Data, Data Warehousing, Data Mining and High Performance Computing. He teaches courses on Enterprise Systems, Designing Database Systems and Data Mining. He also acts as the school liaison person with database and ERP software vendors, Oracle and SAP.

Bjørn Jæger is an Associate Professor with the Department of Economics, Informatics and Social Science at Molde University College, Norway. His M.Sc. is in Nuclear Physics (1989) and PhD in Informatics (2000) from the University of Bergen, Norway. Bjørn teaches courses on Information Assurance, courses on Enterprise Systems and Supply Chain Management using SAP ECC, Microsoft Dynamics NAV and Microsoft Dynamics GP in various assignments. He is the leader of the SCM and IS research group at Molde University College.

Kristine Ludvigsen is a PhD Student at Digital Learning Communities Research Group, Faculty of Psychology, University of Bergen. Her master's degree, completed from the same department in 2009, pertained to conditions offered by virtual-worlds for communication and social interaction in the context of distance education. She works on e-assessment in plenary lectures and in making learning visible through formative assessment and feedback.

Chapter 12
Conclusion

Sue Gregory and Denise Wood

It is now ten years since we witnessed the peak of popularity in the educational use of virtual worlds in higher education and the subsequent decline in interest as educators came to the realisation that much of the hype was based on over-inflated expectations. Yet far from languishing in the "trough of disillusionment", as the authors of this collection show, virtual worlds have now come of age as educators continue to explore the pedagogical affordances of these technologies for engaging students in authentic activities designed to improve their technical and employability skills.

In Chap. 1, "Pedagogy and Learning for Sustainability in a Virtual World Scaffold", Thorne and Macgregor demonstrated how a blended learning approach using the virtual world, a real classroom, and online learning facilitated through a learning management system created an authentic learning environment for learner engagement with sustainability curricula. Drawing on their analysis of students' written, oral and ePortfolio submissions, and evidence gathered through a survey, observations and conversation, the authors concluded that the virtual world assisted students in developing critical thinking and problem-solving skills for real-world sustainability learning. Their findings confirm a high level of learner engagement with the topic, improved student engagement with the subject's learning outcomes, and the development of graduate attributes including information literacy, self-reliance and interpersonal understanding, and proficiency in the use of tools and technologies.

The second chapter, "Intercultural Competence and Virtual Worlds" by Corder and U-Mackey, demonstrated the use of the virtual world to facilitate the

S. Gregory (✉)
University of New England, Armidale, NSW, Australia
e-mail: sue.gregory@une.edu.au

D. Wood
Central Queensland University, Rockhampton, QLD, Australia
e-mail: d.wood@cqu.edu.au

S. Gregory and D. Wood (eds.), *Authentic Virtual World Education*,
https://doi.org/10.1007/978-981-10-6382-4_12

development of students' intercultural competence through authentic learning activities. Corder and U-Mackey's findings drawn from analysis of case studies of student engagement with the virtual world and plotting students' intercultural development using Bennett's (1993) DMIS reported that each student experienced respective shifts in their intercultural competence and developed deeper understanding of their own identities and underlying values and beliefs that influenced their behaviour. However, their findings also suggest that the students varied in the extent to which they applied their understanding to develop strategies and adapt their behaviour, in the virtual world and in real life. They found the virtual world to be unpredictable and fluid in relation to behavioural boundaries, but at the same time a rich and authentic learning environment. Their findings also provide a word of caution that the rich environment does not automatically ensure that students will become competent with their development of intercultural practices. They concluded that there are symbiotic synergies between the affordances of virtual worlds for intercultural competence development and the need to already be interculturally competent for effective engagement and learning to take place. Their findings suggest that students need to be prepared and supported to deal with the technological challenges of the virtual world as well as the emotional and behavioural challenges of virtual cross-cultural interaction.

Jones, Farley and Murphy in Chap. 3 on "Virtual Worlds as Restorative Environments" found that the virtual world could realise the vision of the Australian Government's focus on education to improve health, well-being and economic competitiveness. They explored pre-service teachers and their perceptions of their own personal well-being, sense of belonging, social connectedness, personal creativity and engagement through their experiences in a formal garden setting in the virtual world. The authors analysed students' responses to an online survey comprising eight affective and behavioural measures of attentional fatigue, which provided baseline measures of fatigue for each student. Following 30-min engagement with the virtual restorative environment, students completed a perceived restorativeness scale incorporated into the online survey and were also asked to repeat the attentional fatigue items and open questions about their experiences in the virtual world. Their findings suggest that, providing students are familiar with the virtual environment, it can serve as a restorative environment. However, lack of familiarity with the virtual world led to a negative impact on some students' sense of immersion and the restorativeness of the environment.

Chapter 4, a "Self-guided Exploration of Virtual Learning Spaces", written by Reiners, Wood, Teräs, Teräs, Gregory, Chang, Steurer, McDonald and Fardinpour, explored virtual worlds as a space to create authentic, immersive and high-fidelity experiences for their learners, through the creation of controlled replicas of real life. The experiences they created for their learners enabled the learners to self-pace their learning through a prototype of the nDiVE framework combining authentic learning, gamification, emerging technologies and design principles that are currently being used in the gaming industry to create the spaces for their learners.

The following Chap. 5, written by three of the same authors, Fardinpour, Reiners and Wood, "Action-based Learning Assessment in Virtual Training Environments", continued to explore authentic learning in a virtual world through an Action-based Learning Assessment Method using automated formative assessment. The authors compared recorded actions of a learner in a virtual world with recorded actions by experts. Action-sequences of learners were generated to provide formative feedback to improve learner performance. Their preliminary analysis of experiments showed the validity as well as enhanced opportunity to describe and evaluate training sessions in virtual training environments.

In Chap. 6, “Engagement in Second Life: Language Anxiety and Motivation”, the authors, Grant, Huang and Pasfield-Neofitou, described their use of a virtual world to provide an authentic virtual study abroad program for language learners. The authors found that their students experienced less foreign language anxiety once they had undertaken the virtual world experiences as opposed to their counterparts, who only experienced their learning in a face-to-face classroom. They found that the students’ perceptions of the authenticity of their learning environment contributed to the reduction of foreign language anxiety and motivation.

Further, Chap. 7, “Cognitive Engagement in Virtual Worlds Language Learning” along the same theme with two of the same authors, Henderson, Henderson, Grant and Huang, investigated learner engagement in terms of students’ cognition whilst experiencing their learning in the virtual world. The authors used a simulated recall methodology to discover student’s cognition—affect, strategy planning, evaluating, metacognising and justifying. They explored the relationship between learner cognition, instructional design and other triggers, whilst their students undertook their learning in the virtual world. Their findings revealed a high frequency of cognitive processes stimulated by programmed lessons involving the use of curriculum knowledge and skills to successfully complete in-world tasks. However, some of the thinking processes, despite being related to the task or curriculum, were found to be focussed on meeting the task requirement, suggesting the need to ensure adequate clarity in instructions and supports are provided by the teacher.

The following Chap. 8, “Anticipating Engagement: Pre-Service Teachers Perceptions of Virtual Worlds” by Jacka and Hill, explored student engagement whilst using a virtual world for teaching and learning at the higher education level and also in the classroom of school students from kindergarten to year 12. The authors explored blog posts in relation to student’s perceptions of virtual worlds for learning, and their findings suggest a correlation between engagement and the creative aspects that virtual worlds provide. They found that the design of the learning environment within the virtual world was important when integrating the technologies that are available.

Butler, in Chap. 9, “Utilising Second Life Machinima-Facilitated Narratives to Support Cognitive and Imaginative Engagement across an Undergraduate Curriculum”, described a case study utilising a virtual world to produce machinima videos in the Law School. The machinima was used to enhance engagement and promote authentic learning, using a blended learning approach without requiring students to enter and participate in the virtual world itself. Narratives were facilitated by machinima and linked by a common storyline and recurring characters running throughout the program. Butler explored the pedagogical approach for using machinima and discussed the findings from student responses to end of course survey incorporating a series of Likert scale and open-ended questions. He found that the overwhelming majority of students reported strong agreement to the benefits of the machinima in helping them to understand the application of negotiation principles in real-world practice, providing a realistic setting to understand the principles of negotiation, enabled students to gain an understanding of negotiation theory and practice and was an enjoyable experience as part of their studies. He further found that the qualitative feedback highlighted the authenticity of the approach as one of the most consistent themes emerging from student feedback.

In the final Chap. 10, "Decision Making Supported by Virtual World Systems vis-à-vis Enterprise Systems' Uncertainty and Equivocality", the authors, Rudra, Jæger and Ludvigsen, investigated the potential of the authentic setting of the virtual world for facilitating students' business decision-making using a combination of explicit and tacit. Their findings suggest that virtual worlds have unique properties that support tacit knowledge in a global distributed business environment.

Concluding Remarks

These ten chapters provide some of the leading virtual worlds' research from Australia and New Zealand. They have focussed on the affordances of virtual worlds for facilitating authentic learning, improving learner engagement and developing an understanding of cultural diversity, with a particular focus on the affordances of the virtual world platform for supporting students in the development of technical and generic skills required for professional practice. The chapters reflect a diversity in the ways in which the virtual world was incorporated into the curriculum across a wide range of disciplinary fields, but what is consistent across all the chapters are the strategies employed by educators to maximise the pedagogical affordances of the technology to engage their students in authentic activities.

The findings of evaluation of the efficacy of the approaches employed in the curriculum across the disciplines represented in this book demonstrate the ways in which the virtual world provided a real-world context for students and authentic assessment tasks. The findings also highlight the potential of the virtual world for embedding opportunities for students to experience expert performance, whilst also demonstrating the potential of the virtual worlds for delivering automated feedback, coaching and scaffolding for students.

However, the findings from the studies reported in these chapters remind us that there are also unintended consequences and challenges in utilising any innovative technology in the curriculum. These challenges include technical difficulties and the learning curve associated with navigating and interacting with the virtual world.

Several of the authors have highlighted the importance of mitigating these challenges to maximise the benefits of student engagement in virtual world activities.

Finally, the findings and lessons learned from the experiences of the educators and researchers, whose experiences are documented in this collection of chapters, remind us that technology can never be an educational panacea, and that sound pedagogical practices and research informed evidence are requisites for ensuring that the potential benefits of learning in a virtual world are realised.

The use of virtual worlds in higher education has finally reached "the plateau of productivity", and the authors of this collection demonstrate the strategies educators are employing to provide productive and effective authentic learning opportunities for their students. However, as new technologies emerge, some of which may be integrated or complement virtual world learning, the need for ongoing exploration of the affordances of these technologies to facilitate authentic learning experiences and research to determine the efficacy of the strategies employed by educators to maximise learning outcomes will continue.

Reference

Bennett, M. J. (1993). Towards ethnorelativism: A developmental model of intercultural sensitivity (revised). In R. M. Paige (Ed.), *Education for the intercultural experience*. Yarmouth, ME: Intercultural Press.

The manufacturer's authorised representative in the EU is Springer Nature Customer Service Centre GmbH, Europaplatz 3, 69115 Heidelberg, Germany. If you have any concerns regarding our products, please contact ProductSafety@springernature.com

Printed and bound by CPI Group (UK) Ltd, Croydon, CR0 4YY
25/09/2026
02222869-0005